VEGANIZE IT!

VEGANIZE IT!

EASY DIY RECIPES FOR A
PLANT-BASED KITCHEN

ROBIN ROBERTSON

HOUGHTON MIFFLIN HARCOURT
Boston • New York • 2017

For information about permission to reproduce selections from this book,
write to trade.permissions@hmhco.com or to
Houghton Mifflin Harcourt Publishing Company, 3 Park Avenue,
19th Floor, New York, New York 10016.

www.hmhco.com

Library of Congress Cataloging-in-Publication Data is available.
ISBN 978-0-544-81556-8 (trade paper); 978-0-544-81557-5 (ebk)

Book design by Kara Plikaitis

Printed in China
TOP 10 9 8 7 6 5 4 3 2 1

For all the caring and compassionate people who work to make the world a kinder, gentler place for all sentient beings

And for the animals

INTRODUCTION   1

CHAPTER 1: VEGAN BASICS   5

CHAPTER 2: DIY DAIRY-FREE AND EGG-FREE, TOO

Nut Milk	28
Almost-Instant Nut Milk	29
Coconut Milk	30
Oat Milk	31
Cashew Cream	32
Cashew Sour Cream	33
Easy Vegan Yogurt	34
Creamy Cashew Mayo	35
Easy Vegan Butter	36
Aquafaba Butter	37
Nut Butter	38
Basic White Sauce	39
Cashew Cream Cheese	40
Seasoned Tofu Ricotta	41
Nut-Parm	42
Melty Vegan Cheese	43
Cheddary Sauce	44
Smoky Queso Sauce	45
Say (Veganized) Cheese!	46
Tofu Feta	48
Htipiti (Feta Spread)	49
Spinach-Artichoke Dip	51
Pretzel-Crusted Cheddary Log	52

Bacon-Topped Mac UnCheese	54
Cheesy Broccoli Soup	56
Loaded Baked Potatoes	57
Spinach and Mushroom-Bacon Quiche	60
Spinach-Feta Quesadillas	62
Chickpea Flour Omelets	63
Cheesy Mushroom Scramble	66
Vive la French Toast	67
Breakfast Nachos	69

CHAPTER 3: PLANT-BASED MEATS

Marinated Baked Tofu	74
Burmese Tofu	76
Crispy Tofu	77
Crispy Crumbles	78
Totally Tempting Tempeh	79
Beans from Scratch	80
Smoky Black Bean Soup	82
Iron Kettle Chili	83
Best Bean Burgers	84
Mama's Meatballs	86
White Bean Cutlets	87
Piccata Meatballs with Penne and Asparagus	89
Tuesday Tacos with Avocado Crema	90

CONTENTS

Baked Seitan Roast 92

Oven-Baked Seitan Cutlets 94

Seitan Oscar with Béarnaise Sauce 97

The Wellington 98

BBQ Seitan Ribs 99

CHAPTER 4: VEGAN CHARCUTERIE

Tempeh Bacon 106

Tofu Bacon 107

Coconut Bacon Bits 108

Eggplant Bacon Strips 109

Mushroom Bacon 110

Smoky Chickpeas 111

Hamish Loaf 112

DIY Jerky 113

Banh Mi 115

Handcrafted Pepperoni 116

Spicy Italian Sausage 117

Andouille Sausage 118

Country-Style Pâté 119

Jambalaya 120

Veganized Scrapple 122

Maple Breakfast Sausage 123

Cassoulet 125

No-Meat Loaf 126

Beyond BLT 127

Haute Dogs 128

Haute Dogs Wellington 130

Deviled Hamish Salad 131

Join the Club Sandwich 133

CHAPTER 5: INSTEAD OF SEAFOOD

Clam-Free Chowder 139

Lobster Mushroom Bisque 140

Fish-Free Tacos 142

Vegan Fish and Chips with Tartar Sauce 144

Fish-Free Fillets 146

Fish-Free Sticks 147

See Scallops 148

Palm-Crab Po'boys 149

Hearts of Palm and Artichoke Cakes 150

Creamy Sriracha See Scallops 153

Chickpea and Artichoke Tuna Salad	154
Palm-Crab Imperial	155
Vegan Crab Louis	157

CHAPTER 6: VEGETABLE STEAK-OUT

Baked Eggplant Italian Style	163
Cordon Bleu–Stuffed Portobellos	164
Jumpin' Jackfruit Chili	165
Roasted Cauliflower Piccata	166
Vegetable Shepherd's Pie	169
Mushroom Stroganoff	170
Mashed Potatoes with Sour Cream and Chives	171
Pulled Jackfruit BBQ Sandwiches	172
Eggplant Paprikash	174
Pan-Seared Portobello Strips	175
Cheesy Steak-Out Sandwiches	177

CHAPTER 7: GLOBAL CONDIMENTS, SAUCES, AND DRESSINGS

Vegetable Broth	182
Homemade Vegetable Base	183
Red Wine Sauce with Mushrooms	184
Hollandaise Sauce	185
Vegan Worcestershire Sauce	186
Avocado Crema	187
Remoulade Sauce	188
Fish-Free Nuoc Cham	189

Better Béarnaise Sauce	190
Great Brown Gravy	191
Tapenade	192
Vegan Aioli	193
Basil Pesto	194
Tzatziki Sauce	195
Creamy Ranch Dressing	196
Oven-Roasted Tomato Sauce	197
Mushroom Oyster Sauce	198
Goddess Dressing	199
Hail Caesar Dressing	200
Creamy Pesto Pasta Salad	201
Summer Rolls with Fish-Free Nuoc Cham	203
Seitan Gyros with Tzatziki Sauce	205
Buffalo Cauliflower with Ranch Dressing	206
My Kinda Chef's Salad	208
Easy Kimchi	209
Niçoise Goddess Salad	210
Creamy Coleslaw	212
California Caesar Salad	213

CHAPTER 8: FLOUR POWER

DIY Granola	218
Homemade Pasta	219
Handcrafted Lasagna	221
Fettuccine Bolognese	222
Spaghetti Carbonara	223
Orecchiette with Pistachio Pesto	224

Rotini with Roasted Garlic Alfredo Sauce 226

Pie Dough 228

Easy Artisan Bread 229

Perfect Pot Pie 230

Cheesy Sausage Biscuits 233

Cheesy Crackers 234

Scratch Biscuits 236

All-in-One Cauliflower Pizza 237

Pizza Dough 238

Benedict Pizza 239

Meaty-Cheesy Pizza 240

Loaded Polenta Pizza 242

Cranberry-Walnut Scones 243

CHAPTER 9: SWEETS FROM SCRATCH

Whipped Coconut Cream 248

Cashew Chantilly Cream 249

Date-Caramel Sauce 250

Fudgy Chocolate Sauce 251

Buttercream Frosting 252

Vegan Mascarpone 253

Ganache 254

Veganized Marshmallow Fluff 255

Meringue 256

Lemon Meringue Pie 259

Scratch Cake 260

Tiramisu 261

Strawberry Shortcake 262

Mango Fro-Yo 264

Bellini Trifle 265

Cranberry Oatmeal Cookies 266

Chocolate Truffles 267

Luscious Lava Cakes 269

Chocolate–Chocolate Chip Brownies 271

No-Bake Chocolate Cheesecake 273

No-Bake Nut Lover's Cheesecake 274

Chocolate-Covered Elvis Ice Cream 275

Chocolate–Peanut Butter Milkshake 276

Ice Cream Sundae Cake 278

Banana Split Soft-Serve Sundaes 280

ACKNOWLEDGMENTS 282

INDEX 283

INTRODUCTION

I'd been a restaurant chef for seven years when I went vegan in the late 1980s. I happily immersed myself in cooking fabulous meals made with vegetables, grains, beans, and nuts. Soups, stews, salads, and stir-fries were a cinch.

But making a BLT for lunch or a creamy Alfredo pasta dish for dinner back then presented a challenge. The vegan alternatives to meat and dairy that we have on supermarket shelves today were just a pipe dream.

My husband and I had both been raised on a diet laden with meats, dairy, and eggs. But while we were at peace with our ethical decision to get healthy and stop eating animals, we saw no reason to deprive ourselves of the flavors and textures of dishes we enjoyed that were traditionally made with meat and dairy. If I wanted something meaty or creamy made from plant foods, back in those days, I had to come up with a way to make it myself—I had to figure out how to veganize it.

Before long, veganizing all our favorite foods became second nature. I became skilled at preparing meaty cutlets, sausages, and roasts using beans, vital wheat gluten, and dairy-free versions of sour cream, mayonnaise, and more. I taught others how to do the same and began writing the cookbooks that launched my second career as an author. Nearly thirty years and more than twenty cookbooks later, I continue to develop user-friendly recipes that allow vegans and other health-conscious people to enjoy plant-based versions of foods traditionally made with animal products, while still maintaining the classic flavors and textures loved the world over. I also work at making it easy and inexpensive for home cooks to veganize their favorite dishes.

These days, a wide variety of vegan products are finally available, even in well-stocked supermarkets. So why make our own? There are a lot of reasons. Some of these products, such as vegan cheese, sausages, and burgers, can be expensive, highly processed, full of preservatives, or not to your liking. This book solves these issues by providing fast and economical plant-based solutions for all those favorite dishes that are traditionally made with animal-based ingredients.

In *Veganize It!* my goal is to combine my signature easy-cooking methods and years of experience in global cuisines to create the ultimate guide for making homemade vegan foods from everyday ingredients. Within these pages, you'll find recipes for basics such as Cashew Cream Cheese, Oven-Baked Seitan Cutlets, and Easy Vegan Yogurt, along with specialties such as Handcrafted Pepperoni, Andouille Sausage, and Mama's Meatballs—all made inexpensively, using simple cooking methods and easy-to-find ingredients. But I also wanted the book to showcase a variety of great-tasting classic recipes in which to use the veganized ingredients. For example, with the Cashew Cream Cheese, you'll be able to use it to make Spinach-Artichoke Dip and No-Bake Chocolate Cheesecake. Make the Andouille Sausage, and you're just one step away from an amazing jambalaya.

The more than 150 recipes in *Veganize It!* provide a solid foundation of plant-based basics, such as dairy-free sour cream, mayonnaise, butter, and easy artisanal vegan cheeses, that taste like they took all day to prepare. There are recipes for plant-based meats including roasts, ribs, and loaves made from wheat, soy, and beans. There's even a chapter on fish-free seafood recipes; a charcuterie chapter for making your own sausage, bacon, jerky, and other artisan meats; and a chapter called Vegetable Steak-Out that showcases vegetables prepared in rich, meaty ways.

This collection of recipes is geared to busy home cooks who want to get a great dinner on the table but don't want to spend all day in the kitchen. You'll find recipes for homemade pasta and pizza dough, soups, and crackers, and the chapter Sweets from Scratch has recipes for vegan ice cream, ganache, caramel sauce, and much more. The recipes for international sauces and condiments are also informed by my background as a restaurant chef, which enables me to develop authentic plant-based versions of classic sauces. From Smoky Queso Sauce and my Hollandaise Sauce made without eggs or butter, to Fish-Free Nuoc Cham and Vegan Worcestershire Sauce, vegans can now reach for their own homemade sauces without having to worry about what's in it.

With delicious recipes, variations, helpful tips, and informative sidebars, *Veganize It!* delivers a practical take on getting dinner on the table. With *Veganize It!* in your kitchen, healthy and delicious options are always at your fingertips.

EGAN BASICS

CHAPTER 1

There was a time not many years ago when if you wanted plant-based alternatives to animal foods, you'd have to make them yourself.

These days, however, the vegan way of eating has exploded in North America. Vegan products are now common in small-town grocery stores, and new plant-based foods come out practically by the month. The meat- and dairy-free consciousness is so prevalent now that restaurants that once offered an occasional vegan option now provide a page of vegan choices, and this goes for the sandwich shop as well as the high-end restaurant. Moreover, dedicated and award-winning vegan restaurants are popping up in major cities, where skilled chefs turn out culinary art that even omnivores embrace. We also see the emergence of the vegan "butcher" shop, where top-quality, organic, non-GMO vegetables and plant-based meats are prepared as prime cuts for the discriminating shopper.

Most well-stocked supermarkets offer rows of vegan milks made from almonds, cashews, and soy sitting right next to cow's milk in the dairy case, just as Earth Balance, a vegan buttery spread, perches alongside dairy butter. Tofu varieties abound, as do nondairy ice creams, cheeses, and other dairy-free products, including yogurt, sour cream, and cream cheese. And look at the prepared vegan food now available! Even chain supermarkets and big-box stores carry plant-based products, including sausage, burgers, cold cuts, bacon, meatballs, and vegan seafood.

While many people extoll the convenience and availability of these products, some shun them, saying they're too processed or too expensive. There are others, such as myself, who take a more balanced approach, applying a cost/benefit analysis concerning such foods and deciding on a case-by-case basis which products I want to make at home from scratch and which I'd prefer to buy ready-made. Generally I opt for buying minimally processed foods, such as plant milks, tofu, and tempeh, from the store and make the rest at home, including seitan, cheeses, and sausage.

The premise of this book is a simple one: For reasons of health, ethics, and the environment, food is better when it's made with vegan rather than animal products. That's why I say let's veganize it! If you can enjoy ingredients such as sour cream, cheese, sausage, bacon, and butter without causing ill effects on your body, without harming animals or decimating the environment, why wouldn't you? And if those ingredients could be found in one easy-to-use book, all the better!

It follows that if food is better when it's made vegan than with animal products, then vegan food is better still when it's homemade and not processed. This is, of course, because a whole foods, plant-based diet is better than a vegan diet that relies on processed or ready-made products, not just because fresh homemade foods taste better and are better for you, but also because making your own foods can be more economical as well as fun and easy to prepare.

MAKE IT BETTER — MAKE IT YOURSELF

When I was growing up, cooking everything from scratch was an everyday ritual. My mother made her own pasta, bread, sausage, and more, not just because they were less expensive but also because they tasted better. The fact that she came from a time when convenience foods were virtually nonexistent also played a role. These days, the popularity of selling handcrafted artisan foods has grown in recent years from small-batch jam and locavore soy sauce to artisan breads and bean-to-bar chocolates. In addition to buying handcrafted products from artisanal purveyors, DIY cooking is enjoying a renaissance in home kitchens.

When an ingredient is typically made with animal products, I have developed excellent ways to veganize it. Not only that, but you also have in your hands excellent recipes in which to use them. For example, when you make recipes for vegan mayo and bacon, there's a recipe for Beyond BLTs using both. Likewise, the book contains recipes for Handcrafted Lasagna (made with homemade pasta, sauce, vegan ricotta, and a melty cheese) and others such as Cheesy Sausage Biscuits, Meaty-Cheesy Pizza, and Loaded Baked Potatoes.

What you won't find in this book are recipes that do not traditionally use animal products, such as salsas, jams, and hummus, for the simple reason that they are already plant-based and don't need to be veganized. The only exceptions are the handful of naturally plant-based recipes that are important to a particular recipe, such as pizza dough for the pizza.

If you want to enjoy vegan cheeses, sauces, and proteins without paying the hefty price tags for ready-made versions, then you'll love this book. Not only are homemade foods cheaper, but they also give you an opportunity to customize foods to suit your own taste. Another big reason people favor scratch cooking is to avoid additives and highly processed foods. Plus, store-bought versions of some vegan specialty foods aren't always easy to find, so that gives foods you can make at home a built-in convenience factor.

While some people love to spend hours in the kitchen honing their food-craft, not everyone has that kind of time. That's where *Veganize It!* comes to the rescue with streamlined recipes using easy-to-find ingredients. Within these pages, you get easy and economical recipes for vegan staples as well as recipes that incorporate several of those staple ingredients for a complete vegan cooking experience.

IT TAKES A (WELL-STOCKED) PANTRY

All it takes to make do-it-yourself-vegan staples is a pantry stocked with basic ingredients and some time to make quantities in advance. Most of the ingredients used to make these recipes can be found in well-stocked supermarkets. However, based on my own experience, there are a few ingredients that may be a little more difficult to find if you do not live in a metropolitan area. For such ingredients, I either order them online (many are available on Amazon) or I keep a list going of such ingredients and get them whenever we drive to the metropolitan Washington, D.C., area. Everything else, including agave, sriracha, hearts of palm in jars, and smoked paprika, I am able to find in stores in or near my rural Virginia town (population 5,000), so I will assume that you can find them, too.

Note: You will only need certain of these specialty ingredients if you plan to make particular recipes. For example, the sea vegetables are used primarily in the Instead of Seafood chapter to lend a briny flavor to the plant-based seafood recipes. Likewise for the lobster mushrooms and oyster mushrooms. Other ingredients, such as nutritional yeast and vegetable base powder or paste, are called for throughout the book.

A well-stocked pantry is essential to easy and convenient plant-based cooking. The list below features many of the ingredients used to make the recipes in this book. You may or may not be familiar with some of these ingredients, but they are all available in well-stocked supermarkets, natural foods stores, or Asian markets.

Got Dairy Alternatives?

Contrary to popular belief, milk consumption does not prevent osteoporosis and is not necessary for bone development. Humans are the only animals that drink the milk of other species and continue to drink milk after infancy. Recent studies show that milk consumption can actually contribute to heart disease, some forms of cancer, psoriasis, allergies, and a host of other ailments. The highest incidences of osteoporosis occur in countries where milk consumption is high. So do you ever wonder why "drinking your milk" became the battle cry of moms to their children beginning in the 1950s? Here's why:

The dairy industry developed an "education" program during the 1950s to promote dairy products in American classrooms. Ever since, people have believed that calcium in milk is the only way to grow big and strong. In addition to the dairy industry's inherent animal cruelties, they never revealed another secret —that better sources of calcium can be found in tofu, nuts, broccoli, dark leafy greens, and sea vegetables. And about that vitamin D in dairy products: It's actually a hormone that our bodies create when exposed to sunlight. In other words, it doesn't occur naturally in cow's milk and must be added later (the same is true of vitamin D added to nondairy milks).

When people transition to a plant-based diet, they often find it easier to stop eating meat than dairy products because of their fondness for (some say addiction to) dairy—especially cheese. Fortunately there are plant-based alternatives to replace everything from milk, to cheese, to eggs—and this book is filled with recipes for making them at home.

PANTRY LIST

In addition to the ingredients listed below, you will want to keep on hand a variety of fresh produce, dried and canned beans, grains, pastas, and tomato products, along with condiments such as tahini, salsa, and nut butters, to add variety to your meals. Other necessary pantry ingredients include dried herbs, spices, vinegars, sea salt, and basic seasonings, as well as baking items such as flours, baking powder, baking soda, extracts, and thickeners.

Flours

Chickpea flour

Cornmeal

Semolina flour

Tapioca starch (aka tapioca flour)

Vital wheat gluten

Nuts and Seeds

Almonds

Cashews, raw

Flaxseeds

Peanuts

Pecans

Sesame seeds

Sunflower seeds

Walnuts

Oils

Coconut oil

Dark (toasted) sesame oil

Extra-virgin olive oil

Sunflower oil or grapeseed oil

Seasonings

Creole or Cajun seasoning blend

Filé powder

Kitchen Bouquet or Gravy Master (browning liquid)

Liquid smoke

Old Bay seasoning

Rice vinegar

Smoked paprika

Sriracha sauce

Sun-dried tomatoes

Tamari soy sauce (low-sodium)

Thai chili sauce

Sea Vegetables

Agar-agar powder

Dulse flakes or powder

Soy Foods

Miso paste

Tempeh

Tofu, extra-firm

Tofu, silken

Sweeteners

Agave nectar

Unrefined sugar

Pure maple syrup

Medjool dates

Vegetables, Canned or Jarred

Artichoke hearts, marinated

Capers

Chipotle chiles in adobo

Hearts of palm

Jackfruit (packed in water)

Pimientos, chopped

Pitted Kalamata olives

Tomatoes, whole peeled (San Marzano)

Miscellaneous

Chocolate chips, vegan semi-sweet

Coconut milk, canned, full-fat

Nutritional yeast

Panko bread crumbs

Puff pastry, frozen (Pepperidge Farm brand)

Rice noodles

Rice paper wrappers

Unsweetened flaked coconut

Vegetable base powder, paste, or cubes

INGREDIENTS TO KNOW

SEITAN

Seitan, or "wheat-meat," is made with vital wheat gluten, the protein part of wheat, after the bran and starch have been washed out. This protein is dried and ground into flour known as vital wheat gluten, which is, in turn, mixed with water and seasonings to form a doughlike mass that is then cooked. The cooked gluten, or seitan, is an extremely versatile ingredient owing to its chewy texture and the forms and flavors it can take on. It can be diced, cut into strips for stir-fries, cubed for stews and soups, shredded or ground, stuffed like a roast, thinly sliced, or made into sausage, loaves, and burgers. Making seitan from scratch is a simple process and far less expensive than buying it ready-made. There are several recipes for making and using seitan in this book to create roasts, cutlets, sausages, and other "meaty" foods. Seitan is one of the primary protein-rich plant-based foods that are most often used instead of meat in plant-based versions of traditional recipes. The others are tempeh and tofu, made from soy, and of course, beans.

I recommend making seitan at home because it is easy and economical to prepare and buying ready-made seitan can be expensive. On the other hand, I prefer to buy tofu and tempeh at the store because they are reasonably priced and the preparation process takes more time than most people want to spend.

TOFU

A versatile ingredient and good source of protein, tofu has an uncanny ability to absorb the flavors that surround it. Also known as bean curd, tofu is made from ground, cooked soybeans in a process similar to the way cheese is made. Tofu is available in two main types: regular (Chinese) and silken (Japanese). Both types come in three textures: soft, firm, and extra-firm, each of which lends itself well to various types of dishes.

Extra-firm regular tofu is the sturdiest of the two main types. The firm and extra-firm lend themselves to stir-fries and other dishes in which the tofu must retain its

...MAL INGREDIENTS

...make your own ...y be hidden ...ne of the products ...e vegan. Out of ...onscious people ...f label-readers, due ...r nasty ingre- ...ocessed foods. ..., label-reading ...rtant due to the ...ally found in many ...elatin and lard ...in marshmal- ...nd pastries. Some ...s, even soy cheese, ...ch is obtained from cow's milk, to make it melt better. Other common animal-based ingredients include albumin, whey, lactose, isinglass, lanolin, and suet. As a rule, the more processed a food item is, the more likely it is to contain some form of animal product. Fortunately, for every animal ingredient, there is a plant-based alternative. Look carefully and you will find vegan versions of Worcestershire sauce (the regular product contains ancho- vies) and gelatin-like desserts and pud- dings that use agar-agar or carrageen as thickeners. The safest bet is to go for fresh, whole foods, such as vegetables, grains, beans, and fruits.

shape. Silken tofu, or "Japanese-style," is used when the desired result is smooth and creamy, such as in smoothies, sauces, and puddings. Tofu is most often packed in water-filled tubs, so before using it in a recipe, it is essential to drain, blot, and press out the excess water. To squeeze tofu dry, cut the block into slabs and place the slabs on a baking sheet or cutting board lined with paper towels. Weight down the baking sheet with a heavy skillet or canned goods and let it sit for an hour.

TEMPEH

Tempeh is made from fermented, compressed soybeans and is especially well suited to stews, stir-fries, and sautés because, like tofu, it absorbs the surrounding flavors. Tempeh turns a crisp golden brown when fried and it marinates well.

Originating in Indonesia, tempeh is high in protein with a chewy texture. Tempeh can be found in the refrigerated or freezer sections of natural foods stores, Asian markets, and some supermarkets, and is usually sold in 8-ounce slabs. The slabs can be sliced lengthwise to make thin slices and can also be cut into strips, cubed, or grated. Tempeh requires refrigeration, where it will keep, unopened, for several weeks (check the expiration date). Once it is opened, however, it should be wrapped tightly and used within three days. Tempeh will keep for a month or so frozen. As tempeh can have a strong nutty flavor, I recommend steaming tempeh for 30 minutes before using in recipes, to mellow the flavor and make it more digestible.

Homemade or Store-Bought: Your Choice

To recap, among the "big three" plant-based proteins, I recommend making your own seitan because it's easy to prepare and more economical than buying it, but I suggest that you buy tofu and tempeh ready-made because it is more time-consuming to make at home and reasonably priced to buy. The same goes for plant-based milks. The wide variety, availability, and relatively low cost have made it practical to buy store-bought nondairy milk. However, since they may be more processed than some people would like, I've included recipes for making a few varieties of plant milk for those who prefer to make their own.

It also makes sense to cook your own beans from dried because it is simple and more economical than canned, but it's easy to make a case for keeping a few cans of organic canned beans on hand for quick meals when your stash of frozen beans runs out.

When it comes to more processed ingredients, such as vegan cream cheese or sour cream, or prepared foods such as vegan sausages or burgers, the reasons to make them yourself far outweigh the reasons to buy them ready-made. In fact, the only good reason I can think of to buy these products ready-made is convenience (assuming such products are readily available to you).

BEANS

Beans are an inexpensive source of protein that is easy to prepare, low in fat, and an important component of a well-balanced plant-based diet. The most popular varieties of beans and legumes are chickpeas, black-eyed peas, lentils, black beans, pintos, kidney beans, lima beans, and cannellini beans. With the exception of lentils and split peas, all dried beans require soaking. Soaking rehydrates the beans and shortens their cooking time. It also dissolves some of the complex sugars that cause digestive gas. It's always a good idea to begin by picking through them first in order to remove dust, small stones, and other debris. To soak the beans, place them in a bowl with enough water to cover them by 3 inches. Soak them overnight and drain them before cooking. To quick-soak beans, put them in a pot under 2 to 3 inches of water and boil for 2 minutes. Remove the pot from the stove, cover it, and let it stand for 2 hours. Drain the beans, and they're ready for cooking.

Beans can be cooked in a pressure cooker, slow cooker, oven, or on the stove top. Since I'm trying to limit the special equipment used in this book, here's a simple way to cook beans on the stove top: In a large saucepan, combine 1 cup of beans and 3 cups of water. Salt the water lightly and simmer until tender. Cooking times will vary, usually ranging from 1 to 3 hours, depending on the type, quality, and age of the beans. Altitude and even water quality can also influence the cooking time. The yield for 1 cup of dried beans is 2 to 2½ cups of cooked beans.

PLANT-BASED MILKS

These days supermarket dairy cases share nearly equal space with nondairy milks. Even in the small town where I live, my local grocery store carries milk made from soy, almonds, cashews, and coconut, in plain unsweetened, regular, and vanilla. The decision whether to buy your plant-based milk at the supermarket or make it from scratch is up to you. If convenience is your primary motivation, then store-bought is the way to go. But if you want a milk made from just water and whatever your main ingredient is (with the possible addition of a pinch of salt), instead of a list of additional ingredients, then you may enjoy the pure unadulterated flavor of homemade plant-based milks. Whichever you decide, it's important that you use "plain unsweetened" milk for cooking. Any milks that include a sweetener or flavoring should be reserved for drinking or making desserts (although plain unsweetened is good for those uses as well).

Experiment with different types of plant milks to decide which you like best. My favorite choice for cooking is plain unsweetened almond milk because I think it has the most neutral flavor for cooking. You may prefer another almond or soy milk. Coconut milk is another popular plant milk, though it is the thick full-fat culinary coconut milk sold in cans that is called for in my recipes (not the thin coconut milk from the dairy case). Oat milk is more difficult to find commercially, but easy to make at home. It has a rather bland flavor but makes a serviceable milk for cooking, especially when you don't have another type of plant milk on hand.

VEGETABLE BROTH

Vegetable broth is an important ingredient for cooking, especially when making soups and sauces. It's easy to make homemade broth using the recipe on page 182. Making your own broth is far less expensive than commercial broths, and it will taste better, too. If you don't have time to make homemade broth, but you don't want to buy it ready-made, you can use vegetable soup base powder or paste or vegetable bouillon cubes. The salt content in these products varies, so find one you like and adjust seasonings in recipes accordingly. My favorite commercial brand of vegetable base paste is Better Than Bouillon. I also provide a recipe for a homemade vegetable base on page 183.

THE WELL-MEATED VEGAN

Although the word meat is usually associated with animal flesh, the original meaning of the word was "meal." In fact, the correct meaning of meat is food in general: anything eaten for nourishment, either by man or beast. Meat is the edible part of anything, as in the meat of a crab, a nut, or a tomato.

This was the meaning of meat for Chaucer as well as in the King James Bible (Genesis 1:29) where it states that Adam was intended to have a vegan diet.

Not long ago, it was called to "sit at meat" when it was time for dinner, regardless of what type of food was on the table. Therefore, when you enjoy a nutritious plant-based meal, you are "well-meated."

Whether you use a refined white sugar or a natural sweetener in your cooking is a matter of personal preference. One reason to avoid refined sugar is because it is often filtered using charred animal bones. I prefer using a naturally processed granulated cane sugar, which is sold under various brand names, including Sucanat and Florida Crystals. These can be substituted in equal measure for white table sugar. Date sugar is another good option.

Honey is not vegan, so when you need a liquid sweetener, two good alternatives to honey are agave nectar and pure maple syrup, though maple will add a bit of its distinct flavor to your recipe. Date syrup can also be used in recipes where its color and flavor will be welcome.

Other Ingredients to Know and Love

There are a few ingredients that are used throughout the book that, while fairly common and easy to find, may be new to you. In case you're not familiar with them, here's a rundown.

COCONUT OIL

Because it is solid at room temperature, coconut oil is a good alternative to butter in recipes. It can also be used for cooking and has a high smoke point, making it a good choice for high-heat cooking. You can easily find coconut oil in supermarkets. It is available two ways: unrefined, extra-virgin, which retains a slight coconut flavor, and refined, which has little to no discernable coconut flavor. Either can be used in recipes, depending on your personal preference.

FLAXSEEDS

Flaxseeds are available whole or ground, and golden or brown. The recipes in this book call for ground golden flaxseeds, but you can buy them whole, if you prefer, and grind them yourself. Flaxseeds are rich in omega-3 fatty acids and are used as a binder (when combined with warm water) in recipes.

NUTRITIONAL YEAST

Known for the complex nutty or cheesy flavor it adds to foods, this deactivated yeast is high in protein and vitamin B. It is available at natural foods stores or online. It is an important ingredient in many recipes in this book that require a "cheesy" flavor.

SEA VEGETABLES

Sea vegetables (aka seaweed) are loaded with vitamins, minerals, and antioxidants. They also add a "taste of the sea" to plant-based recipes. Most people are familiar with nori, the dark wrapper on sushi rolls, but there are lots more varieties where that came from. My favorite (and the one called for in a few recipes in this book) is dulse. I prefer dulse over the others because I think it has the best flavor (mild, yet salty-smoky). You can find it in natural foods stores and online. It comes dried in large pieces, flakes, or powder. The only other sea vegetable called for in one or two recipes in this book is agar-agar, which is known for its gelling power and is a plant-based alternative to gelatin. It is white in color and comes in powder, flakes, and bars.

TAMARI

Tamari is a high-quality soy sauce usually made without wheat or other additives. It has a deeper flavor than regular soy sauce and is available in a reduced-sodium variety, which is what I recommend.

TAPIOCA STARCH OR FLOUR

Tapioca starch (sometimes labeled tapioca flour) is the dried ground root of the cassava plant. It is used to thicken liquids, bind ingredients, and add a bit of stretch to melty vegan cheese.

LIQUID SMOKE

Available in supermarkets, liquid smoke is a concentrated liquid seasoning that adds a deep smoky flavor to foods. It is a key ingredient in the plant-based bacon recipes in this book.

Equipment

To help streamline these recipes, it was important to me as I developed the book that the only special equipment called for be a food processor or high-speed blender. That's it. If you don't have a high-speed blender, you can use a regular blender or food processor to make those recipes, too, although the results may not be as smooth.

Using the recipes in this book, you can make yogurt without a yogurt maker, ice cream without an ice cream maker, and pasta without a pasta machine. It's more important to spend your money on a few good pieces of cookware and knives than fancy or specialized equipment or gadgets. Here's a list of what I consider "must-have" kitchen equipment:

FOOD PROCESSOR: A food processor is essential for making pesto, pureeing vegetables, chopping nuts, and making bread crumbs. It is also great for making pie dough, chopping vegetables, and numerous other mixing and chopping tasks. The trick is knowing when it will be faster to cut, whisk, or chop by hand, and that can usually be determined by the quantity of food involved. Some people have a large-capacity processor as well as a smaller model that they use for smaller tasks.

MISE EN PLACE

Mise en place is the French term for getting your ingredients and equipment ready before beginning a recipe. It's a handy thing to remember and will streamline the cooking process immensely. Before starting any recipe, read the recipe through like it's a newspaper article, and then read it again, making notes of any ingredients you do not have on hand. This becomes your shopping list. Once you have all the ingredients you need, gather them together along with any equipment you may need. The process of mise en place includes preheating your oven as well as chopping and premeasuring ingredients in the quantities required. It can help you avoid missing ingredients, finish cooking faster, and enjoy the cooking process more.

INGREDIENT SENSITIVITIES

For those of you with sensitivities or allergies to ingredients such as gluten, soy, and peanuts, there are a few easy ways to make these recipes suitable to your diet, often with just a simple ingredient swap.

For example, in recipes that call for pasta, flour, or bread, simply use a gluten-free version of those ingredients. You can substitute extra-firm tofu or tempeh for recipes that use seitan. Be sure to use wheat-free tamari and certified gluten-free oats.

Likewise, recipes that call for soy foods can be made with a variety of soy-free alternatives, depending on the recipe. For example, coconut aminos can replace tamari; seitan can replace extra-firm tofu; and thick cashew cream can be used in recipes calling for silken tofu.

If you avoid oils, feel free to water-sauté ingredients instead of sautéing them in oil.

BLENDER: While it's possible to get by with just a food processor to make these recipes, a high-powered blender (such as a Vitamix or Blendtec) can be a wise investment if you do a lot of cooking at home. I use both blender and food processor for different purposes. The blender is reserved for smoothies, sauces, soups, and anything I want to make super-smooth and creamy very quickly. I use the food processor for chopping, shredding, and mixing dough. Other handy blenders are the immersion (stick) blender, which is handy for pureeing soups and sauces right in the pot, and a personal-size blender, which is great for small amounts of liquids such as salad dressings and sauces.

KNIVES: No need for a whole set! You can accomplish any task with just three knives: a paring knife for peeling and trimming; a long serrated knife for slicing bread, tomatoes, and other fragile foods; and a good (8- or 10-inch) chef's knife for virtually everything else. Buy the best-quality knives you can afford and keep them sharp. You can chop more quickly and safely with sharp knives than with dull ones.

POTS AND SAUCEPANS: A 5- to 6-quart pot or Dutch oven with a lid can be used for soups and stews or as a pasta pot. A 1- and 2-quart saucepan (with a steamer insert) can take care of the rest.

SKILLETS: A good 12-inch skillet can handle most needs. It can be used to sauté, stir-fry, and braise. I find a good nonstick skillet to be indispensable. I also love my cast-iron skillet for certain things, such as cornbread, but it's heavy for everyday use. A smaller skillet is also handy when you have only a small amount of ingredients to cook.

OTHER KITCHEN TOOLS: You'll also need the various items used to prepare foods, including a cutting board, mixing bowls, baking pans, measuring cups and spoons, whisks, spatulas, vegetable peeler, and colander. It's also handy to have a box grater, salad spinner, a hand mixer or stand mixer, parchment paper, and cheesecloth.

WHAT'S IN A NAME?

There is an ongoing debate among vegans regarding the use of animal product descriptors to describe plant-based foods. One school of thought subscribes to the idea that plant-based foods should not be referred to as meat, milk, bacon, sausage, cheese, and so on. Others (myself included) believe that the animal agriculture industry doesn't own those words—many of them are, in fact, used to describe plant foods such as nut meats, coconut milk, and so on. The fact is, a lot of times these words are used as a simple way to help people know what to expect or how to use a particular plant food.

Let's take the word meat, for example. It was used in the Bible to mean "sustenance" and was literally referring to plant-based foods: "And God said, Behold, I have given you every herb bearing seed, which is upon the face of all the earth, and every tree, in which is the fruit of a tree yielding seed; to you it shall be for meat" (Genesis 1:29).

Meatloaf, meatballs, and sausage, for example, are all foods made by seasoning ingredients in a certain way and then shaping and cooking them. The seasoned ingredients can be made from ground animal flesh, or it can be made with plant-based ingredients. The appearance, texture, and flavor will be similar but, more importantly, the use will be the same—whether made with animal or plant, meatballs will still be served with pasta and tomato sauce, meatloaf will still be served with potatoes and gravy, and sausage will still fry up with onions and peppers for a great sandwich. As vegans, we simply choose to make these foods with plant-based ingredients. Plant-based meats abound—they are not "fake meats"—they are simply "plant meats." Plant-based milks are widely available now, and several cutting-edge companies are producing cultured plant-based cheeses, rich and creamy mayonnaise, and even vegan eggs.

Naysayers may claim that we enjoy such foods because we "miss the meat" (i.e., animal products) when the reality is that we simply appreciate the flavor, texture, and variety that can be enjoyed with plant-based ingredients. We also have a right to enjoy the traditions and comfort foods of our heritage without the need for animal flesh.

It's also a convention of communication to be able to quickly "shorthand" a description of what's for dinner. For example, if I'm cooking sautéed patties made with shredded hearts of palm combined with celery, onion, and seasonings, it's much easier to say "we're having palm-crab cakes" because they will have a similar texture and appearance to seafood crab cakes, and while not tasting the same, they have a pleasant flavor that goes well with the same sauces and sides you'd enjoy with traditional crab cakes.

USING THE RECIPES

The recipes in the book are organized primarily according to what type of animal products they replace in a vegan diet, such as dairy products, meat, charcuterie, seafood, and condiments. There is also a flour chapter featuring recipes for pie dough, bread, and biscuits, and a dessert chapter where you'll find recipes in categories that typically contain animal products, such as tiramisu, cheesecake, and lemon meringue pie. The Vegetable "Steak-Out" chapter features recipes in which certain vegetables, such as jackfruit, cauliflower, and portobello mushrooms, are the resident veganizers.

The recipes in the chapters can be divided into two groups: the basic ingredient or food that typically contains animal products, followed by recipes that incorporate these foods to make a veganized dish. For example, the Handcrafted Lasagna recipe contains instructions for assembling and baking the various components that make up the lasagna, with page references to recipes for each of the components, including homemade tomato sauce, pasta, and three kinds of cheese. If you make all of the components from scratch, it will take several hours to get the lasagna on the table. Not all of us have that kind of time, so it's important to know that you can use store-bought alternatives for any or all of the components of this recipe and you'll still have a delicious lasagna. In my own kitchen, I may not always have the time to make my own pasta dough, but I always make my own ricotta and melty cheese, and usually I make my own sauce as well, but I always have a few jars of marinara in the pantry for emergencies.

The same holds for the other recipes in this book that call for basics such as nondairy milk, vegan butter, and so on. Like many of us, you may not have time to make these basic ingredients yourself, especially the ones that are easy and economical to buy in the store. That's perfectly fine. Just knowing that you can make everything from scratch if you want to can be empowering in its own right.

The recipes in this book were developed to appeal to cooks of all skill levels and abilities, from seasoned cooks to novices, using easy-to-find ingredients. With an emphasis on fresh whole foods, the recipes are cholesterol-free, low in saturated fat, and high in fiber and complex carbohydrates. Most importantly, these delicious recipes offer endless variety that will help make menu planning easier than ever. With these recipes, I hope you will feel empowered knowing you can make virtually anything you want to eat in a kinder, gentler, and healthier way. So dig in, have fun, and Veganize It!

CHAPTER 2

DAIRY-FREE AND EGG-FREE, FREE, TOO

Once upon a time, not too many years ago, nondairy milks were found only in natural foods stores in aseptic containers. Nowadays, virtually every supermarket dairy case is lined with cartons of plant-based milks made from soy, almonds, cashews, coconut, and more. The once hard-to-find vegan sour cream, cream cheese, mayo, and butter alternatives are easy to locate as well.

Even with this availability, there are still people who prefer to make these ingredients from scratch and others who find the cost of the commercial products to be prohibitive (although, while some are more expensive, there are others that are actually cheaper or comparable in price to their homemade counterparts).

In this chapter, I provide veganized recipes for the most popular dairy products while also noting my favorite commercial plant-based brands, where applicable, for those who are interested. Many of the staple recipes in this chapter are used to make other recipes throughout the book, such as Meaty-Cheesy Pizza, Spinach-Feta Quesadillas, and vegan cheesecakes, as well as the mayonnaise-based sauces in chapter 7.

There are also a few recipes in this chapter for veganized egg dishes, including a frittata, a scramble, and an omelet (see sidebar, page 28); however, egg replacers that are used in baking are detailed on page 257 in the dessert chapter.

NUT MILK   28

ALMOST-INSTANT
NUT MILK   29

COCONUT MILK   30

OAT MILK   31

CASHEW CREAM   32

CASHEW SOUR CREAM   33

EASY VEGAN YOGURT   34

CREAMY CASHEW MAYO   35

EASY VEGAN BUTTER   36

AQUAFABA BUTTER   37

NUT BUTTER   38

BASIC WHITE SAUCE   39

CASHEW CREAM CHEESE   40

SEASONED TOFU RICOTTA   41

NUT-PARM   42

MELTY VEGAN CHEESE   43

CHEDDARY SAUCE   44

SMOKY QUESO SAUCE   45

SAY (VEGANIZED) CHEESE!   46

TOFU FETA   48

HTIPITI (FETA SPREAD)   49

SPINACH-ARTICHOKE DIP   51

PRETZEL-CRUSTED
CHEDDARY LOG   52

BACON-TOPPED MAC
UNCHEESE   54

CHEESY BROCCOLI SOUP   56

LOADED BAKED POTATOES   57

SPINACH AND MUSHROOM-
BACON QUICHE   60

SPINACH-FETA
QUESADILLAS   62

CHICKPEA FLOUR OMELETS   63

CHEESY MUSHROOM
SCRAMBLE   66

VIVE LA FRENCH TOAST   67

BREAKFAST NACHOS   69

NUT MILK

MAKES ABOUT 4 CUPS

1 cup almonds or cashews, soaked overnight, then drained

3 cups water

Pinch of salt

Almond milk is my favorite all-purpose nondairy milk, although you can use cashews in this recipe, if you prefer.

1   Combine all the ingredients in a high-speed blender and blend until smooth. Strain the mixture through a fine-mesh strainer or a nut milk bag.

2   Transfer the milk to a glass bottle or jar with a tight-fitting lid and chill until ready to serve. It will keep well in the refrigerator for up to 3 days.

VEGAN ALTERNATIVES TO EGGS

There are several ways to veganize eggs in your cooking, but the egg alternative you choose has everything to do with the function of the egg in any given recipe. For example, if you are looking to replace eggs in an egg-centered dish such as an omelet or frittata, the choice would be vastly different from the egg alternatives that are used in baking. For a list of egg replacers used in baking, please refer to the sidebar on page 257. If you're looking for great egg-free eggy dishes, this chapter features the following recipes: Chickpea Flour Omelets (page 63), Cheesy Mushroom Scramble (page 66), and Spinach and Mushroom-Bacon Quiche (page 60).

ALMOST-INSTANT NUT MILK

MAKES ABOUT 2 CUPS

Whether you make your own nondairy milk or buy it at the store, there are still times when you run out and don't have time to make a new batch or go to the store. This almost-instant nut milk can save the day.

2 tablespoons almond butter or cashew butter, store-bought or homemade (page 38)

2 cups water

1 Combine the nut butter and water in a high-speed blender and blend until smooth.

2 Transfer the milk to a glass bottle or jar with a tight-fitting lid and chill until ready to serve. It will keep well in the refrigerator for up to 3 days.

COCONUT MILK

1 cup unsweetened shredded coconut

3 cups water

Pinch of salt

Coconut milk is delicious and a good choice if you are nut-sensitive, as coconut is a drupe (not a nut).

1   Combine all the ingredients in a high-speed blender and blend until smooth. Strain the mixture through a nut milk bag.

2   Transfer the milk to a glass bottle or jar with a tight-fitting lid and chill until ready to serve. It will keep well in the refrigerator for up to 3 days.

DAIRY DOUBLES

Dairy milk can easily be replaced with non-dairy milk in a one-to-one ratio. Whether you make your own nondairy milk or buy it ready-made from among the wide variety of nondairy milks on the market, the choice is yours. I like cashew milk or almond milk for a creamy, light flavor, or coconut milk for its richness. Opt for unsweetened varieties so you can use them in both sweet and savory recipes. Full-fat canned coconut milk or soy creamer is a great stand-in for heavy cream. To replace buttermilk, combine 1 tablespoon fresh lemon juice or cider vinegar and 1 cup nondairy milk, whisk to blend, and let sit for 10 minutes.

OAT MILK

Oat milk is a little bland for drinking but is a good choice to use in cooking such as creamy soups or casseroles. It is a bit thicker than soy milk because of the fiber in the oats.

Note: Be sure to use certified gluten-free oats if you have a gluten sensitivity.

½ cup old-fashioned rolled oats

1½ cups water

Pinch of salt

1   Combine the oats, water, and salt in a high-speed blender and blend until smooth.

2   Transfer the milk to a glass bottle or jar with a tight-fitting lid and chill until ready to serve. It will keep well in the refrigerator for up to 3 days.

CASHEW CREAM

1 cup raw cashew pieces, soaked in boiling hot water for 30 minutes, then drained

½ cup water, or more if needed

Cashew cream is made the same way you make cashew milk, only using less water. The thick creamy goodness that is cashew cream is a revelation and makes magic happen in many vegan recipes. As written, the cashew cream will be very thick, ideally suited to make Cashew Chantilly Cream (page 249) and other recipes where a thick cream is needed. To make a thinner cream, just add more water, a little at a time, until it is your desired consistency.

1 Transfer the drained cashews to a high-speed blender. Add the water and blend until completely smooth and creamy. The cashew cream should be very thick. For a thinner cream, add a little more water, 1 tablespoon at a time.

2 Transfer to a bowl with a tight-fitting lid and chill until ready to serve. It will keep well in the refrigerator for up to 3 days.

CASHEW SOUR CREAM

MAKES
ABOUT
1 CUP

This plant-based sour cream delivers a creamy texture and a just-tart-enough flavor. Use it to top baked potatoes or in any recipe calling for sour cream.

1 Combine the drained cashews, milk, vinegar, melted coconut oil, and salt in a high-speed blender and blend until very smooth.

2 Transfer the mixture to a container, cover tightly, and refrigerate for at least 2 hours to chill and thicken before use. Keep refrigerated for up to 5 days.

¾ cup raw cashews, soaked in hot water for 30 minutes, then drained

⅓ cup plain unsweetened almond milk, store-bought or homemade (page 28)

2 tablespoons rice vinegar

1½ tablespoons refined coconut oil, melted

⅛ teaspoon salt

EASY VEGAN YOGURT

⅓ cup raw cashew pieces, soaked in hot water for 30 minutes, then drained

⅓ cup plain unsweetened almond milk, store-bought or homemade (page 28)

¼ cup fresh lemon juice

½ teaspoon sugar

Pinch of salt

1 (12.3-ounce) box extra-firm silken tofu, drained and crumbled

If you want a yogurty flavor but don't have a yogurt maker, try this easy shortcut recipe. For a fruity yogurt, blend in your favorite fruit-sweetened jam.

1   In a high-speed blender, combine the drained cashews, almond milk, lemon juice, sugar, and salt and blend until very smooth. Add the tofu and blend until smooth and creamy. Taste and adjust the seasonings, if needed.

2   Transfer the mixture to a bowl or jar with a tight-fitting lid. Cover and refrigerate for at least 3 hours or overnight to chill and thicken before use. Stir before using. The yogurt will keep well in the refrigerator for up to 5 days.

CREAMY CASHEW MAYO

MAKES
1½ CUPS

Personally I never liked the "eggy" flavor of traditional mayonnaise, but if you do, then add a pinch of kala namak (Himalayan black salt) to the mixture.

⅔ cup raw cashews, soaked in hot water for 30 minutes, then drained

½ cup plain unsweetened almond milk, store-bought or homemade (page 28)

2 tablespoons rice vinegar

1 tablespoon fresh lemon juice

¾ teaspoon salt

½ teaspoon mustard powder

¼ cup olive oil

1 Combine the drained cashews, milk, vinegar, lemon juice, salt, and mustard powder in a high-speed blender and blend until smooth. Let the mixture sit for 5 minutes.

2 With the machine running, slowly pour in the olive oil in a thin stream, blending until very smooth. Taste and adjust the seasonings, if needed. Transfer the mixture to a bowl or jar with a tight-fitting lid and refrigerate for at least 30 minutes to thicken. This mayo will keep well in the refrigerator for about 1 week.

EASY VEGAN BUTTER

¼ cup plain unsweetened almond milk, store-bought or homemade (page 28)

1 teaspoon rice vinegar

½ teaspoon salt

⅛ teaspoon ground turmeric

¾ cup refined coconut oil

¼ cup grapeseed or sunflower oil

Be sure to use refined coconut oil to avoid giving the butter a coconut flavor. If making homemade butter is not your thing, try Earth Balance Buttery Spread, available in most supermarkets.

Note: For a firmer texture, add 1 teaspoon soy lecithin liquid or 2 teaspoons soy lecithin granules to the mixture.

1   In a blender or food processor, combine the milk, vinegar, salt, and turmeric and let it sit for 10 minutes.

2   Heat the coconut oil in a microwave-safe bowl in the microwave until it is just melted. Let it cool slightly, then add it to the mixture in the blender or food processor, along with the grapeseed oil. Blend until smooth and thoroughly combined.

3   Transfer to a container or butter mold and refrigerate to set and firm up, at least 1 hour. Keep tightly covered in the refrigerator for 3 to 4 weeks or wrap tightly and store in the freezer for up to 6 months.

AQUAFABA BUTTER

Aquafaba (water-bean) is the name given to the liquid poured off cooked or canned chickpeas or white beans that, when beaten, can be used to make everything from a vegan meringue to butter. Other recipes for aquafaba butter call for special ingredients such as lecithin, but I prefer to keep it simple, using only everyday supermarket ingredients. For a softer butter, bring to room temperature for 10 to 15 minutes before using.

⅓ cup refined coconut oil (measured when solid)

1 tablespoon grapeseed or sunflower oil

2½ tablespoons white bean aquafaba, at room temperature

¾ teaspoon rice vinegar

¼ teaspoon salt

Pinch of turmeric (for color)

1 Melt the coconut oil in a small saucepan over low heat until it is nearly all liquid. Remove from the heat and stir in the grapeseed oil.

2 Combine the aquafaba, vinegar, salt, and turmeric in a small blender or in a bowl, if using an immersion blender or whisk. Blend until smooth and frothy. With the blender running (or while whisking), slowly pour in the oil mixture, incorporating after each addition. Continue blending for a few minutes until thickened.

3 Transfer the mixture to a small container such as a ramekin. Refrigerate until firm, about 2 hours. The butter is now ready to use. Store tightly covered in the refrigerator for up to a week.

NUT BUTTER

3 cups dry almonds or cashews

Organic raw almond or cashew butter can be expensive to buy, so if you buy nuts in bulk at a good price, it can save you money to make your own. This easy preparation works in any recipe calling for almond or cashew butter, in this book or any other. Because cashews are naturally softer than almonds, cashew butter takes slightly less time to make than almond butter.

1   Place the nuts into a food processor and pulse into small crumbs. Turn the machine on and let it run for 12 to 15 minutes, stopping frequently (every 1 to 2 minutes) to scrape down the sides of the bowl with a spatula. The butter is ready when the nuts have released their oils and the mixture is smooth and creamy.

2   Transfer to a glass jar or small container and store at room temperature for up to 2 weeks or in the refrigerator for up to 6 months.

BASIC WHITE SAUCE

This rich-tasting sauce can be used as an all-purpose white sauce. It also makes a great base for casseroles or as a nice alternative topping to cheese on lasagna.

2 tablespoons sunflower or grapeseed oil

2 tablespoons unbleached all-purpose flour

2 cups plain unsweetened almond milk, store-bought or homemade (page 28)

½ teaspoon salt

¼ cup raw cashews, soaked in boiling water for 30 minutes, then drained

1   Heat the oil in a medium saucepan and whisk in the flour. Whisk it over medium heat for a minute or two to cook the raw taste from the flour. Do not let it brown. Stir in 1½ cups of the milk and cook, stirring, until it comes to a boil. Decrease the heat to a simmer, add the salt, and cook 3 minutes longer, then remove from the heat and set aside.

2   In a high-speed blender, combine the drained cashews with the remaining ½ cup milk and blend until very smooth.

3   Scrape the mixture from the saucepan into the blender and blend for a few seconds, then pour the mixture back into the same saucepan. Cook, stirring, over medium-high heat until it comes to a boil, then decrease the heat to a simmer and cook, stirring, until thickened.

VARIATIONS

Make it cheesy Add 2 tablespoons nutritional yeast.

Make it curry Add 1 to 2 teaspoons curry powder or paste.

Make it hot and spicy Add 1 to 2 tablespoons sriracha sauce or pureed canned chipotle in adobo sauce.

Make it pumpkin-y Replace ½ cup of the nondairy milk with ½ cup pumpkin puree; add 2 tablespoons nutritional yeast and ½ teaspoon pumpkin pie spice.

CASHEW CREAM CHEESE

¾ cup raw cashews, soaked in hot water for 30 minutes, then drained

3 tablespoons refined coconut oil, melted

1 tablespoon plain unsweetened almond milk, store-bought or homemade (page 28)

1 tablespoon rice vinegar

1 tablespoon fresh lemon juice

½ teaspoon salt

Use in recipes calling for cream cheese. For an herbed cream cheese, add 1 to 2 tablespoons chopped fresh herbs (I like a combination of parsley, chives, and dill) and serve as a dip or spread. For a fruity spread, add 2 to 3 tablespoons of your favorite jam to the chilled cream cheese.

1 Combine all the ingredients in a high-speed blender and blend until completely smooth and creamy.

2 Transfer the mixture to a bowl or jar with a tight-fitting lid. Cover and refrigerate for at least 2 hours to chill and thicken before use. It will keep well in the refrigerator for up to 5 days.

SEASONED TOFU RICOTTA

MAKES ABOUT 2 CUPS

This makes a firm-style ricotta already seasoned for use in lasagna or other savory dishes.

Crumble the tofu in a bowl or a food processor. Add the remaining ingredients and mash or pulse until well mixed. Don't overmix. Taste and adjust the seasonings, if needed. Use immediately or cover and refrigerate until needed. It will keep well in the refrigerator for up to 5 days.

1 (12- to 16-ounce) package firm tofu, drained and well pressed

3 tablespoons minced fresh parsley

3 tablespoons nutritional yeast

2 tablespoons olive oil

1 tablespoon rice vinegar

1 teaspoon garlic powder

1 teaspoon onion powder

1 teaspoon dried oregano

1 teaspoon dried basil

1 teaspoon salt

½ teaspoon ground black pepper

NUT-PARM

½ cup slivered raw almonds

½ cup raw walnut pieces

¼ cup nutritional yeast

¾ teaspoon salt

This is an easy and tasty alternative to Parmesan cheese. Use it as a topping on pasta dishes, salads, or anywhere else you want a salty, cheesy flavor.

1 Combine all the ingredients in a food processor and process until finely ground.

2 Transfer to a covered container or shaker and keep refrigerated for up to 2 weeks.

MELTY VEGAN CHEESE

MAKES ABOUT 2 CUPS

The secret to a "melty" vegan cheese is tapioca starch. Use this to top the pizzas on pages 237 and 240, the lasagna on page 221, or anywhere else you want a nice melty cheese.

1 cup raw cashews, soaked in hot water for 30 minutes, then drained

2 cups water

5 tablespoons tapioca starch

2 tablespoons nutritional yeast

2 teaspoons light-colored miso paste

2 teaspoons rice vinegar

2 teaspoons fresh lemon juice

1 teaspoon salt

1 Combine the cashews and water in a high-speed blender or food processor. Add the tapioca, nutritional yeast, miso, vinegar, lemon juice, and salt. Blend until completely smooth.

2 Transfer the mixture to a saucepan and cook for 2 to 3 minutes over medium-high heat, stirring constantly. Watch carefully so the mixture doesn't burn. Decrease the heat to medium and continue cooking and stirring until thickened, about 2 minutes longer. It is now ready to use in recipes.

VARIATION

Melty Cheddary Cheese Increase the nutritional yeast to 4 tablespoons; add 1 teaspoon smoked paprika and ½ teaspoon ground turmeric.

CHEDDARY SAUCE

1¼ cups raw cashews, soaked in hot water for 30 minutes, then drained

⅓ cup nutritional yeast

2 tablespoons jarred chopped pimientos or roasted red bell pepper, drained and blotted dry

1 tablespoon beer, white wine, or dry sherry (optional, but recommended)

1 tablespoon rice vinegar

1½ teaspoons light-colored miso paste

1 teaspoon salt

½ teaspoon smoked paprika

½ teaspoon onion powder

½ teaspoon prepared yellow mustard

¼ teaspoon turmeric

1 cup plain unsweetened almond milk, or more, store-bought or homemade (page 28)

Use this creamy, flavorful sauce anytime you want to add an exclamation point to whatever you're serving. I use this sauce to make mac uncheese or as a topping for baked potatoes and steamed or roasted vegetables. With the addition of some spices and a little heat, it can also be used to top nachos and enchiladas. Even more remarkable, just omit the nondairy milk and add melted coconut oil and you have the makings of a fantastic cheddary cheese log (page 47). If not using beer or sherry, add an extra ½ teaspoon of miso paste.

Combine all the ingredients in a high-speed blender. Process until the mixture is pureed and smooth, scraping down the sides as needed. The sauce is now ready to use in recipes. Use as is, or heat gently in a saucepan for a minute or two, if desired, stirring in a little more milk, if needed, for a thinner sauce. Store leftovers in the refrigerator in a tightly sealed container for up to 5 days.

SMOKY QUESO SAUCE

This easy-cheesy sauce is great for nachos or folded into cooked pasta for a zesty mac and cheese. If chopped pimientos are unavailable, you can substitute 3 tablespoons chopped roasted red bell pepper.

1 Combine all the ingredients in a blender and blend until smooth.

2 Transfer to a saucepan and cook over medium heat, stirring constantly, until thickened, about 5 minutes. Taste and adjust the seasonings, if needed. Use as desired.

1 (2-ounce) jar chopped pimientos, drained

1 teaspoon canned chipotle chiles in adobo sauce

⅓ cup nutritional yeast

3 tablespoons cornstarch

½ teaspoon smoked paprika

½ teaspoon mustard powder

½ teaspoon onion powder

½ teaspoon garlic powder

1 teaspoon salt

1 tablespoon olive oil

2 teaspoons fresh lemon juice

2 teaspoons rice vinegar

1½ cups plain unsweetened almond milk, store-bought or homemade (page 28), or water

SAY (VEGANIZED) CHEESE!

MAKES
ABOUT
1½ CUPS

1½ cups raw cashews, soaked in hot water for 30 minutes, then drained

⅓ cup nutritional yeast

3 tablespoons melted coconut oil

2 tablespoons fresh lemon juice

1 tablespoon dry white wine or water

1 teaspoon white miso paste

½ teaspoon onion powder

¼ teaspoon salt

Coating of choice: Fresh or dried herbs of choice; paprika; ground walnuts

Create your own vegan cheese board beginning with this super-basic cheesy wheel and then riff off the variations that follow for your own favorite selection of flavors and shapes. Just add crackers (and wine, if you like) and it's a party!

1 Line a 4- x 2-inch springform pan or a 2-cup ramekin with plastic wrap, draping the ends over the sides.

2 Combine all the ingredients (except the coating) in a food processor, pulsing until smooth. Scrape down the sides as needed. Scoop the mixture into the prepared pan and bring up the sides of the plastic wrap to cover the top of the cheese mixture. Press down on the cheese mixture to spread it evenly in the pan and flatten the top. Refrigerate for 3 hours, then remove from the refrigerator and remove from the springform pan.

3 Remove the film wrap and dredge the cheese wheel in your choice of coatings until covered, pressing the coating into the cheese. Transfer the coated cheese wheel to a plate, cover, and refrigerate until ready to serve.

Two-for-One Cheesy Wheels It's easy to make two 1-inch layers out of your 2-inch-high cheesy wheel. First, place 3 toothpicks as markers around the 1-inch point at the back and side edges to use as a guide. Next, place a piece of dental floss (about 2 feet long) around the edge of the cheese wheel, setting the floss on top of the toothpicks. With the floss wrapped around the perimeter of the cheese wheel, cross the ends of the floss and hold each end in each hand. Pull each end out and away from the cheese, allowing the floss to cut through the center of the cheese as the circle of floss tightens. This will create two cheese wheels, 1 inch high.

Cheese Log Scoop the mixture into the center of a sheet of plastic wrap and twist to form a log. Coat with your choice of crushed pretzels, toasted nuts, or minced fresh herbs.

Cheese Ball Scoop the mixture into the center of a sheet of plastic wrap and twist to form a ball. Coat with your choice of crushed pretzels, toasted nuts, or minced fresh herbs.

Creamy Chive Cheese Add 1 to 1½ tablespoons dehydrated minced chives and 1 tablespoon vegan cream cheese or sour cream to the cheese mixture, then proceed with the recipe. Coat the chilled cheese wheel in dehydrated minced chives.

Holiday Cheese Shape the cheesy mixture into your choice of a wheel, log, or ball.

Coat with minced fresh parsley or crushed pistachios and stud with small pieces of chopped pimientos (if using parsley) or dried cranberries (if using pistachios).

Porcini Cheese Add 2 teaspoons porcini powder to the cheese mixture, then proceed with the recipe. Coat the chilled cheese wheel with porcini powder.

Cheesy Christmas Tree Place a sheet of parchment paper or plastic wrap on a small cutting board. Scoop the cheesy mixture into the center of the plastic wrap and top with a sheet of plastic wrap, then use your hands to shape the mixture into a triangle shape to make your tree. It should be about 1 inch thick. Top the cheesy mixture with another small cutting board (or other flat object) to be sure the "tree" is even. Refrigerate for 2 to 3 hours. Remove from the fridge, remove the plastic wrap, and smooth the tree shape, using a knife to even up the sides and bottom. Shape a small amount of the cheese mixture that you trimmed from the tree into a small piece of trunk and attach it at the bottom of the tree. Press your choice of minced fresh parsley or crushed pistachios evenly into the cheesy tree, on the top and on the sides, then place bits of pimiento (if using parsley) or dried cranberries (if using pistachios) onto the "tree" to represent holiday ornaments. Use a thin, wide metal spatula to transfer to a plate or cheese board and chill until ready to serve.

TOFU FETA

6 tablespoons olive oil

3 tablespoons rice vinegar

3 tablespoons fresh lemon juice

1 teaspoon light miso paste

1 teaspoon salt

½ teaspoon dried oregano

1 (12- to 16-ounce) package extra-firm tofu, drained, well pressed, and blotted dry

When you marinate extra-firm tofu with just the right ingredients, the result tastes amazingly like feta.

In a bowl, combine the oil, vinegar, lemon juice, miso, salt, and oregano, stirring to mix well. Cut the tofu into ½-inch dice and add it to the marinade, turning gently to coat well. Cover and set aside at room temperature for 1 hour. If not using right away, refrigerate until needed. It will keep well in the refrigerator for up to 5 days.

THICKENERS BEYOND CORNSTARCH

Cornstarch is a common binder and thickener, but there are other options as well, including the following:

Agar-agar (powder or flakes) is a thickener made from seaweed that can be used as a replacement for gelatin.

Arrowroot powder can be used in recipes calling for cornstarch.

Kuzu root starch is a natural thickener that can be found at natural foods stores.

Tapioca flour or starch is a lighter option than either cornstarch or arrowroot.

HTIPITI (FETA SPREAD)

MAKES
1 CUP

Serve this flavorful dip with toasted pita chips or raw veggies. It also makes a great spread for a wrap sandwich or crostini. If you prefer a smoother dip, you can blend the ingredients in a food processor. You can also make it into a sauce by adding a few tablespoons of nondairy milk and processing the mixture until smooth.

Mash the tofu in a bowl. Add the minced pepperoncini, garlic, oil, lemon juice, oregano, red pepper flakes, and black pepper. Stir to mix well. The mixture should be well blended, but with some texture. Cover and chill for 1 to 2 hours before serving. Store in the refrigerator for up to 3 days.

1 cup Tofu Feta (page 48)

1 pepperoncini pickled pepper, finely minced

1 garlic clove, finely minced

2 tablespoons olive oil

1 tablespoon fresh lemon juice

1 teaspoon chopped fresh oregano

¼ teaspoon red pepper flakes

⅛ teaspoon ground black pepper

SPINACH-ARTICHOKE DIP

As a lover of all things artichoke, I find this is my favorite dip. It even makes a great pasta sauce when thinned out with some plant-based milk and a little extra salt and pepper.

1 Preheat the oven to 400°F. Microwave the spinach in a bowl for 45 seconds or steam it for 1 minute until limp. Set aside.

2 In a food processor, combine the cream cheese, mayo, lemon juice, garlic, salt, and pepper. Blend until very smooth.

3 When the spinach is cool enough to handle, squeeze the liquid from it and add it to the mixture in the food processor, along with the artichokes. Pulse to combine, leaving some texture. Do not overprocess. Transfer to an ovenproof baking dish, and bake uncovered for 15 minutes, or until hot and bubbly. Remove and let cool slightly.

1 bag (9 ounces) baby spinach

1 cup vegan cream cheese, store-bought or homemade (page 40)

3 tablespoons vegan mayo, store-bought or homemade (page 35)

2 tablespoons fresh lemon juice

2 large garlic cloves, crushed

¾ teaspoon salt

⅛ teaspoon ground black pepper

2 jars (12 ounces each) marinated artichoke hearts, well drained

PRETZEL-CRUSTED CHEDDARY LOG

1⅓ cups raw cashews, soaked in boiling water for 30 minutes, then drained

3 tablespoons jarred chopped pimientos or roasted red bell pepper, drained and blotted dry

1 tablespoon rice vinegar

1½ teaspoons light-colored miso paste

½ teaspoon Dijon mustard

¼ cup nutritional yeast

1 teaspoon salt

½ teaspoon onion powder

½ teaspoon smoked paprika

¼ teaspoon turmeric

½ cup refined coconut oil, melted

1 cup crushed pretzels

VARIATIONS

Omit the smoked paprika and turmeric for a lighter color and flavor. Instead of rolling the log in crushed pretzels, roll it in your choice of minced fresh parsley, snipped chives, chopped dried cranberries, or toasted ground walnuts.

My favorite mac and cheese sauce was the inspiration (and base) for this creamy, flavorful, cheesy log. By eliminating the nondairy milk and adding melted coconut oil, the sauce that everyone said was "good enough to drink" transformed into a cheesy log that was good enough to eat! Everyone loves it —even non-vegans. Best of all, it takes only minutes of hands-on time—the rest of the time is spent letting the cashews soak and allowing the cheese log to firm up. Serve with your favorite crackers.

1   In a high-speed blender or food processor, combine the cashews, pimientos, vinegar, miso, and mustard. Process until the mixture is a smooth paste. Add the nutritional yeast, salt, onion powder, paprika, and turmeric. Process until smooth, scraping down the sides as needed.

2   Add the melted coconut oil and process until completely smooth, scraping the sides as needed. Transfer the soft mixture to a shallow bowl or plate lined with a sheet of plastic wrap, folding the sides in to loosely shape the mixture into a log about 6 inches long. Cover and refrigerate for 2 to 3 hours, or until firm.

3   Pick up the cheese with the plastic wrap from the bowl and transfer it to a flat work surface. Use your hands to shape the cheese into a smooth log. Roll the log in the crushed pretzels, pressing to make them adhere. Transfer the log to a plate and refrigerate until very firm, 3 hours or longer.

BACON-TOPPED MAC UNCHEESE

SERVES
4 TO 6

2 teaspoons olive oil

½ cup finely chopped vegan bacon, store-bought or homemade (pages 106–107)

8 to 12 ounces elbow macaroni or other bite-size pasta shape

1½ cups plain unsweetened almond milk, store-bought or homemade (page 28)

⅓ cup raw cashew pieces, soaked in hot water for 30 minutes, then drained

2 tablespoons cornstarch, tapioca flour, or arrowroot

⅓ cup nutritional yeast flakes

1 tablespoon light-colored miso paste

1 heaping tablespoon tomato paste

2 teaspoons cider vinegar or fresh lemon juice

½ teaspoon liquid smoke

½ teaspoon smoked paprika

½ teaspoon mustard powder

½ teaspoon onion powder

½ teaspoon garlic powder

¼ teaspoon ground turmeric

½ teaspoon salt, or more to taste

A touch of smoky bacony flavor makes everyone's favorite comfort food even better. Serve with a crisp green salad or roasted veggies or add your favorite cooked vegetable to the mac uncheese to make it a one-dish meal. If you don't have homemade nut milk on hand, use store-bought almond or cashew milk—just be sure it's unsweetened. Plain, unsweetened soy or oat milk may also be used instead.

1   Heat the oil in a small skillet over medium heat. Add the chopped bacon and cook, stirring occasionally, until crisp and browned, about 5 minutes. Be careful not to burn. Set aside.

2   Cook the pasta in a pot of boiling salted water until al dente, or follow package directions. Drain and leave in the strainer.

3   In a blender, combine the milk, cashews, cornstarch, yeast flakes, miso, tomato paste, vinegar, liquid smoke, paprika, mustard powder, onion powder, garlic powder, turmeric, and salt. Blend until smooth and creamy.

4   Pour the sauce into the pot in which the pasta was cooked and cook over medium-high heat, stirring, until the sauce is hot, bubbly, and thickened, about 4 minutes.

5   Return the pasta to the pot and stir gently to combine with the sauce and heat through. Serve hot, sprinkled with the chopped cooked bacon.

CHEESY BROCCOLI SOUP

1 tablespoon olive oil or water

1 yellow onion, coarsely chopped

1 russet potato, peeled and finely chopped or shredded

1 pound broccoli, trimmed and coarsely chopped

3 cups vegetable broth, store-bought or homemade (page 182)

Salt and ground black pepper

2 cups Cheddary Sauce (page 44)

This easy, cheesy soup proves that you don't need dairy cream to have a creamy soup and you don't need dairy cheese to add a cheesy flavor.

1 In a large soup pot, heat the oil over medium heat. Add the onion, cover, and cook until softened, about 5 minutes. Add the potato and broccoli and stir in the broth. Season with salt and pepper to taste. Bring to a boil, then decrease the heat to low and simmer, uncovered, until the vegetables are tender, about 20 minutes.

2 Use an immersion blender to puree the soup directly in the pot or transfer to a high-speed blender or food processor and puree, in batches if necessary, then return to the pot. Stir in the sauce, then taste and adjust the seasonings, if needed. Reheat the soup over low heat until hot. To serve, ladle soup into bowls and serve hot.

LOADED BAKED POTATOES

SERVES 4

Depending on how much you "load" them (and what you load them with!), these baked potatoes can be a meal in themselves. Start with the classic version in the main recipe, or venture into some of the more exotic variations that follow the recipe. Consider making a double batch to freeze some for another meal—just thaw, cover with foil, and reheat in a 375°F oven for about 30 minutes, or until hot. You could also use small potatoes for an appetizer version.

4 russet potatoes, well scrubbed and dried

1 cup Cheddary Sauce (page 44)

1 cup Coconut Bacon Bits (page 108)

½ cup vegan sour cream, store-bought or homemade (page 33)

2 tablespoons snipped fresh chives or 2 scallions, minced

½ teaspoon salt

¼ teaspoon ground black pepper

1 Preheat the oven to 400°F. Line a baking sheet with parchment paper or aluminum foil.

2 Pierce the potatoes in several places with a fork. Arrange the potatoes directly on the center rack and bake until tender, 50 to 60 minutes. Remove the potatoes from the oven and set aside for 10 minutes or until cool enough to handle.

3 Cut the baked potatoes in half lengthwise and scoop the insides into a bowl, leaving about ¼ inch of the potato with the skin so they're sturdy enough to stuff. To the bowl, add half of the cheesy sauce, half of the bacon bits, the sour cream, chives, salt, and pepper and mash well to combine. Fill the potato skins evenly with the potato mixture. Top each potato half evenly with the remaining cheesy sauce and bacon bits. Arrange the stuffed potatoes on the prepared baking sheet and bake until the filling is hot, 10 to 15 minutes.

OMIT the cheesy sauce, bacon bits, sour cream, and chives. REPLACE WITH any of the following combinations and proceed with the recipe:

Artichoke-Hummus Potatoes Heat 2 teaspoons olive oil in a skillet over medium heat. Add 4 chopped scallions and 1 teaspoon thyme. Drain 1 (12-ounce) jar of marinated artichoke hearts and chop well. Add the artichokes to the skillet, stirring to mix. Transfer the artichoke mixture to the bowl with the scooped-out potato, add ½ cup hummus and ¼ cup nondairy milk, and mix well. Taste and adjust the seasonings, if needed. Fill the potato skins with the mixture. Sprinkle with some panko crumbs, if desired. Arrange the stuffed potatoes on the prepared baking sheet and bake until the filling is hot, about 10 minutes.

Indian Samosa Potatoes Heat 2 teaspoons olive oil in a skillet over medium heat. Add 1 chopped onion, 1 tablespoon curry powder, 2 teaspoons grated ginger, and ½ teaspoon mustard seeds and cook, stirring, until the onion is tender, about 5 minutes. Cut the baked potatoes in half lengthwise and scoop the insides into a bowl. Add the onion mixture, ¼ cup chopped cilantro, and 1 cup peas, and mash well. Stuff the mixture into the skins. Arrange the stuffed potatoes on the prepared baking sheet and bake until the filling is hot, 10 to 15 minutes. Top with vegan yogurt.

Creamy Spinach Potatoes Heat 2 tablespoons olive oil in a skillet. Add 2 chopped shallots and cook until tender. Stir in 2 tablespoons all-purpose flour and cook, stirring, for 2 minutes. Add 1 (10-ounce) box thawed frozen chopped spinach (squeezed dry), 1 cup almond or cashew milk, and a pinch of nutmeg; cook for 5 minutes. Season with salt and pepper to taste. Cut the potatoes in half lengthwise and scoop the insides into a bowl. Combine with the spinach mixture and stuff the mixture into the skins. Arrange the stuffed potatoes on the prepared baking sheet and bake until the filling is hot, 10 to 15 minutes.

POTATO TOPPERS

For a tasty treat even easier than stuffed potatoes, try topping baked potatoes with a potato topper. Instead of scooping out the potatoes, simply cut open the baked potatoes and top them with any of the following combos:

Chili-Cheesy 1 cup warm vegan chili (page 83 or 165) + ½ cup Cheddary Sauce (page 44).

Guacamole and Salsa Mash 2 ripe avocados, 1 tablespoon each fresh lime juice, chopped red onion, and chopped cilantro, ½ teaspoon minced jalapeño, and salt. Top with your favorite tomato salsa.

Greens with Feta and Pecans 1 cup sautéed kale or spinach + ¼ cup Tofu Feta (page 48) + 2 tablespoons toasted pecan pieces.

Tapenade–Sour Cream 4 tablespoons Tapenade (page 192) + 4 tablespoons Cashew Sour Cream (page 33) + 1 tablespoon finely chopped fresh parsley.

SPINACH AND MUSHROOM-BACON QUICHE

1 (9-inch) vegan pie dough, store-bought or homemade (page 228)

1 tablespoon olive oil

½ cup minced onion

1 cup chopped cooked Mushroom Bacon (page 110)

1 cup chopped cooked fresh or frozen spinach

Salt and ground black pepper

12 to 14 ounces extra-firm tofu, drained, squeezed, and crumbled

½ cup thick cashew cream, vegan mayo, or vegan sour cream, store-bought or homemade (pages 32, 35, or 33)

3 tablespoons plain unsweetened almond milk, store-bought or homemade (page 28)

1 tablespoon white miso

1 tablespoon fresh lemon juice

1 teaspoon Dijon mustard

¼ cup nutritional yeast

2 tablespoons cornstarch

1 teaspoon onion powder

½ teaspoon smoked paprika, plus more for garnish

⅛ teaspoon ground turmeric

This easy-to-make quiche reheats well, making it a wonderful do-ahead dish for brunch. It can be eaten warm, cold, or at room temperature. I like to make it the day before I need it and then cover with foil and reheat in a 375°F oven for 20 to 30 minutes, or until warm.

1   Preheat the oven to 425°F. Roll the dough out into a circle on a lightly floured surface. Arrange the dough in a quiche pan or pie plate, pressing evenly with your fingers to fit it into the pan, trimming and fluting the edges. Prick the bottom of the crust with the tines of a fork. Cover the edges of the crust with aluminum foil to protect from browning and bake the crust for 10 minutes. Remove the foil and set the crust aside to cool. Lower the oven temperature to 400°F.

2   Heat the oil in a skillet over medium-high heat. Add the onion and cook for 5 minutes to soften. Remove from the heat and stir in the cooked chopped bacon and the cooked chopped spinach. Season to taste with salt and pepper. Set aside to cool.

3   In a food processor, combine the tofu, cashew cream, milk, miso, lemon juice, and mustard. Process until smooth. Add the nutritional yeast, cornstarch, onion powder, paprika, turmeric, 1 teaspoon salt, and black pepper to taste. Blend until completely smooth, then transfer to a bowl and stir in the mushroom and spinach mixture. Scrape the mixture into the reserved cooled pie crust. Spread the filling evenly and smooth the top with a rubber spatula. Cover the pie edges with foil again and sprinkle the top with a little smoked paprika. Bake

for about 40 minutes, or until slightly browned on top. Remove the foil and bake for 10 more minutes, until the crust is golden. Cool for 15 minutes before slicing. If not using right away, allow to cool to room temperature, then cover and refrigerate until needed. You can then cover the top with foil and reheat it in a 375°F oven for 20 to 30 minutes, or until warm.

VARIATIONS

Broccoli and Sausage Quiche Substitute 1 cup chopped cooked broccoli and 1 cup chopped cooked breakfast sausage (page 123) for the spinach and mushrooms.

Mediterranean Quiche Substitute 1 cup chopped cooked zucchini, ¾ cup chopped cooked pepperoni (store-bought or homemade, page 116), and ½ cup chopped roasted red bell pepper for the spinach and mushrooms.

Asparagus and Ham Quiche Substitute 1 cup chopped cooked asparagus, ¾ cup chopped Hamish Loaf (page 112), and 2 tablespoons capers for the spinach and mushrooms.

SPINACH-FETA QUESADILLAS

SERVES 2 TO 4

1 tablespoon olive oil

2 garlic cloves, minced

3 scallions, chopped

8 cups chopped fresh baby spinach or 10 ounces frozen chopped spinach, thawed

1 cup cooked or canned cannellini beans, drained, rinsed, and mashed

1 teaspoon dried basil or oregano

Salt and ground black pepper

1 cup Tofu Feta (page 48) or Htipiti (Feta Spread) (page 49)

2 (10-inch) flour tortillas

These tasty wedges are reminiscent of spanakopita, if spanakopita were made with tortillas instead of phyllo dough. This recipe serves two for a light meal or four as a snack, but can be easily doubled.

1 Heat the oil in a large nonstick skillet over medium heat. Add the garlic and scallions and cook for 30 seconds to soften. Add the spinach, stirring to wilt. Stir in the mashed beans, basil, and salt and pepper to taste. Cook off or drain any liquid from the spinach mixture and transfer to a bowl. Add the feta, stirring to combine.

2 Arrange the tortillas on a flat work surface. Divide the mixture among the tortillas and spread evenly. Fold the tortillas over, pressing down to hold them together.

3 Wipe out the same large nonstick skillet and place over medium heat. Add one or two of the quesadillas (depending on the size of your pan) and cook until golden brown on one side, about 3 minutes. Carefully flip over and brown the other side, about 2 minutes longer. Remove from the skillet, cut into wedges, and serve hot.

CHICKPEA FLOUR OMELETS

MAKES 4 (6-INCH) OMELETS

Inspired by the Indian chickpea pancakes, these chickpea flour omelets are amazingly versatile, depending on how you season them. You can add ingredients to cook within the omelet, as is done in an Italian frittata, or make a filling to fold inside, like a traditional French omelet. The omelets are also delicious topped with a spoonful of Hollandaise (page 185) or Cheddary Sauce (page 44).

1 cup cold water

1 cup chickpea flour

2 tablespoons nutritional yeast

1 tablespoon fresh lemon juice or dry white wine

½ teaspoon salt

½ teaspoon garlic powder

½ teaspoon baking powder

¼ teaspoon mustard powder

¼ teaspoon ground black pepper

¼ teaspoon turmeric

½ cup finely chopped scallion

3 tablespoons minced fresh parsley or other fresh herb of choice

4 teaspoons grapeseed oil or cooking oil spray

1   In a bowl, food processor, or blender, combine the water, chickpea flour, nutritional yeast, lemon juice, salt, garlic powder, baking powder, mustard powder, black pepper, and turmeric and whisk or blend until smooth. Stir in the scallion and parsley. Allow to stand and thicken for 5 to 10 minutes. The mixture should resemble pancake batter. If it is too thick, add a little more water, 1 tablespoon at a time, until the batter is pourable.

2   Add 1 teaspoon of the oil to an 8-inch nonstick skillet or spray it with cooking spray. Heat over medium heat. When the skillet is hot, pour or ladle about ⅓ cup of the mixture into the hot skillet and move the skillet to spread the omelet evenly in the pan. Cover tightly and cook until the bottom is lightly browned and there are little holes on top, about 4 minutes. Carefully loosen it with a very thin spatula. Flip and cook for another 3 minutes. Transfer the omelet to an ovenproof platter, cover, and keep warm in a low oven while you cook the remaining omelets, using the remaining oil. Continue to make more omelets until all of the batter is used. Serve hot.

LOADED FRITTATA

Chopped pitted Kalamata olives

Minced soft sun-dried tomatoes

Chopped roasted red bell pepper

Sautéed chopped spinach or thinly sliced zucchini

Sautéed sliced mushrooms

Shredded vegan cheese

1 Preheat the oven to 400°F. Add 1 cup total of the ingredients (in any combination) to the omelet mixture.

2 Transfer the omelet mixture to an oiled ovenproof skillet or pie plate and smooth it evenly into the pan. Bake for about 30 minutes, or until firm and lightly browned along the edges. Remove from the oven and let sit for 5 to 10 minutes before serving.

FRENCH-STYLE ASPARAGUS OMELET

Filling

1½ cups sliced asparagus, cut into 1-inch pieces, roasted with 2 minced shallots and seasoned with 2 teaspoons fresh or dried tarragon and salt and pepper to taste.

Spoon one-quarter of the filling just off-center of each omelet while in the skillet, fold the other half of the omelet over the filling, cover, and cook for 2 minutes longer.

CHEESY MUSHROOM SCRAMBLE

SERVES
4 TO 6

1 tablespoon grapeseed or sunflower oil, or more if needed

1 small red or yellow onion, chopped

½ red bell pepper, cored, seeded, and chopped

1 garlic clove, minced

8 ounces mushrooms (any kind), cleaned, dried, and thinly sliced or chopped

¼ teaspoon liquid smoke

Salt and ground black pepper

12 to 16 ounces extra-firm tofu, drained and crumbled

2 tablespoons nutritional yeast

1 teaspoon onion powder

¼ teaspoon turmeric

¼ teaspoon smoked paprika

½ cup Cheddary Sauce (page 44)

Toast or English muffins, for serving

My husband and I could eat this scramble morning, noon, or night—and we often do! The best thing about a tofu scramble (besides being protein rich, delicious, and easy to prepare) is that it is infinitely versatile—try some of the variations listed at the end of the recipe, or create your own combination.

1   Heat the oil in a large nonstick skillet over medium heat. Add the onion and bell pepper and cook, stirring occasionally, for 5 minutes to soften. Add the garlic and mushrooms and cook until tender, about 4 minutes. Drizzle on the liquid smoke and season with salt and pepper to taste.

2   Place the crumbled tofu in a mixing bowl. Add the nutritional yeast, onion powder, 1 teaspoon salt, turmeric, and paprika. Mix well.

3   Push the vegetables to the sides of the skillet or, if your skillet is not large enough, transfer the vegetables to a plate. Add a teaspoon or so of oil, if needed, and reheat the skillet over medium heat. Add the tofu mixture and cook, stirring, until heated through and golden. Incorporate the vegetables into the tofu and continue to cook. Mix in the sauce and continue cooking for a few minutes longer. Taste and adjust the seasonings, if needed. Serve hot with toast.

VARIATIONS   Sauté any of the following with the onion and garlic:

2 plum tomatoes, chopped

1 small zucchini, sliced

1 cup chopped vegan sausage

1 cup chopped cooked potato

If desired, omit the cheesy sauce and sprinkle the scramble with chopped fresh chives, basil, or other fresh herb just before serving.

VIVE LA FRENCH TOAST

French toast without eggs? You bet! Aquafaba (page 257) makes a great egg alternative in this flavorful French toast batter. Top with a drizzle of pure maple syrup or your choice of toppings.

1 Preheat the oven to 250°F. In a mixing bowl, combine the Aquafaba, milk, sugar, vanilla, nutmeg, cinnamon, and salt. Use a whisk to mix until well blended and frothy.

2 Lightly oil a nonstick skillet or spray it with cooking spray and heat it over medium heat. Place a slice of bread into the batter, coating both sides. Let it sit for a few seconds to absorb some of the batter, then allow the excess batter to drip off. Place the battered bread in the hot skillet and cook for 1 to 2 minutes on each side, flipping with a thin spatula, until lightly browned on both sides. Repeat with the remaining bread and batter. Depending on the size of your skillet (and the size of your bread), you can cook two or more slices of bread at the same time, without crowding. Place the cooked pieces of French toast on a heatproof platter or baking pan and keep them warm in the oven while you cook the rest. Serve hot with your choice of toppings.

1 cup Aquafaba (page 257)

⅔ cup nondairy milk, store-bought or homemade (page 28)

¼ cup sugar

1 tablespoon pure vanilla extract

⅛ teaspoon ground nutmeg

⅛ teaspoon ground cinnamon

⅛ teaspoon salt

8 to 12 slices Easy Artisan Bread (page 229) or your favorite bread

Toppings: Your choice of vegan butter (store-bought or homemade, page 36), pure maple syrup, confectioners' sugar, berries, sliced bananas, whipped cream (page 248)

BREAKFAST NACHOS

SERVES 4

Nachos for breakfast is a fun way to start the day. Make the queso sauce in advance and the nachos will come together quickly.

1 Heat the oil in a large nonstick skillet over medium-high heat. Add the onion and cook for 3 minutes, then add the garlic and scallions and cook 2 minutes longer. Add the tofu and salt, and cook, stirring, for 5 minutes. Stir in the nutritional yeast, cumin, and turmeric. Taste and adjust the seasonings if needed. Stir in the beans, cover, and keep warm.

2 In a medium bowl, combine the tomato, jalapeño, cilantro, and lime juice. Season with salt to taste and mix well. Gently stir in the avocado.

3 To assemble, spoon a thin layer of the sauce on the bottom of a large plate. Place half of the chips on top of the sauce. Spoon half of the sauce on top of the chips, followed by half of the tofu and beans, and then half of the salsa. Top with the remaining chips and repeat with the remaining ingredients. Serve immediately, garnished with additional cilantro, if using.

1 tablespoon olive oil

1 small yellow onion, minced

2 garlic cloves, minced

3 scallions, chopped

12 ounces extra-firm tofu, drained and diced

½ teaspoon salt

2 tablespoons nutritional yeast

½ teaspoon ground cumin

¼ teaspoon turmeric

1½ cups cooked or 1 (15-ounce) can black beans, drained and rinsed

1 large tomato, diced

1 jalapeño, seeded and minced

¼ cup chopped cilantro, plus more for garnish (optional)

1 tablespoon fresh lime juice

1 ripe avocado, peeled, pitted, and diced

1 recipe Smoky Queso Sauce (page 45), kept warm

1 (13-ounce) bag restaurant-style tortilla chips

CHAPTER 3

PLANT-BASED MEATS

The word *meat* can mean more than beefsteak and pork chops. Protein-rich plant-based meats such as tofu, tempeh, and seitan all have long culinary histories in ancient China, Japan, and Indonesia. And, of course, beans are a primary source of protein in many parts of the world to this day.

This chapter shows you how to get the most flavor from tofu, tempeh, and beans, and includes several recipes using these ingredients, including Iron Kettle Chili, Tuesday Tacos with Avocado Crema, Marinated Baked Tofu, Smoky Black Bean Soup, Best Bean Burgers, and White Bean Cutlets.

There is also a recipe for making seitan from scratch that can, in turn, be used to make roasts, cutlets, and meatballs, as well as the classy Seitan Oscar with Béarnaise Sauce and down-home BBQ Seitan Ribs.

MARINATED BAKED TOFU   74

BURMESE TOFU   76

CRISPY TOFU   77

CRISPY CRUMBLES   78

TOTALLY TEMPTING TEMPEH   79

BEANS FROM SCRATCH   80

SMOKY BLACK BEAN SOUP   82

IRON KETTLE CHILI   83

BEST BEAN BURGERS   84

MAMA'S MEATBALLS   86

WHITE BEAN CUTLETS   87

PICCATA MEATBALLS
WITH PENNE AND
ASPARAGUS   89

TUESDAY TACOS WITH
AVOCADO CREMA   90

BAKED SEITAN ROAST   92

OVEN-BAKED SEITAN
CUTLETS   94

SEITAN OSCAR WITH
BÉARNAISE SAUCE   97

THE WELLINGTON   98

BBQ SEITAN RIBS   99

MARINATED BAKED TOFU

¼ cup tamari

¼ cup pure maple syrup, agave, or brown sugar

3 tablespoons fresh lemon juice

2 garlic cloves, pressed

1 tablespoon nutritional yeast

1 teaspoon onion powder

1 (12- to 16-ounce) package extra-firm tofu, drained, cut into ¼-inch-thick slices

Marinated baked tofu is widely available in markets, but it can be expensive. It's easy to make your own using extra-firm or super-firm regular tofu (not silken). This recipe uses a basic teriyaki-inspired marinade, but you can change up the marinade to suit your own tastes. For example, add 2 teaspoons grated ginger, swap out the lemon juice for orange juice, or try one of the marinade variations on the next page. Enjoy the baked tofu as is or use it in recipes where you need a flavorful tofu, such as in a salad or sandwich.

1   In a small bowl or personal blender, combine the tamari, maple syrup, lemon juice, garlic, nutritional yeast, and onion powder. Mix or blend until well combined.

2   Arrange the tofu slices in a single layer in a large glass or ceramic baking dish. Pour the marinade over the tofu, spreading the marinade with the back of a spoon to cover the tofu. Gently turn the tofu to make sure it is all coated with the marinade. Cover and refrigerate for several hours or overnight.

3   Preheat the oven to 400°F. Lightly oil a large baking sheet or cover with parchment paper. Arrange the tofu slices on the prepared baking sheet, pouring the remaining marinade on top of the tofu. Bake for about 30 minutes, or until the tofu is golden brown on both sides, turning once halfway through. Watch carefully near the end of the baking time so the marinade does not burn or smoke. Use immediately or cool to room temperature and transfer to a glass or ceramic container, cover, and refrigerate until needed.

For a different flavor profile, substitute either of the following marinades for the one above and proceed with the recipe:

HOME-STYLE MARINADE

1 teaspoon dried thyme

1 teaspoon ground sage

1 teaspoon dried basil

1 teaspoon paprika

1 teaspoon garlic powder

1 teaspoon onion powder

1 teaspoon nutritional yeast

¼ teaspoon ground black pepper

⅓ cup vegetable broth, store-bought or homemade (page 182)

¼ cup dry white wine or additional vegetable broth

2 tablespoons tamari

In a small bowl or personal blender, combine all the ingredients and mix or blend until well combined.

GARLICKY MUSTARD MARINADE

¼ cup water

2 tablespoons Dijon mustard

2 tablespoons vegan mayo, store-bought or homemade (page 35)

2 garlic cloves, pressed

1 teaspoon dried basil

¼ teaspoon salt

¼ teaspoon ground black pepper

In a small bowl or personal blender, combine all the ingredients and mix or blend until well combined.

BURMESE TOFU

1¼ cups chickpea flour

½ teaspoon salt

2 cups cold water

Burmese tofu is not tofu as we know it because it is not made from soy bean curd. Rather, it is made from chickpea flour blended with water. After it is chilled, it can be sliced or cut into cubes or strips and used in stir-fries, or it can be sautéed or baked in recipes calling for firm or extra-firm tofu. Since Burmese tofu doesn't marinate well, you can add extra seasoning to the mixture as it cooks; however, if adding liquid, you'd need to adjust the amount of water accordingly.

1 Lightly oil a small glass loaf pan or baking dish and set it aside. In a medium saucepan over medium heat, combine the chickpea flour, salt, and cold water, and whisk until completely smooth. Cook, stirring constantly, until very thick, about 4 minutes.

2 Use a spatula to spread the tofu immediately into the prepared container and set aside to cool at room temperature for 30 minutes, then cover and refrigerate it for at least 2 hours to allow it to firm up before using. It will keep well covered in the refrigerator for up to 5 days.

CRISPY TOFU

Since tofu is already vegan, it doesn't need to be veganized. However, it can be used in place of animal products in stir-fries, sandwiches, and other dishes such as tonkatsu, tacos, and more. And for that, it should not only taste good but also have a firm, crispy texture. As with all tofu recipes (except those calling specifically for silken tofu or a soft tofu), use an extra-firm (or super-firm, if you can find it) tofu that has been packed in water in plastic or a plastic tub.

1 (12- to 16-ounce) package extra-firm or super-firm tofu, drained

2 tablespoons sunflower oil or other neutral oil

Salt

1   After draining the tofu, cut the tofu block into ½-inch slabs. Depending on how you wish to use it, you can leave it as slabs or cut it into strips or cubes. Place a clean kitchen towel or a few thicknesses of paper towel on a work surface. Arrange the tofu in a single layer on the towel. Put another clean kitchen towel on top and pat well to remove any moisture. This will help it get brown and crispy.

2   Heat a large (preferably cast-iron) skillet over medium-high heat. When it is hot, add the oil, tilting the pan to spread the oil. Arrange the tofu in the hot skillet in a single layer, working in batches, if needed. Do not crowd the pan or allow the tofu pieces to touch. Cook the tofu on one side until golden brown, 4 to 5 minutes, then flip with a thin metal spatula and brown the other side, 4 to 5 minutes longer. When both sides are browned and crispy, transfer the tofu to a plate and season with salt to taste. The tofu can now be used in recipes: enjoyed in a sandwich, topped with a sauce, or added to a stir-fry. If not using right away, allow to cool to room temperature, then cover and refrigerate for up to 5 days.

3   If using in a stir-fry: Keep the crispy tofu aside on a plate until you stir-fry the vegetables and sauce. Add the tofu into the stir-fry just before serving, just long enough to reheat and lightly coat with sauce.

> **VARIATION**
>
> **Oven-Fried Crispy Tofu** Preheat the oven to 400°F. Line a baking sheet with parchment paper or coat it with cooking spray. Drain, cut, and dry the tofu as you would for pan-frying above. Arrange the tofu in a single layer on the prepared baking sheet. Spray very lightly with cooking spray, if desired. Bake the tofu until browned and crisp, about 30 minutes, flipping halfway through. Remove from the oven and season with salt to taste. The tofu can now be used in recipes.

CRISPY CRUMBLES

1 (12- to 16-ounce) package extra-firm tofu, drained

1 tablespoon olive oil

2 teaspoons agave

1 tablespoon smoked paprika

1 teaspoon salt

1 teaspoon onion powder

½ teaspoon garlic powder

¼ teaspoon black pepper

¼ teaspoon cayenne pepper (optional)

2 tablespoons cornstarch

Tofu is the master of disguise. In this recipe it transforms into tasty crispy crumbles that can be used in recipes such as tacos, sloppy Joes, or chili. They also make a great addition to a salad!

1 After draining the tofu, cut it into quarters and use your hand to squeeze any moisture out of each piece, then finely crumble the tofu into a large bowl. If your tofu is too firm to crumble well, finely chop it. Preheat the oven to 375°F. Line a baking sheet with parchment paper.

2 Coat the tofu with the oil and agave, then add the paprika, salt, onion powder, garlic powder, pepper, and cayenne, if using, tossing to coat evenly. Sprinkle the cornstarch on top, then mix well until all of the tofu is coated with cornstarch.

3 Spread the tofu evenly on the prepared baking sheet. Bake until golden brown, turning once, 20 to 30 minutes. Remove from the oven and set aside to cool. Use immediately or transfer to a container and cool to room temperature, then cover and refrigerate until needed.

TOTALLY TEMPTING TEMPEH

MAKES
8 OUNCES

Braising tempeh in a liquid helps mellow the flavor and makes it more digestible. When you add delicious seasonings to the braising liquid, it makes the tempeh totally tempting.

1 (8-ounce) package tempeh

2 tablespoons grapeseed or sunflower oil

½ cup minced onion

3 garlic cloves, minced

¼ cup tamari

½ cup water

1   Cut the tempeh in half to make two ½-inch-thick cutlets. Cut each cutlet in half crosswise to create four ¼-inch-thick cutlets. Heat the oil in a large skillet over medium-high heat. Add the tempeh and cook until golden brown on both sides, about 4 minutes per side. Add the onion and garlic. Sauté until the onion is softened, about 4 minutes.

2   Add the tamari and water. Cover with a lid and decrease the heat to medium-low. Braise the tempeh for about 10 minutes, turning occasionally. The liquid will reduce and the tempeh will become infused with flavor. Transfer the tempeh to a plate. The tempeh can now be used in recipes or cooled to room temperature, then covered and refrigerated for up to a week.

BEANS FROM SCRATCH

MAKES 6 CUPS COOKED BEANS

1 pound dried beans

6 to 8 cups water

2 bay leaves

2 garlic cloves, crushed

1 to 2 teaspoons salt (optional)

One pound of dried beans produces about 6 cups cooked. When cooking dried beans it makes sense to make up a pound at a time, since they take so much time (and energy) to cook. Since they freeze well, they are ideal for portioning and freezing to use as needed. This is a generic recipe—the actual cooking times will vary, depending on the size, type, and age of the beans used.

1 Soak the beans overnight in enough water to cover. Drain the beans and put them in a large pot with the 6 to 8 cups fresh water (older and larger beans will require the higher amount of water). Put a lid on the pot and bring to a boil. Decrease the heat to a simmer, add the bay leaves and garlic, and cook until the beans are tender, 1 to 3 hours, or longer, depending on the beans. Add more water if needed to keep the beans covered while cooking. About halfway through cooking, add the salt, if using.

2 When the beans are tender, divide them into 2-cup containers and set aside to cool. Once cool, cover with tight-fitting lids and refrigerate some to use right away and freeze the rest.

CANNED VERSUS HOME-COOKED BEANS

Although canned beans are relatively inexpensive and infinitely convenient, they still cost about three times as much as the same amount of cooked dried beans. If you cook a different pot of beans each week and freeze them in measured portions, you'll soon have a convenient stockpile of different beans at your fingertips. Still, canned beans are very handy to keep in the pantry for those times when you're caught without a supply of cooked beans and no time to prepare them. I choose the best of both worlds by cooking dried beans regularly to portion and freeze and I also keep a stash of several varieties of canned beans in the pantry. The recipes in this book call for cooked or canned beans, so you can use whatever you have on hand.

SMOKY BLACK BEAN SOUP

SERVES 4

1 tablespoon olive oil

1 large onion, finely chopped

1 carrot, finely chopped

3 garlic cloves, minced

1 teaspoon ground cumin

1 teaspoon smoked paprika

½ teaspoon dried oregano

½ teaspoon chipotle chile powder
(or to taste)

Salt and ground black pepper

4 cups vegetable broth, store-
bought or homemade (page 182)

3 cups cooked or 2 (15-ounce)
cans black beans, drained and
rinsed

½ teaspoon liquid smoke

½ cup chopped Tempeh Bacon
(page 106) or Smoky Chickpeas
(page 111)

Vegan sour cream, store-bought or
homemade (page 33), for serving
(optional)

2 tablespoons minced fresh cilantro
(optional)

Black bean soup is a hearty, economical meal that doesn't need the addition of a ham hock or bacon to make it smoky-rich. Just a splash of liquid smoke and a little vegan bacon provide the smoky accent we love in this soup. The optional dollop of sour cream sends it over the top.

Heat the oil in a large saucepan over medium-high heat. Add the onion and carrot and cook for 5 minutes to soften. Add the garlic, cumin, paprika, oregano, chipotle powder, and salt and pepper to taste. Cook, stirring, for 1 minute, then add the broth and beans and bring to a boil. Decrease the heat to a simmer and cook for 30 minutes, or until the vegetables are soft and the flavors are well blended. Just before serving, stir in the liquid smoke, then taste and adjust the seasonings, if needed. Ladle into bowls and serve hot topped with the bacon and sour cream and cilantro, if using.

VARIATION

Add 2 tablespoons uncooked quinoa when you add the spices.

IRON KETTLE CHILI

I call this "iron kettle" chili because of its deep rich flavor that tastes like it's been simmering all day. In reality, this hearty chili can be enjoyed in less than an hour from start to finish. Its rich flavor comes from the addition of barbecue sauce, fire-roasted tomatoes, and smoked paprika.

Heat the oil in a large pot over medium heat. Add the onion and cook for 5 minutes to soften. Stir in the bell pepper and garlic, then add the chili powder, paprika, cumin, oregano, salt, and pepper. Cook for about 5 minutes, stirring occasionally, until the vegetables are softened. Add the tomatoes with their juice, the beans, seitan (if using), and barbecue sauce. Bring to a simmer, then cover and cook on medium-low until the flavors are blended, 30 minutes or longer. During the last 10 minutes of cooking, stir in the corn. Taste and adjust the seasonings, if needed.

1 tablespoon olive oil

1 large yellow onion, finely chopped

1 red bell pepper, cored, seeded, and finely chopped

4 garlic cloves, minced

2 tablespoons chili powder

1 teaspoon smoked paprika

1 teaspoon ground cumin

1 teaspoon dried oregano

1 teaspoon salt

¼ teaspoon ground black pepper

2 (14.5-ounce) cans fire-roasted diced tomatoes, undrained

2 (15-ounce) cans dark red kidney beans, drained and rinsed

1 (15-ounce) can black beans, drained and rinsed

2 cups chopped seitan or tempeh, store-bought or homemade (optional)

½ cup barbecue sauce, store-bought or homemade (page 101)

1 cup fresh or frozen corn kernels

BEST BEAN BURGERS

¾ cup chopped walnuts

¾ cup old-fashioned rolled oats

1½ cups cooked or 1 (15-ounce) can black beans, drained and rinsed

½ cup minced onion

½ cup bread crumbs

2 tablespoons vital wheat gluten (optional)

1 flax egg (see Note below)

1 tablespoon tamari

½ teaspoon gravy browner, such as Gravy Master or Kitchen Bouquet (optional)

½ teaspoon garlic powder

½ teaspoon paprika

½ teaspoon salt

¼ teaspoon ground black pepper

2 tablespoons olive oil

4 burger rolls

Condiments of choice

This is my go-to veggie burger. It has a firm texture and holds up well whether cooked in a skillet, in the oven, or on the grill. I prefer them cooked in a skillet. These burgers can be seasoned according to your own taste, so feel free to add your favorite herbs and spices to "have it your way."

Note: The optional wheat gluten will make firmer burgers.

1   In a food processor, combine the walnuts and oats and process until finely ground. Add the beans, onion, bread crumbs, wheat gluten (if using), flax egg, tamari, gravy browner (if using), garlic powder, paprika, salt, and pepper. Process to mix well. Transfer the mixture to a work surface and divide into 6 balls (or more or less, depending on how large you like your burgers). If the mixture is too soft, add a little more vital wheat gluten or bread crumbs. Use your hands to firmly shape each ball into a thin burger, pressing the mixture well to hold the burger together. Set the burgers aside on a plate and refrigerate for 30 minutes or longer.

2   Heat the oil in a large nonstick skillet over medium heat. Add the burgers and cook for 5 minutes. Use a spatula to flip the burgers and cook for 5 minutes longer. Serve hot on burger rolls with your favorite condiments.

VARIATION

To make a flax egg Combine 1 tablespoon ground flaxseed and 3 tablespoons warm water in a small bowl. Mix and set aside for 5 to 10 minutes.

MAMA'S MEATBALLS

1 tablespoon ground flaxseed

3 tablespoons hot water

2 garlic cloves, crushed

1 cup coarsely chopped mushrooms

1 tablespoon olive oil

1 tablespoon tomato paste

1 tablespoon tamari

1½ cups cooked or 1 (15-ounce) can cannellini beans, drained and rinsed

2 tablespoons vital wheat gluten

¾ cup dry bread crumbs

¼ cup nutritional yeast

2 tablespoons minced fresh parsley

1 teaspoon dried basil

¾ teaspoon dried oregano

½ teaspoon paprika

½ teaspoon salt

¼ teaspoon ground black pepper

Try these flavorful orbs in the Piccata Meatballs with Penne and Asparagus on page 89, or serve them with pasta and Oven-Roasted Tomato Sauce (page 197). They're also great in a sub roll with a little tomato sauce and melty cheese.

1 In a small bowl, combine the ground flaxseed and hot water, stirring to mix. Set aside for 5 to 10 minutes.

2 In a food processor, process the garlic until finely minced. Add the mushrooms and pulse until finely chopped, but not pureed. Heat the oil in a skillet over medium heat. Add the mushroom mixture and cook for a few minutes, stirring until the mushrooms release their liquid and the liquid evaporates. Stir in the tomato paste and tamari, then remove from the heat.

3 Pulse the cannellini beans in the same food processor (no need to clean it out), then add them to the mushroom mixture. Sprinkle on the vital wheat gluten, then add the bread crumbs, nutritional yeast, parsley, flax mixture, basil, oregano, paprika, salt, and pepper and mix well. Set aside to cool for a few minutes.

4 Preheat the oven to 375°F. Lightly oil a large baking sheet or line it with parchment paper. When the mixture is cool enough to handle, use your hands to press the mixture together. If it's too wet, add additional bread crumbs. If it's too dry, add a little water, 1 tablespoon at a time. Pinch off a small piece of the mixture, press it together in your hand, and then roll between your palms to make a 1½- to 2-inch ball. Repeat until the mixture is used up, arranging the meatballs in rows on the prepared baking sheet. Bake for 25 to 30 minutes, or until firm and nicely browned, turning once about halfway through. If not using right away, transfer to a container and cool completely at room temperature, then cover tightly and refrigerate or freeze until needed.

WHITE BEAN CUTLETS

MAKES
8 CUTLETS

Make a batch of these cutlets and then cool and refrigerate some to use right away and freeze the rest for future use. These versatile cutlets can be sautéed and sauced in a variety of ways. Try them with the Great Brown Gravy on page 191.

Broth

6 cups water

¼ cup tamari

1 yellow onion, quartered

3 garlic cloves, crushed

1 tablespoon vegetable base, store-bought or homemade (page 183)

Cutlets

½ cup cooked white beans

2 tablespoons tamari

½ cup cold vegetable broth, store-bought or homemade (page 182)

1¼ cups vital wheat gluten

⅓ cup nutritional yeast

1 teaspoon garlic powder

½ teaspoon onion powder

1   **Broth:** In a large pot, combine the water, tamari, onion, garlic, and vegetable base, and bring to a simmer.

2   **Cutlets:** Combine the beans and tamari in a food processor and process until smooth. Add the broth and process until blended. Add the vital wheat gluten, nutritional yeast, garlic powder, and onion powder, and process until well combined into a soft dough. Add a little more broth, 1 tablespoon at a time, if the dough is too dry. Turn the dough out onto a floured surface and knead for a minute or two. Place the dough between two sheets of parchment paper or plastic wrap and flatten with your hands, then roll it out into a rectangle using a rolling pin or wine bottle until it is about ¼ inch thick. Remove the top sheet of parchment paper and cut the flattened dough into 8 pieces. Add the cutlets to the simmering broth. Cover and simmer for 1 hour, turning the cutlets about halfway through. Do not allow the broth to boil.

3   Remove from the heat and allow the cutlets to cool in the broth. Remove the cutlets from the broth and transfer to a plate or container. Cover and refrigerate until needed for up to 5 days or wrap individually and transfer to a freezer bag to freeze for up to 3 months. The cutlets can be sautéed in a small amount of oil until golden brown and topped with a sauce or cut into strips or chunks to use in recipes.

PICCATA MEATBALLS WITH PENNE AND ASPARAGUS

I came up with this recipe one night when my husband wanted pasta and meatballs and I was in the mood for asparagus and something with a piccata sauce. This dish combined all those elements and satisfied us both deliciously. If you want to use less or no oil, you can add a little vegetable broth to the sauce to replace the oil.

8 ounces penne

1 pound asparagus, cut into 1-inch pieces

3 tablespoons olive oil

Salt and ground black pepper

1 tablespoon vegan butter, store-bought or homemade (page 36)

3 scallions, minced

8 to 12 Mama's Meatballs (page 86), cooked

2 tablespoons capers

3 tablespoons dry white wine

3 tablespoons fresh lemon juice

2 tablespoons minced fresh parsley

1 Preheat the oven to 425°F. Lightly oil a large baking pan or line it with parchment paper.

2 Cook the pasta in a pot of boiling salted water until just tender, about 10 minutes, or according to package directions. Drain and return to the pot.

3 While the pasta is cooking, toss the asparagus pieces with 1 tablespoon of the olive oil and salt and pepper to taste. Transfer the asparagus to the prepared baking pan and arrange in a single layer. Roast until tender and lightly browned, 8 to 12 minutes, depending on the thickness of the asparagus.

4 Heat the remaining 2 tablespoons oil and the butter in a skillet over medium heat. Add the scallions and the cooked meatballs and heat until hot. Add the capers, white wine, and lemon juice, and cook for 1 minute to cook off the alcohol. When the pasta is drained and returned to the pot, add the roasted asparagus, the cooked meatballs, and the piccata mixture. Add the parsley and season with salt and pepper to taste. Toss gently to combine, then taste and adjust the seasonings, if needed.

TUESDAY TACOS WITH AVOCADO CREMA

4 cups shredded green cabbage

3 tablespoons chopped cilantro leaves

3 tablespoons rice vinegar

1 teaspoon sugar

½ teaspoon salt

¼ teaspoon ground cumin

¼ teaspoon ground coriander

1 tablespoon olive oil

4 scallions, minced

1 recipe Crispy Crumbles (page 78)

½ teaspoon chili powder

¼ teaspoon smoked paprika

6 (7-inch) flour tortillas

1 recipe Avocado Crema (page 187)

Tomato salsa, to serve (optional)

The Crispy Crumbles from page 78 combine with a crunchy cabbage slaw and an avocado crema for a delicious meal on Taco Tuesdays. Make the crumbles and slaw ahead of time (up to 3 days ahead) for quick and easy assembly. Allow two tacos per serving.

1 In a bowl, combine the cabbage, cilantro, vinegar, sugar, salt, cumin, and coriander. Set aside or, if not using right away, cover and refrigerate until needed.

2 Heat the oil in a medium skillet over medium-high heat. Add the scallions and cook for 3 minutes. Stir in the Crispy Crumbles and season with the chili powder and smoked paprika, stirring to coat and heat through. Keep warm.

3 Warm the tortillas, then spoon the crumbles inside the tortilla. Add some of the slaw and top with the crema and salsa, if using. Serve immediately.

BAKED SEITAN ROAST

Seitan

1½ cups vital wheat gluten flour

¼ cup chickpea flour or tapioca starch

2 tablespoons nutritional yeast

1 teaspoon smoked paprika

1 teaspoon onion powder

½ teaspoon garlic powder

½ teaspoon salt

¼ teaspoon ground black pepper

1 cup cold water

2 tablespoons tamari

1 tablespoon miso paste

1 tablespoon olive oil

1 teaspoon gravy browner, such as Gravy Master or Kitchen Bouquet (optional)

Cooking Broth

3 cups cold water

2 tablespoons tamari or 1 teaspoon vegetable broth powder

This recipe uses vital wheat gluten to make a simple, protein-rich seitan roast that can be enjoyed as is; as a pot roast; or cut into slices, chunks, or strips for sautés, stews, stir-fries, and more, including The Wellington on page 98. You can portion and freeze this seitan in airtight containers, with or without the cooking broth.

1 **Seitan:** In a food processor or bowl, combine the vital wheat gluten, chickpea flour, nutritional yeast, paprika, onion powder, garlic powder, salt, and pepper and pulse or stir to mix. Add the water, tamari, miso, oil, and gravy browner, if using. Process or stir to mix well until the mixture forms a dough ball. If the mixture is too dry, add a tablespoon or so of water and process to absorb all the flour. If the mixture is too wet, add a tablespoon of vital wheat gluten and process to incorporate. Transfer the dough from the food processor and knead for about 2 minutes by hand. Cover the dough ball and set aside to rest for a few minutes while you prepare the cooking broth.

2 **Cooking broth:** In a measuring cup, combine 1 cup of the water with the tamari and set aside. Preheat the oven to 350°F.

3 Form the smooth dough into a log about 3 inches wide x 8 inches long. Place the roast on a sheet of aluminum foil sprayed with cooking spray and tightly wrap the foil around the roast so it holds its shape. Place the roast in a pan large enough to hold the roast. Pour in the remaining 2 cups cold water. Cover the roasting pan tightly with aluminum foil. Bake for 45 minutes, then remove the pan from the oven and uncover the pan. Remove the foil from around the roast, leaving the roast in the pan.

4   Add the reserved cooking broth to the baking pan. Cover the pan again with the foil, and continue to bake for 45 minutes longer. The cooked seitan should be firm to the touch. If using right away, transfer the seitan to a platter or cutting board and slice with a long serrated knife. If not using right away, allow it to cool, then cover and refrigerate until needed. The seitan can be cut or sliced to use in recipes. It can be refrigerated for up to 4 days or tightly wrapped and frozen for up to 3 months.

SEITAN IN A SLOW COOKER

A slow cooker is a great way to cook seitan if you don't want to use the oven. For the seitan roast, oil the inside of a large oval slow cooker. Pour 1 cup of the hot cooking broth into the bottom of the pot, then place the loaf-shaped seitan dough in it. Pour in the rest of the broth. Cover with the lid and cook on Low for 6 to 8 hours or on High for 4 hours, turning once halfway through. The cooked seitan should be firm to the touch. Cool the seitan completely before using in recipes.

OVEN-BAKED SEITAN CUTLETS

MAKES 16 CUTLETS

Wet Mix

1½ cups canned or cooked cannellini beans, drained and rinsed very well

½ cup cold water

¼ cup tamari

1 tablespoon dark miso paste

1 tablespoon olive oil

1 teaspoon gravy browner, such as Gravy Master or Kitchen Bouquet (optional, for color)

Dry Mix

2 cups vital wheat gluten

½ cup chickpea flour

¼ cup nutritional yeast

1 teaspoon onion powder

1 teaspoon garlic powder

1 teaspoon smoked paprika

Cooking Broth

3 tablespoons tamari

2 garlic cloves, crushed

1 tablespoon vegetable broth powder or paste, store-bought or homemade (page 182)

1 tablespoon olive oil

3 cups cold water

In this recipe the seitan is cooked as cutlets to use for grilling or sautéing. They are great topped with brown gravy (page 191) or sautéed in a piccata sauce (page 89). They are the main component in the Seitan Oscar with Béarnaise Sauce recipe on page 97. The cutlets can also be cut into chunks or strips for stews, stir-fries, or other recipes. For best results, make the seitan ahead of time so you can chill before using to firm up the texture. This seitan freezes well in airtight containers, frozen with or without the cooking broth. In addition, the cooking broth can be reused for another batch of seitan or used as broth to make sauces.

1   **Wet mix:** In a food processor, combine the beans, water, tamari, miso, oil, and gravy browner, if using, and process until smooth and well blended.

2   **Dry mix:** In a large bowl, combine the vital wheat gluten, chickpea flour, nutritional yeast, onion powder, garlic powder, and paprika. Mix well. Add the dry mix ingredients to the food processor with the wet ingredients and pulse to mix well, then process until it forms a dough ball. If the mixture is too dry, add a tablespoon of water and process to absorb all the flour. If the mixture is too wet, add a tablespoon of vital wheat gluten and process to incorporate. Pulse for a minute or two, then remove from the food processor and knead for 2 to 3 minutes by hand. Cover the dough ball and set aside to rest while you prepare the cooking broth.

3 **Cooking broth:** In a 9- x 13-inch baking dish, combine the tamari, garlic, broth powder, and oil. Mix well, then pour in 2 cups of the cold water and stir to blend.

4 Preheat the oven to 300°F. Wet your hands to make the dough easier to handle. Form the smooth dough into a log and slice it into 16 equal pieces. Wet your hands and flatten the pieces one at a time by stretching the dough with the palm of your hand on a damp flat surface. Don't use flour. Make the cutlets as thin as possible because they will expand when cooked. Arrange the cutlets in the baking dish, overlapping only very slightly, if needed. Pour the remaining 1 cup cold water over the cutlets. Cover tightly with aluminum foil and bake for 60 to 70 minutes. Allow the cooked cutlets to cool in the water for about 30 minutes, then arrange the cooked cutlets on a platter and allow them to cool completely before using. They should be firm to the touch. They can be portioned and stored in covered containers or freezer bags with a piece of parchment paper between each cutlet to separate them for easy use, then refrigerated for up to a week or frozen for up to 3 months.

SEITAN OSCAR WITH BÉARNAISE SAUCE

This recipe is a plant-based version of an old-time restaurant favorite. For best results, prepare the seitan, cakes, and béarnaise sauce ahead of time (even a day or so beforehand) and dinner will come together quickly. Serve with your favorite potatoes or grain dish on the side. You'll only need about half of the béarnaise sauce for this recipe, but it's so delicious (and reheats well) that you'll want to make the whole batch to enjoy over cooked veggies, roasted potatoes, or a tofu scramble.

4 Oven-Baked Seitan Cutlets (page 94), sautéed

4 Hearts of Palm and Artichoke Cakes (page 150), sautéed

1 pound asparagus, trimmed

1 tablespoon olive oil

Salt and ground black pepper

½ recipe Better Béarnaise Sauce (page 190)

1 Prepare the seitan cutlets and hearts of palm patties and keep them warm. Preheat the oven to 425°F. Lightly oil or spray a baking sheet with cooking spray or line it with parchment paper. Toss the asparagus with the oil and season with salt and pepper to taste. Arrange the asparagus in a single layer on the baking sheet and roast until tender, 8 to 12 minutes, depending on the thickness of the asparagus. If you haven't prepared your béarnaise sauce in advance, do it now.

2 Arrange a warm seitan cutlet on each of 4 dinner plates. Top each with a warm hearts of palm patty, followed by 3 or 4 asparagus spears, more or less, depending on the thickness of the asparagus. (If you have trouble stacking the asparagus, you can nestle them alongside the seitan.) Spoon the béarnaise sauce on top and serve hot.

THE WELLINGTON

8 ounces white mushrooms, cleaned, trimmed, and halved lengthwise

4 shallots, halved lengthwise

2 garlic cloves, crushed

2 teaspoons chopped fresh thyme or 1 teaspoon dried thyme

1 tablespoon olive oil, plus more for the pan

Salt and ground black pepper

1 Baked Seitan Roast (page 92), cooled to room temperature

1 sheet Pepperidge Farm Puff Pastry or other vegan puff pastry, thawed

1 recipe Red Wine Sauce with Mushrooms (page 184) or Great Brown Gravy (page 191)

The ultimate fancy dinner entrée is best served topped with Red Wine Sauce with Mushrooms (page 184). Roasted potatoes and asparagus make good accompaniments.

1   In a food processor, combine the mushrooms, shallots, garlic, and thyme. Pulse until finely minced. Heat the oil in a large skillet over medium heat. Add the mushroom mixture and cook, stirring, until most of the liquid has evaporated, about 10 minutes. Season with salt and pepper to taste. Set aside to cool. This mushroom mixture is known as duxelles.

2   Heat a thin layer of oil in a large skillet over medium-high heat. Add the seitan roast and sear it on all sides until nicely browned, then remove it from the skillet and set aside to cool completely. Preheat the oven to 425°F.

3   Roll out the puff pastry sheet between two sheets of parchment paper or plastic wrap to thin out the dough and to smooth the seams. Remove the top sheet of parchment from the pastry. Spread the duxelles in a line down the center of the pastry, about the length of the seitan log. Place the seitan on top of the duxelles mixture. Fold up the pastry around the seitan to enclose it. Brush a little water on the edge of the pastry to help seal it, tucking in the ends and sealing in the seitan.

4   Place the Wellington on a baking sheet, seam-side down. Cut two or three slits on the top of the puff pastry for the steam to escape. Bake until nicely browned, about 30 minutes. To serve, transfer the Wellington to a cutting board. Use a serrated knife to cut it into ½-inch-thick slices. Serve hot with the sauce.

BBQ SEITAN RIBS

SERVES
6 TO 8

These lip-smacking strips of deliciousness are messy and fun to eat. I like to serve them out on the deck with potato salad and coleslaw.

1 In a food processor or large bowl, combine the almond butter, 2 tablespoons of the barbecue sauce, nutritional yeast, garlic powder, onion powder, smoked paprika, salt, pepper, 1 cup of the water, tamari, and 1 tablespoon of the olive oil. Process or stir until smooth and well blended. Add the vital wheat gluten and process or mix until well combined. Add up to ⅓ cup additional water if needed to hold the mixture together. Transfer the dough to a work surface and knead lightly until well combined and the dough feels elastic. Preheat the oven to 350°F. Grease a 9- x 13-inch baking dish.

2 Flatten the dough into a rectangle about ½ inch thick. Cut the dough into 2-inch strips, then cut in half crosswise and arrange them in the prepared baking dish. In a bowl, combine 1 cup of the barbecue sauce with 1 cup of the water and mix well. Pour the sauce mixture over the seitan and cover tightly with aluminum foil. Bake for about 60 minutes, or until the seitan is firm and the sauce has reduced. When the seitan ribs are done baking, remove the baking dish from the oven and increase the oven temperature to 400°F.

3 Heat the remaining 1 tablespoon oil in a large skillet over medium-high heat. Arrange 3 or 4 seitan ribs in the skillet and sear on both sides, about 2 minutes per side. Do not crowd the pan. Return the seared ribs to the baking dish and sear the remaining seitan. When all the seitan has been seared and returned to the baking dish, pour the remaining 2 cups barbecue sauce over the seitan, turning to coat. Return the pan to the oven and bake, uncovered, until the seitan is nicely glazed with the sauce, about 10 minutes. Serve hot.

2 tablespoons almond butter, store-bought or homemade (page 38)

3 cups plus 2 tablespoons barbecue sauce, store-bought or homemade (page 101)

2 tablespoons nutritional yeast

1 tablespoon garlic powder

1 tablespoon onion powder

2 teaspoons smoked paprika

½ teaspoon salt

¼ teaspoon ground black pepper

2⅓ cups water

3 tablespoons tamari

2 tablespoons olive oil

2 cups vital wheat gluten

BARBECUE SAUCE

MAKES
ABOUT
3 CUPS

1 tablespoon grapeseed or
sunflower oil

1 yellow onion, minced

3 garlic cloves, minced

1 (28-ounce) can tomato sauce or
puree

1 canned chipotle chile in adobo
sauce, minced

⅓ cup pure maple syrup or dark
brown sugar

¼ cup water

¼ cup cider vinegar

¼ cup tamari

½ teaspoon salt

½ teaspoon ground black pepper

½ teaspoon liquid smoke

Heat the oil in a saucepan over medium heat. Add the onion and garlic and cook for 5 minutes, until the vegetables soften. Add the tomato sauce, chipotle, maple syrup, water, vinegar, tamari, salt, and pepper, stirring to mix well. Simmer for 20 minutes, or until the sauce reduces to the desired consistency. Near the end of the cooking time, stir in the liquid smoke, then taste and adjust the seasonings, adding more salt, maple syrup, or vinegar if needed to balance the flavors.

VEGAN CHARCUTERIE

CHAPTER 4

Charcuterie (from the French for "cooked flesh") is a term to describe prepared and cured meats, such as sausage, bacon, ham, and pâtés, the process of which was originally developed as a way to preserve meats without refrigeration.

This chapter is all about vegan charcuterie. From DIY cold cuts to several sausage variations, it also features recipes for vegan jerky, pepperoni, pâté, and scrapple, as well as six ways to make vegan bacon using ingredients such as tempeh, tofu, eggplant, mushrooms, and coconut. Recipes using these staples feature several world-class sandwiches, including a tempting BLT, a hearty club sandwich, and my personal favorite, a delicious banh mi sandwich. There are also haute dogs (a classy version of the hot dog) and comfort-food favorites including jambalaya, cassoulet, and a satisfying meatloaf.

If you needed an especially compelling reason to veganize prepared meat products, consider this: the World Health Organization recently released a report concluding that processed meats such as bacon, sausage, and hot dogs cause cancer and are, in fact, now ranked alongside cigarettes and asbestos in terms of causing cancer.

TEMPEH BACON   106

TOFU BACON   107

COCONUT BACON BITS   108

EGGPLANT
BACON STRIPS   109

MUSHROOM BACON   110

SMOKY CHICKPEAS   111

HAMISH LOAF   112

DIY JERKY   113

BANH MI   115

HANDCRAFTED PEPPERONI   116

SPICY ITALIAN SAUSAGE   117

ANDOUILLE SAUSAGE   118

COUNTRY-STYLE PÂTÉ   119

JAMBALAYA   120

VEGANIZED SCRAPPLE   122

MAPLE BREAKFAST
SAUSAGE   123

CASSOULET   125

NO-MEAT LOAF   126

BEYOND BLT   127

HAUTE DOGS   128

HAUTE DOGS WELLINGTON   130

DEVILED HAMISH SALAD   131

JOIN THE CLUB SANDWICH   133

TEMPEH BACON

MAKES 12 TO 16 STRIPS

1 (8-ounce) package tempeh, cut lengthwise into thin strips

3 tablespoons tamari

3 tablespoons pure maple syrup or agave syrup

2 tablespoons cider vinegar

2 tablespoons water

1 teaspoon liquid smoke

½ teaspoon smoked paprika

½ teaspoon ground black pepper

2 tablespoons olive oil

In the vegan food world, "bacon" means smoky, salty, savory, crispy, chewy goodness—no animal flesh needed. Tempeh happens to be a great vehicle for everything we love about bacon. Best of all, it's high in protein and can be easily cut into thin slices for convenience. Use your favorite brand of tempeh —my current fave is Trader Joe's Organic 3-Grain Tempeh.

1 Arrange the tempeh slices in a shallow baking dish, overlapping slightly if necessary. In a small saucepan, combine the tamari, maple syrup, vinegar, water, liquid smoke, paprika, and pepper and heat over medium heat until hot. Pour the hot marinade over the tempeh slices and set aside for 15 to 20 minutes to allow the tempeh to absorb the marinade.

2 Heat the oil in a large skillet over medium-high heat. Add the tempeh, in batches if needed, and cook, turning once, until the tempeh is nicely browned. Pour any remaining marinade onto the tempeh as it cooks and allow it to evaporate.

TOFU BACON

Extra-firm tofu can be used to make tasty bacon slices that are great in sandwiches.

1 Preheat the oven to 350°F. In a 9- x 13-inch glass baking dish, combine the tamari, water, sugar, ketchup, nutritional yeast, liquid smoke, and oil. Mix well.

2 Arrange the tofu slices in the marinade in a single layer, overlapping as little as possible. Carefully turn over the tofu to coat with the marinade. Bake for 30 minutes, then carefully turn over the tofu slices with a thin metal spatula. Return them to the oven and continue cooking until nicely browned, 20 to 30 minutes longer.

Quick trick: For crispy bacon that's ready sooner than later, remove the bacon from the oven after the first 30 minutes and pan-fry it in a lightly oiled nonstick skillet for about 2 minutes per side.

¼ **cup tamari**

¼ **cup water**

1 **tablespoon brown sugar**

1 **tablespoon ketchup**

1 **tablespoon nutritional yeast flakes**

1½ **teaspoons liquid smoke**

½ **teaspoon dark (toasted) sesame oil**

1 **(12- to 16-ounce) package extra-firm tofu, drained, pressed, and cut lengthwise into ⅛-inch strips**

COCONUT BACON BITS

1 tablespoon pure maple syrup

1 tablespoon liquid smoke

1 tablespoon tamari

1 tablespoon water

1½ cups unsweetened flaked coconut (large flakes)

Be sure to use the large flake unsweetened coconut for this recipe—some brands may label them as "chips." These tasty morsels are an ideal topping for salads, soups, and casseroles.

Preheat the oven to 325°F. In a medium bowl, combine the maple syrup, liquid smoke, tamari, and water. Add the coconut and toss gently to coat. Spread the coconut mixture evenly in a single layer on a nonstick baking sheet or one lined with parchment paper. Bake for about 20 minutes, turning the coconut with a thin metal spatula every 5 minutes to help it cook evenly and prevent burning. Watch carefully during baking as the coconut can burn easily.

EGGPLANT BACON STRIPS

Eggplant is a good choice for making vegan bacon because it's easy to cut into long strips, it absorbs the seasonings very well, and it gets nice and crispy. If you know someone who isn't an eggplant fan, this may just win them over. Long thin eggplants work best for this recipe.

1 pound eggplant

3 tablespoons tamari

2 tablespoons pure maple syrup or agave syrup

1 teaspoon liquid smoke

½ teaspoon smoked paprika

Salt and ground black pepper

1   Cut the ends off the eggplant, then use a vegetable peeler to remove the skin. Cut the eggplant in half lengthwise, then cut each half into long thin strips, about ⅛ inch thick.

2   Arrange the eggplant slices in a single layer on a baking sheet and spray the eggplant with cooking spray. Bake for 6 to 8 minutes, or until lightly browned, then remove from the oven and flip the eggplant slices. If any of the eggplant strips are too browned, transfer them to a plate.

3   In a shallow bowl, combine the tamari, maple syrup, liquid smoke, paprika, and salt and pepper to taste. Add the eggplant strips, turning to coat evenly. Set aside to marinate for 1 hour at room temperature or cover and refrigerate to marinate for 2 to 3 hours or overnight.

4   Preheat the oven to 325°F. Line a large baking sheet with parchment paper and spray it with cooking spray. Arrange the eggplant strips in a single layer on the prepared baking sheet. Bake for 30 minutes, then remove from the oven and flip the eggplant. Return to the oven and bake 30 minutes longer, or until browned and slightly crisped on the edges. Remove from the oven. If the strips are not as crisp as you'd like, allow them to cool completely, then sauté for a minute or two in a hot skillet when ready to use.

MUSHROOM BACON

8 ounces portobello mushroom caps or shiitake mushroom caps, thinly sliced, or king oyster mushroom stems, cut lengthwise into ⅛-inch slices

3 tablespoons grapeseed oil

Salt and ground black pepper

1 tablespoon tamari

1 tablespoon pure maple syrup

1 teaspoon liquid smoke

¼ teaspoon garlic powder

¼ teaspoon smoked paprika

¼ teaspoon light brown sugar

If you love mushrooms and the smoky, sweet, saltiness of bacon, then this recipe is for you. I usually make mushroom bacon with portobellos when I want slices or shiitakes when I want small pieces, but when I'm lucky enough to find king oyster mushrooms, they are my first choice, hands down. Their large stems when cut lengthwise into thin slices make perfect mushroom bacon strips.

1 Preheat the oven to 350°F. Line a rimmed baking sheet with parchment paper and spray it with cooking spray. Arrange the mushroom slices on the prepared baking sheet in a single layer (you may need two baking sheets). Brush 2 tablespoons of the oil onto the mushrooms, using a pastry brush to coat evenly. Season lightly with salt and pepper. Bake for 15 minutes, then carefully turn over the mushroom slices with a thin metal spatula. Return them to the oven and continue cooking until well browned and crisp on the edges, 10 to 15 minutes longer, depending on the type of mushrooms. (Mushrooms will quickly overcook; watch carefully so they don't burn.)

2 In a shallow bowl, combine the tamari, maple syrup, liquid smoke, garlic powder, paprika, sugar, and remaining 1 tablespoon oil. Remove the mushrooms from the oven and add them to the bowl, tossing gently to coat with the marinade. Return the mushrooms to the baking sheet in a single layer and continue baking for about 5 minutes longer, or until the mushrooms are nicely glazed. These taste best when eaten right after baking as the texture tends to soften after they cool down.

SMOKY CHICKPEAS

Cooked chickpeas take on a smoky bacony flavor from the marinade and become firm and crunchy when baked. Enjoy them as a snack or use them on top of soups or salads, added to grain or noodle dishes, or as a filling ingredient for wrap sandwiches.

Preheat the oven to 400°F. Blot the chickpeas dry in order to help them become crunchy. In a medium bowl, combine the tamari, maple syrup, oil, liquid smoke, paprika, and salt. Add the chickpeas and toss gently to coat. Spread the chickpea mixture evenly in a single layer on a nonstick baking sheet or one lined with parchment paper. Bake for about 30 minutes, stirring the chickpeas every 10 minutes to allow them to cook evenly and prevent burning. The chickpeas should become nicely browned. Remove from the oven and serve warm or at room temperature. These are best eaten right away as they lose their crunchiness after being stored and refrigerated.

1½ cups cooked or 1 (15-ounce) can chickpeas, drained and rinsed

2 tablespoons tamari

1 tablespoon pure maple syrup

1 tablespoon olive oil

1 teaspoon liquid smoke

¼ teaspoon smoked paprika

¼ teaspoon salt

HAMISH LOAF

1 cup cooked or canned white beans, drained and rinsed

1 cup tomato juice

3 tablespoons tamari

1 tablespoon olive oil

1 teaspoon liquid smoke

1½ cups vital wheat gluten

½ cup all-purpose flour

¼ cup nutritional yeast

2 tablespoons tapioca flour

2 teaspoons onion powder

1 teaspoon garlic powder

1 teaspoon smoked paprika

½ teaspoon ground coriander

½ teaspoon sugar

½ teaspoon salt

¼ teaspoon ground black pepper

⅛ teaspoon ground nutmeg

⅛ teaspoon ground allspice

This versatile loaf can be chilled and thinly sliced to use in sandwiches and sautés or chopped or diced to use in stews, stir-fries, or scrambles. If you prefer to mix the dough by hand instead of in a food processor, you can blend the wet ingredients in a blender and then combine in a bowl with the dry ingredients.

1   Preheat the oven to 350°F. In a food processor, combine the beans, tomato juice, tamari, oil, and liquid smoke and blend until smooth. Add the vital wheat gluten, flour, nutritional yeast, tapioca flour, onion powder, garlic powder, smoked paprika, coriander, sugar, salt, pepper, nutmeg, and allspice. Process to combine and form a soft dough. If the mixture is too wet, add a little more vital wheat gluten, 1 tablespoon at a time. If the mixture is too dry, add a little more tomato juice, 1 tablespoon at a time. Transfer to a work surface and knead for 3 minutes, then shape into a loaf about 9 inches long.

2   Place the loaf on an oiled sheet of aluminum foil and enclose it in the foil. Place the loaf in a 10-inch baking dish, seam-side up. Add an inch of water to the baking dish and cover the entire pan tightly with foil. Bake until firm, about 1 hour and 45 minutes. Uncover and allow to cool to room temperature, then refrigerate to firm up for 2 to 3 hours before slicing to use in recipes.

> ## VARIATION
>
> **Glazed Hamish Loaf** While the loaf is baking, combine ¼ cup peach jam with 1 tablespoon packed brown sugar and 2 teaspoons tamari in a small bowl. Mix well and set aside. About 40 minutes before the loaf is finished baking, remove it from the oven. Remove the loaf from the baking dish, unwrap it, and brush the glaze over the loaf. Drain the water from the baking dish, then return the glazed, uncovered loaf to the baking dish and return to the oven to finish baking.

DIY JERKY

This produces tangy, flavorful tofu jerky that makes a great protein-rich snack.

1   In a shallow bowl, combine the tamari, barbecue sauce, brown sugar, maple syrup, garlic powder, liquid smoke, and pepper, and mix until well blended.

2   Cut the pressed tofu into ¼-inch-thick slices and add them to the marinade, turning to coat both sides. Cover and refrigerate for 2 hours.

3   Preheat the oven to the lowest temperature (about 200°F). Place the oven rack in the lowest position in the oven. Line a large baking sheet with parchment paper. Place the tofu slices on the parchment in a single layer. Bake for about 8 hours, turning over the tofu slices once about halfway through. When the tofu is hard and uniformly dark in color, it is ready.

3 tablespoons tamari

3 tablespoons barbecue sauce, store-bought or homemade (page 101)

2 teaspoons brown sugar

2 teaspoons pure maple syrup

1 teaspoon garlic powder

½ teaspoon liquid smoke

½ teaspoon ground black pepper

1 (12- to 16-ounce) package extra-firm tofu, drained and well pressed

HOW TO PRESS TOFU

Place the tofu block between paper towels on a plate. Set another plate on top, and put a weight on top of the plate, such as a can, to press the water from the tofu while you prepare the sauce.

BANH MI

Crusty French bread is the vehicle for the flavorful banh mi sandwich filling of hoisin-glazed plant protein combined with crisp veggies, fragrant cilantro, creamy-spicy mayo, and sriracha.

1 In a small bowl, combine the shredded carrot, vinegar, sugar, and salt. Mix well and set aside.

2 Heat the oil in a skillet over medium heat. Add the hamish slices and cook until lightly browned, turning frequently, about 5 minutes. Add the hoisin, turning to coat, and glaze the slices for another minute or two. Remove from the heat and set aside to cool.

3 To assemble, spread the inside of each roll with mayo and drizzle with sriracha to taste. Arrange 2 hamish slices on the bottom half of each baguette. Top each with the cucumber slices, cilantro, jalapeños, and reserved pickled carrot. Close up the sandwiches and serve at once.

1 cup shredded carrot

2 tablespoons rice vinegar

1 teaspoon sugar

¼ teaspoon salt

1 tablespoon neutral vegetable oil

8 thin slices Hamish Loaf (page 112) or seitan or extra-firm tofu

2 tablespoons hoisin sauce

4 (6-inch) sub rolls or 1 or 2 baguettes, cut into 4 (6-inch) pieces, split

½ cup vegan mayo, store-bought or homemade (page 35)

1 to 2 tablespoons sriracha, or to taste

1 cucumber, peeled, seeded, and thinly sliced

1 cup cilantro leaves

2 tablespoons chopped bottled jalapeño slices

HANDCRAFTED PEPPERONI

MAKES
2 (8-INCH)
LOGS

1 cup vital wheat gluten

¼ cup nutritional yeast

3 tablespoons tapioca starch

2 teaspoons smoked paprika

1 teaspoon ground fennel seed

¾ teaspoon garlic powder

¾ teaspoon onion powder

½ teaspoon whole fennel seeds

½ teaspoon red pepper flakes

½ teaspoon cayenne pepper

½ teaspoon salt

¼ teaspoon ground black pepper

¾ cup water

2 tablespoons tomato paste

2 tablespoons olive oil

1 tablespoon tamari

1 teaspoon liquid smoke

Growing up in an Italian-American household, I cut my teeth on pepperoni. While I'm happy that vegan pepperoni is available commercially, the flavor isn't even close to the pepperoni I grew up with—and the price tag is sure to induce sticker shock. Try my DIY recipe for an inexpensive and delicious alternative.

1 Preheat the oven to 350°F. In a mixing bowl or food processor, combine the vital wheat gluten, nutritional yeast, tapioca starch, and spices. Mix or pulse to combine. Add the water, tomato paste, oil, tamari, and liquid smoke, and mix or process well to combine thoroughly.

2 Transfer to a work surface, then knead the dough for a few minutes. Divide the dough in half and roll into 2 logs about 8 inches long. Lightly oil two sheets of aluminum foil large enough to wrap each of the logs. Place a pepperoni log on each sheet of foil and wrap it tightly, twisting the ends to seal.

3 Place the foil-wrapped logs in a 9-inch baking pan, seam-side up. Add about ½ inch of water to the pan and cover tightly with foil. Bake for 1 hour, turning halfway through. Unwrap and cool for about 15 minutes, then refrigerate to firm up, 1 to 2 hours. Use a serrated knife to cut into thin slices. Use as is or pan-fry as needed. If not using right away, wrap tightly and refrigerate for up to 5 days or freeze for up to 3 months.

SPICY ITALIAN SAUSAGE

MAKES
6 (6-INCH)
LINKS

This riff on my mother's homemade Italian sausage tastes remarkably like the original. They can be sliced or chopped and used as a pizza topping or added to a scramble. Try them in a sub roll with ketchup, fried onions, and peppers. Testers pronounced these links better tasting than leading brands of vegan sausage and at a fraction of the cost. If you prefer less heat, omit the cayenne, and/or cut back on the red pepper flakes.

1 (15-ounce) can kidney beans, drained and rinsed

3 tablespoons water

2 tablespoons tamari

3 tablespoons olive oil

1 cup vital wheat gluten, or more if needed

2 tablespoons tapioca starch

1 tablespoon nutritional yeast

2 teaspoons smoked paprika

1 teaspoon whole fennel seeds

1 teaspoon ground fennel seeds

1 teaspoon red pepper flakes

1 teaspoon garlic powder

1 teaspoon onion powder

½ teaspoon cayenne pepper

½ teaspoon salt

¼ teaspoon ground black pepper

1 Preheat the oven to 350°F. Lightly oil a shallow baking pan. In a food processor, combine the kidney beans, water, tamari, and 2 tablespoons of the olive oil and process until well mixed. Add the vital wheat gluten, tapioca starch, nutritional yeast, paprika, whole and ground fennel seeds, red pepper flakes, garlic powder, onion powder, cayenne, salt, and pepper and process until a soft dough is formed. If the dough is too wet, add more vital wheat gluten, 1 tablespoon at a time. If the dough is too dry, add more water, 1 tablespoon at a time.

2 Transfer the dough to a work surface and knead gently for 2 minutes. Divide the dough into 6 equal pieces. Roll each piece into a link, 6 inches long. Place each sausage link on a small sheet of aluminum foil and enclose it in the foil, twisting the ends to seal. Place the foil-wrapped sausage links, seam-side up, in a large baking pan (I use a lasagna pan). Add about ½ inch of water to the pan and cover tightly with foil. Bake for 1 hour, turning halfway through. Unwrap and cool for about 15 minutes, then refrigerate to firm up, about 1 hour.

3 To cook, heat the remaining 1 tablespoon oil in a skillet over medium heat. Add the sausage links and cook until hot and browned all over, 3 to 5 minutes total.

ANDOUILLE SAUSAGE

MAKES 6 LINKS

1 cup cooked or canned black-eyed peas, drained, rinsed, and blotted dry

2 tablespoons tamari

1 tablespoon coconut oil, melted

2 teaspoons smoked paprika

1 teaspoon garlic powder

1 teaspoon salt

½ teaspoon black pepper

½ teaspoon onion powder

½ teaspoon dried thyme

½ teaspoon dried oregano

½ teaspoon ground cumin

½ teaspoon filé powder

½ teaspoon chili powder

½ teaspoon cayenne pepper

½ teaspoon red pepper flakes

¾ teaspoon liquid smoke

⅔ cup tomato juice

1¼ cups vital wheat gluten

3 tablespoons tapioca starch

1 tablespoon olive oil

This is a medium-spicy, smoky sausage made with black-eyed peas as an homage to the Southern roots of this popular staple in the Cajun cooking of Louisiana. If you prefer a very spicy sausage, increase the cayenne pepper or red pepper flakes slightly.

1   Preheat the oven to 350°F. In a food processor, combine the black-eyed peas, tamari, coconut oil, paprika, garlic powder, salt, pepper, onion powder, thyme, oregano, cumin, filé powder, chili powder, cayenne, red pepper flakes, and liquid smoke. Add the tomato juice and process until blended.

2   Add the vital wheat gluten and tapioca starch and process until well mixed and a soft dough is formed. Transfer the dough to a work surface and knead gently for 2 minutes. Divide the dough into 6 equal pieces. Roll each piece into a link. Place each sausage link on a small sheet of aluminum foil and enclose it in the foil, twisting the ends to seal. Place the foil-wrapped sausage links, seam-side up, in a large baking pan (I use a lasagna pan). Add about ½ inch of water to the pan and cover tightly with foil. Bake for 1 hour. Unwrap and cool for about 15 minutes, then refrigerate to firm up, about 1 hour.

3   To cook, heat the olive oil in a skillet over medium heat. Add the sausage links and cook until hot and browned on all sides.

COUNTRY-STYLE PÂTÉ

The deep, rich flavor of this pâté makes it a favorite at gatherings. It's good spread onto celery sticks, toast, crackers, crostini, bruschetta, or pita crisps. It also makes a great sandwich filling.

1   Preheat the oven to 350°F. Lightly oil a 6-cup loaf pan or pâté mold.

2   Heat the oil in a large skillet over medium heat. Add the onion and cook until softened, about 5 minutes. Add the garlic and mushrooms and cook, stirring, for 3 minutes. Add the parsley, thyme, marjoram, tamari, brandy, miso paste, tomato paste, and sesame oil. Stir to mix well. Cook until all the liquid evaporates, 2 to 3 minutes. Remove from the heat.

3   In a food processor, grind the walnuts and sunflower seeds. Add the chickpea flour, nutritional yeast, salt, pepper, and nutmeg. Process until well combined. Add the reserved mushroom mixture and the flaxseed mixture and process until combined but not pureed, leaving some texture. Taste and adjust the seasonings, if needed. Spoon the mixture into the prepared pan and smooth the top evenly. Spray or brush the top of the pâté with olive oil, then cover the pan tightly with aluminum foil and place the pan inside a large baking dish with about an inch of hot water in the bottom. Bake until firm, about 1 hour. Let the pâté cool in the pan, then refrigerate until well chilled for easier slicing. When ready to serve, carefully loosen the edges of the pâté with a knife, if necessary, and invert onto a serving platter. Serve at room temperature. Store leftovers in the refrigerator, tightly wrapped. The pâté can also be wrapped well with plastic wrap and foil, then frozen for up to 3 months.

1 tablespoon olive oil

1 large onion, chopped

2 garlic cloves, minced

4 cups fresh mushrooms (any kind or in combination), rinsed, patted dry, and chopped

2 tablespoons chopped fresh parsley

1 teaspoon dried thyme

1 teaspoon dried marjoram

2 tablespoons tamari

2 tablespoons brandy

1 tablespoon miso paste

1 tablespoon tomato paste

1 tablespoon dark (toasted) sesame oil

1 cup toasted walnuts or pecans

½ cup sunflower seeds

½ cup chickpea flour

¼ cup nutritional yeast

½ teaspoon salt

¼ teaspoon ground black pepper

Pinch of ground nutmeg

2 tablespoons ground flaxseed blended with 2 tablespoons warm water

JAMBALAYA

1 tablespoon olive oil

4 to 6 Andouille Sausage links (page 118) or store-bought vegan sausage links, cut into ½-inch slices

1 yellow onion, chopped

½ cup chopped celery

1 green bell pepper, cored, seeded, and chopped

3 garlic cloves, minced

½ cup water

2 tablespoons tomato paste

1 (14.5-ounce) can fire-roasted diced tomatoes, undrained

1 teaspoon dried thyme

½ teaspoon filé powder (optional)

½ teaspoon salt

¼ teaspoon cayenne pepper

1½ cups cooked or 1 (15-ounce) can dark red kidney beans, drained and rinsed

1 teaspoon Tabasco sauce

Cooked brown rice, for serving

A combination of red beans and vegan sausage provides the protein in this vegan jambalaya, made with the culinary holy trinity of onion, green bell pepper, and celery, and simmered in a spicy tomato broth. This is one of those dishes where you'll want to have some hot cooked rice ready to spoon the jambalaya on top.

Heat the oil in a large pot over medium heat. Add the sausage and cook until browned, about 5 minutes. Remove the sausage from the pot. Return the pot to the heat and add the onion, celery, bell pepper, and garlic. Add the water and cook, stirring occasionally, for 10 minutes, or until the vegetables begin to soften. Stir in the tomato paste, then add the tomatoes, thyme, filé powder (if using), salt, cayenne, and beans. Cover and simmer for 20 minutes, or until the vegetables are tender. A few minutes before serving time, stir in the Tabasco and the reserved sausage. Taste and adjust the seasonings, if needed. Serve hot over rice.

VEGANIZED SCRAPPLE

SERVES 6

3 cups vegetable broth, store-bought or homemade (page 182)

1 cup coarse yellow cornmeal

1 teaspoon dried sage

1 teaspoon dried thyme

1 teaspoon salt

½ teaspoon ground black pepper

12 ounces extra-firm tofu, drained and pressed

2 tablespoons tamari

1 tablespoon olive oil, plus more for cooking

½ cup old-fashioned rolled oats

1 cup cooked or canned chickpeas, mashed well

2 tablespoons cornstarch

1 teaspoon garlic powder

1 teaspoon onion powder

½ teaspoon smoked paprika

⅛ teaspoon allspice

½ cup all-purpose flour, for dredging

The Pennsylvania Dutch specialty known as scrapple made regular appearances at the breakfast table when I was a child. Considering the traditional ingredients, it was surprisingly easy to make a plant-based version, which appeared in my 2002 book, *The Vegetarian Meat and Potatoes Cookbook*. This is my latest (and best) version of veganized scrapple. Serve topped with ketchup or maple syrup, as desired.

Note: It is important to chill the scrapple before slicing and frying it.

1   Spray a loaf pan with cooking spray. Bring the broth to a boil in a medium saucepan. In a bowl, whisk together the cornmeal, sage, thyme, salt, and pepper. Slowly whisk the cornmeal mixture into the broth, stirring until smooth. Bring to a boil, stirring constantly. Decrease the heat to low, and continue cooking for 15 minutes, or until thick, stirring frequently. Remove from the heat.

2   Squeeze any excess water from the pressed tofu and place it in a food processor. Add the tamari, oil, oats, chickpeas, cornstarch, garlic powder, onion powder, paprika, and allspice. Process until well blended. Add the tofu mixture to the cornmeal mixture and mix until well combined. Press the mixture evenly into the prepared pan, smoothing the top. Refrigerate for at least 4 hours to firm up.

3   Run a thin-bladed knife around the edge of the loaf pan to loosen the scrapple. Invert the loaf pan onto a cutting board to remove the scrapple from the pan and cut it into ½-inch-thick slices. You should get 12 slices. Place the flour in a shallow bowl. Dredge the slices in the flour, tapping off any excess. Heat a thin layer of oil in a nonstick skillet over medium heat. Add the scrapple, in batches if needed. Cook, turning once, to brown on both sides, about 5 minutes per side.

MAPLE BREAKFAST SAUSAGE

MAKES
6 TO 8
PATTIES

These savory breakfast patties have just the right touch of sweetness. They make a great accompaniment to pancakes or waffles, or try them in a breakfast sandwich.

1   Preheat the oven to 350°F. Lightly oil a large shallow baking pan (I use a lasagna pan).

2   In a food processor, combine the vital wheat gluten, tapioca starch, onion powder, sage, thyme, salt, pepper, coriander, paprika, and nutmeg. Pulse to mix. In a bowl, coarsely mash the pinto beans, then add them to the food processor. Pour in the water, maple syrup, tamari, and coconut oil and process until well mixed and a soft dough is formed.

3   Transfer the dough to a work surface and knead gently for 2 minutes. Divide the dough into 6 to 8 equal pieces and shape them into patties about ¼ inch thick. Place each patty on a small sheet of aluminum foil (about 6 inches long) and enclose it in the foil. Place the foil-wrapped sausage patties, seam-side up, in a single layer in the prepared baking pan. Add about ½ inch of water to the pan and cover tightly with foil. Bake for 30 minutes, turning the patties about halfway through. Unwrap and cool for about 15 minutes, then refrigerate to firm up, about 1 hour. To cook, heat the olive oil in a skillet over medium heat. Add the sausage patties and cook until hot and browned on both sides, about 3 minutes each side.

1 cup vital wheat gluten

3 tablespoons tapioca starch or cornstarch

1 teaspoon onion powder

1 teaspoon ground sage

1 teaspoon dried thyme

1 teaspoon salt

½ teaspoon ground black pepper

½ teaspoon ground coriander

½ teaspoon smoked paprika

¼ teaspoon ground nutmeg

⅔ cup cooked or canned pinto beans

¾ cup water

2 tablespoons pure maple syrup

2 tablespoons tamari

1 tablespoon coconut oil, melted

1 tablespoon olive oil

CASSOULET

This classic country French peasant dish is great made with the Haute Dogs on page 128, but you can use any smoky vegan sausage you like. Cassoulet is traditionally cooked for several hours in the oven, but with this plant-based version, the cooking time is shortened. It can also be made on the stove top or in a slow cooker.

1   Preheat the oven to 350°F. Lightly oil a large (2-quart) casserole dish.

2   Heat 1 tablespoon of the olive oil in a large skillet over medium heat. Add the sausage slices and cook until browned, about 5 minutes. Remove from the skillet. Return the skillet to the heat, add the remaining 1 tablespoon oil, and heat until hot. Add the onion and carrots and cook until slightly softened, about 5 minutes. Stir in the garlic and cook, stirring, until fragrant, about 30 seconds. Stir in the miso mixture, tamari, and mustard. Add the thyme, marjoram, paprika, bay leaf, salt, and pepper.

3   Place the beans, tomatoes and their juice, and broth in the prepared casserole dish. Add the vegetable mixture, reserved sausage, and liquid smoke, and stir to mix well. Cover tightly and bake until the vegetables are tender, about 1 hour. Serve hot, sprinkled with the parsley.

2 tablespoons olive oil

4 Haute Dogs (page 128) or other vegan sausage links, cut into 1-inch slices

1 large yellow onion, chopped

2 large carrots, thinly sliced

3 garlic cloves, minced

1 tablespoon mellow white miso paste dissolved in 2 tablespoons hot (not boiling) water

1 tablespoon tamari

2 teaspoons Dijon mustard

1 teaspoon dried thyme

1 teaspoon dried marjoram

½ teaspoon smoked paprika

1 large bay leaf

½ teaspoon salt

¼ teaspoon ground black pepper

3 cups cooked or 2 (15-ounce) cans cannellini beans, drained and rinsed

1 (14.5-ounce) can petite diced fire-roasted tomatoes, undrained

½ cup vegetable broth, store-bought or homemade (page 182), or water

1 teaspoon liquid smoke

2 tablespoons chopped fresh parsley

NO-MEAT LOAF

1 tablespoon olive oil

1 large onion, chopped

4 garlic cloves, minced

2 cup chopped mushrooms

1 tablespoon tamari

1 tablespoon tomato paste

¼ cup chopped fresh parsley

1 cup old-fashioned rolled oats

½ cup walnuts

½ cup sunflower seeds

2 tablespoons cornstarch or tapioca
starch

1 teaspoon dried thyme

½ teaspoon ground sage

1 teaspoon salt

¼ teaspoon ground black pepper

2 cups cooked lentils or kidney
beans, cooled and mashed

3 cups cooked brown rice, quinoa,
or other grain, cooled

Lentils and brown rice (or your choice of beans or grains)
combine with oats, nuts, and seasonings to make a delicious
no-meat loaf that is terrific sliced and served with brown gravy
(page 191) and accompanied by roasted potatoes and carrots.
Leftovers make fantastic sandwiches.

1   Preheat the oven to 350°F. Lightly oil a loaf pan or line it with
parchment paper.

2   Heat the oil in a large saucepan or Dutch oven over medium heat.
Add the onion and cook until softened, about 5 minutes. Add the
garlic and mushrooms and cook until softened, stirring occasionally,
about 5 minutes longer. Stir in the tamari, tomato paste, and parsley
and set aside to cool.

3   In a food processor, combine the oats, walnuts, and sunflower
seeds and process until finely ground. Add the cornstarch, thyme,
sage, salt, and pepper and pulse to mix.

4   Add the mashed lentils and rice to the onion mixture, then add the
oat mixture and mix well to combine thoroughly. Transfer the mixture
to the prepared pan and press the mixture evenly and firmly into the
pan, smoothing the top. Cover with foil and bake for 45 minutes, then
uncover and bake for 15 minutes longer to brown the top. Remove
from the oven and let stand for about 10 minutes to firm up.

5   To serve, carefully loosen the edges of the loaf with a knife, if
necessary, and invert onto a serving platter. Use a long serrated knife
to slice.

Optional glaze: In a small bowl, combine ½ cup ketchup with
3 tablespoons brown sugar and 1 tablespoon cider vinegar. Mix well,
then spread the glaze evenly on top of the loaf before baking.

BEYOND BLT

My go-to recipe for BLT sandwiches is beyond the traditional version in several ways, not the least of which is a plant-based bacon. To this delicious yet nutritious sandwich favorite I add sliced avocado and swap in spinach leaves for lettuce. Hearty whole-grain sandwich bread, lightly toasted and slathered with vegan mayo, seals the deal.

4 tablespoons vegan mayo, store-bought or homemade (page 35)

4 slices whole-grain sandwich bread, lightly toasted

8 baby spinach leaves

1 small ripe Hass avocado, peeled, pitted, and sliced

8 slices Tempeh Bacon (page 106) or your favorite vegan bacon

1 small ripe tomato, thinly sliced

Salt and ground black pepper

1   Spread 1 tablespoon of the mayo on each slice of toasted bread. Arrange 4 spinach leaves on top of 2 bread slices. Top each with avocado slices, followed by 4 bacon slices. Arrange tomato slices on top of the bacon and season with salt and pepper to taste.

2   Top each sandwich with the remaining bread slices. Cut each sandwich in half diagonally and serve immediately.

HAUTE DOGS

8 ounces firm tofu, well drained

¼ cup water

2 tablespoons tamari

3 tablespoons olive oil

1 tablespoon smoked paprika

1 teaspoon garlic powder

1 teaspoon onion powder

1 teaspoon ground coriander

1 teaspoon ground mustard

1 teaspoon sugar

1 teaspoon salt

½ teaspoon ground black pepper

½ teaspoon ground cardamom

¼ teaspoon allspice

1 cup vital wheat gluten

⅓ cup oat or almond flour (or make your own by finely grinding old-fashioned rolled oats or slivered almonds)

1 teaspoon cornstarch, tapioca starch, or arrowroot

Hot dog buns, for serving

Condiments: Mustard, ketchup, relish

Casual comfort food at its best—the iconic hot dog has been transformed into a healthy link of deliciousness using plant-based ingredients. Haute dog!

1 Preheat the oven to 350°F. Crumble the tofu into a food processor. Add the water, tamari, and oil, and process to blend.

2 Add the paprika, garlic powder, onion powder, coriander, mustard, sugar, salt, pepper, cardamom, and allspice and process until smooth. Add the vital wheat gluten, almond flour, and cornstarch and pulse until well combined and thoroughly mixed to form a soft dough. Transfer the dough to a work surface and knead gently for 2 minutes. Divide the dough into 8 equal pieces. Roll each into a hot dog–shaped log, about 6 inches long. Place each hot dog on a small sheet of aluminum foil and enclose it in the foil, twisting the ends to seal.

3 Place the foil-wrapped hot dogs, seam-side up, in a large baking pan (I use a lasagna pan). Add about ½ inch of water to the pan and cover tightly with foil. Bake for 1 hour. Unwrap and cool for about 15 minutes, then refrigerate to firm up, about 1 hour.

4 To cook, simmer in water for 5 minutes to heat through, or fry in a skillet until browned, or cook on the grill until hot. Serve on buns with your favorite hot dog condiments. If not using right away, cover the hot dogs tightly and refrigerate for up to 4 days or freeze for 2 to 3 weeks.

HAUTE DOGS WELLINGTON

SERVES 4

2 tablespoons olive oil

4 Haute Dogs (page 128) or store-bought vegan hot dogs

½ cup chopped onion

1 cup ground seitan or vegan burger crumbles

⅓ cup ketchup

4 tablespoons prepared yellow mustard

1 teaspoon chili powder

Salt and ground black pepper

1 sheet vegan puff pastry, thawed

Cook up some Haute Dogs (page 128) or your favorite brand of vegan hot dogs and slather them with some mustard and chili, then wrap them in puff pastry and bake. This haute cuisine way to enjoy hot dogs has become a Fourth of July tradition at my house.

1   Heat 1 tablespoon of the oil in a skillet over medium heat. Add the hot dogs and cook until browned all over, about 5 minutes. Transfer to a plate to cool. Heat the remaining 1 tablespoon oil in the same skillet over medium heat. Add the onion and cook until softened, about 5 minutes. Add the seitan and cook until nicely browned, about 5 minutes. Stir in the ketchup, 1 tablespoon of the mustard, and the chili powder. Season with salt and pepper to taste and cook, stirring to blend the flavors. Remove from the heat and set aside to cool. The hot dogs and chili must be completely cool before wrapping in the pastry, so refrigerate them, if necessary, to speed the cooling process.

2   Preheat the oven to 400°F. Line a baking sheet with parchment paper. Place the thawed pastry on a flat work surface and cut it into 4 equal squares. Spread about 2 teaspoons of mustard down the center of each pastry square and place a cooled hot dog on top of the mustard. Spread a line of about 3 tablespoons of the cooled chili alongside each hot dog. Roll up the pastry to enclose the hot dog and chili, folding in the ends and pinching the seam to close tightly. Arrange the pastry-wrapped hot dogs on the prepared baking sheet and bake for 20 to 25 minutes, or until the pastry is nicely browned. Serve hot.

DEVILED HAMISH SALAD

MAKES
ABOUT
2½ CUPS

Reminiscent of the homemade ham salad my mother used to make, this spread is terrific on crackers or as a sandwich filling.

1 In a food processor, combine all of the ingredients and pulse to make a spread with a little texture remaining. Taste and adjust the seasonings, if needed.

2 Transfer to a bowl. The spread is now ready to use in sandwiches or on crackers. If not using right away, cover tightly and refrigerate for up to 5 days.

8 ounces Hamish Loaf (page 112) or your favorite vegan ham, cut into 1-inch chunks

1 celery rib, coarsely chopped

1 tablespoon chopped onion (optional)

⅓ cup vegan mayo, store-bought or homemade (page 35)

3 tablespoons sweet pickle relish

1 tablespoon prepared yellow mustard

½ teaspoon Tabasco sauce

Salt and ground black pepper

JOIN THE CLUB SANDWICH

Although club sandwiches often contain three slices of bread, tradition holds that it was originally made with two slices. With this club, you can enjoy vegan ham, bacon, and mayo, all in one delicious sandwich. The recipe is easily doubled to make more sandwiches. The amount of ham you use will depend on how thinly you slice it and personal preference.

1 In a small bowl, combine the mayo with the mustard until blended. Spread about 1 tablespoon on one side of each slice of bread.

2 Place 2 of the toasted bread slices on a work surface, mayo-side up, and top each with a lettuce leaf, followed by 2 or 4 slices of ham, then 2 tomato slices, salt and pepper, avocado slices, and 2 bacon slices. Top each sandwich with the remaining lettuce leaf and the remaining toast (mayo-side down). Secure each sandwich with long toothpicks and cut each sandwich into 4 triangles.

¼ cup vegan mayo, store-bought or homemade (page 35)

1 teaspoon Dijon mustard

4 slices bread, toasted

4 lettuce leaves

4 to 8 thin slices Hamish Loaf (page 112) or other vegan ham

4 slices tomato

Salt and ground black pepper

1 ripe avocado, peeled, pitted, and thinly sliced

4 slices cooked vegan bacon, store-bought or homemade (pages 106–107)

INSTEAD OF SEAFOOD

SEAFOOD

CHAPTER 5

Hearts of palm features prominently in making many of these vegan seafood recipes. Vegan Crab Louis and Creamy Sriracha See Scallops are among the tantalizing recipes you can make using these DIY seafood ingredients. As with many of the other recipes, the dishes in this chapter are not meant to be replicas of seafood. Rather, they provide plant-based alternatives that are similar enough in taste, texture, and appearance that they work well in traditional seafood preparations so that you can enjoy the same sauces and seasonings and other elements of a particular dish.

CLAM-FREE CHOWDER   139

LOBSTER MUSHROOM
BISQUE   140

FISH-FREE TACOS   142

VEGAN FISH AND CHIPS WITH
TARTAR SAUCE   144

FISH-FREE FILLETS   146

FISH-FREE STICKS   147

SEE SCALLOPS   148

PALM-CRAB PO'BOYS   149

HEARTS OF PALM AND
ARTICHOKE CAKES   150

CREAMY SRIRACHA
SEE SCALLOPS   153

CHICKPEA AND ARTICHOKE
TUNA SALAD   154

PALM-CRAB IMPERIAL   155

VEGAN CRAB LOUIS   157

CLAM-FREE CHOWDER

Oyster mushrooms star in this vegan interpretation of New England clam chowder made with diced potatoes, onion, and celery with a creamy, cashew-based broth. If oyster mushrooms are unavailable, substitute white button mushrooms, chanterelles, or a combination of both.

1   Heat 1 tablespoon of the butter in a large pot over medium heat. Add the mushrooms and cook for 5 minutes. Remove from the pot with a slotted spoon. Add the remaining 1 tablespoon butter to the same pot over medium heat. Add the onion, celery, and garlic and cook, stirring occasionally, for 5 minutes, or until softened. Stir in the potatoes, bay leaves, dulse, thyme, Old Bay, salt, pepper, and vegetable broth. Bring to a boil and then decrease the heat to low and cook for 30 minutes, or until the potatoes are just tender. Remove the bay leaves and stir in the liquid smoke.

2   While the soup is simmering, blend the cashews and 1 cup of the almond milk in a high-speed blender until smooth. When the vegetables are tender, stir in the cashew mixture and the remaining 1 cup almond milk. Stir in the reserved mushrooms and heat the soup for a minute or two until hot. Taste and adjust the seasonings, if needed. Serve hot, garnished with the parsley.

2 tablespoons vegan butter, store-bought or homemade (page 36)

8 ounces oyster mushrooms, chopped

1 yellow onion, chopped

1 celery rib, minced

1 garlic clove, minced

2 cups peeled and diced potatoes

2 bay leaves

1 teaspoon dulse or nori flakes

½ teaspoon dried thyme

½ teaspoon Old Bay seasoning

1 teaspoon salt

¼ teaspoon ground black pepper

2 cups vegetable broth, store-bought or homemade (page 182)

¼ teaspoon liquid smoke

½ cup raw cashews, soaked in hot water for 1 hour, then drained

2 cups unsweetened almond milk, store-bought or homemade (page 28)

1 tablespoon minced fresh parsley

LOBSTER MUSHROOM BISQUE

2 cups lobster mushrooms, fresh or reconstituted from dried (see headnote)

2 tablespoons olive oil

1 yellow onion, minced

1 celery rib, minced

2 garlic cloves, minced

3 cups vegetable broth, store-bought or homemade (page 182)

2 teaspoons tomato paste

¼ cup brandy or dry white wine

Salt and ground black pepper

1 cup Cashew Cream (page 32)

1 tablespoon minced fresh chives

The reddish-orange color of lobster mushrooms looks a lot like cooked lobster. Fresh lobster mushrooms can be difficult to find (but worth trying, if you can). The dried ones can be easier to locate at specialty food stores or online. If using dried mushrooms, combine them with the 3 cups of broth in a medium pot and bring it to a boil. Then decrease the heat and simmer for 30 minutes until the mushrooms are reconstituted; use this enriched broth in the recipe to add flavor to the bisque. Regular white mushrooms or oyster mushrooms may be substituted for up to half of the lobster mushrooms.

1   Trim the fresh or reconstituted mushrooms. Reserve 4 pieces of the reddish part of the lobster mushrooms for garnish and set aside. Cut the rest of the mushrooms into thin slices. Heat 1 tablespoon of the oil in a large pot over medium heat. Add the onion, celery, and garlic, and cook until softened, about 5 minutes, adding a little broth if the vegetables begin to stick. Add the mushrooms and cook for 3 minutes longer. Stir in the tomato paste and mix well. Cook, stirring, for 2 minutes, then remove the pan from the heat and stir in the brandy. Return the pan to the heat and cook, stirring, to scrape the bottom of the pan. Add the broth and salt and pepper to taste. Bring to a boil, then decrease the heat to low and simmer for 20 minutes.

2 Transfer the mushroom mixture to a high-speed blender or a food processor and blend until smooth. Return the mixture to the pot and stir in the cream. Bring just to a boil, then decrease the heat to low and simmer for another 15 to 20 minutes.

3 While the soup is simmering, thinly slice the reserved mushroom pieces. Heat the remaining 1 tablespoon oil in a small skillet over medium heat, add the mushrooms, and cook, turning as needed, until crisped. Season with salt and pepper to taste. Taste the bisque and adjust the seasonings, if needed. Ladle the hot soup into bowls and serve hot, garnished with the mushroom slices and chives.

VARIATIONS

If lobster mushrooms are unavailable, use oyster mushrooms to make oyster bisque. If you can't find either lobster or oyster mushrooms, use any other type of mushrooms, alone or in combination, to make a delicious mushroom bisque.

FISH-FREE TACOS

Slaw

4 cups shredded green cabbage

½ cup chopped fresh cilantro

2 tablespoons olive oil

2 tablespoons fresh lime juice

2 teaspoons ancho chile powder

Salt and ground black pepper

Salsa

3 large plum tomatoes, cored and halved

2 jalapeños, stems and seeds removed, then minced

1 small red onion, finely diced

3 tablespoons red wine vinegar

¼ cup chopped fresh cilantro

1 teaspoon dried oregano

Salt and ground black pepper

To assemble

1 recipe Fish-Free Sticks (page 147)

4 soft wheat tortillas

1 ripe Hass avocado, peeled, pitted, and chopped or sliced

I love the vibrant flavors in these delicious tacos inspired by the fish tacos of Veracruz. The slaw and salsa can be made ahead of time and refrigerated until ready to serve.

1 **Slaw:** In a bowl, combine the cabbage and cilantro. Drizzle with the olive oil and lime juice and sprinkle on the ancho powder and salt and pepper to taste. Toss to combine, then set aside until needed.

2 **Salsa:** In a separate bowl, combine the tomatoes, jalapeños, onion, vinegar, and cilantro. Add the oregano and salt and pepper to taste. Mix well, then set aside until needed.

3 **To assemble:** Prepare the fish sticks according to the recipe. Place 2 fish sticks end to end inside each tortilla. Top with the slaw, salsa, and avocado. Serve immediately.

VEGAN FISH AND CHIPS WITH TARTAR SAUCE

SERVES 4

2 large russet potatoes, halved lengthwise and cut lengthwise into ¼-inch slices

2 tablespoons olive oil

½ teaspoon salt

½ teaspoon paprika

½ teaspoon garlic powder

¼ teaspoon ground black pepper

1 recipe Fish-Free Fillets (page 146)

½ cup vegan mayo, store-bought or homemade (page 35)

1 tablespoon sweet pickle relish

½ to 1 teaspoon fresh lemon juice

This healthier alternative to fish and chips features baked (not fried) potatoes and tofu fish fillets along with a creamy vegan tartar sauce.

1   Preheat the oven to 425°F. Line a baking sheet with parchment or spray it with cooking spray.

2   In a bowl, combine the potato slices, olive oil, salt, paprika, garlic powder, and pepper. Toss to coat the potatoes. Arrange the potato slices in a single layer on the prepared baking sheet. Bake until golden brown and tender, turning occasionally, about 30 minutes total. When the potatoes are about halfway done, bake the fillets according to the recipe directions.

3   In a small bowl, combine the mayonnaise, pickle relish, and lemon juice. Mix well and refrigerate until ready to serve. When the potatoes and fillets are done, serve hot with the tartar sauce.

FISH-FREE FILLETS

1 (12- to 16-ounce) package extra- or super-firm tofu, drained

3 tablespoons olive oil

2 tablespoons tamari

1 tablespoon fresh lemon juice

¾ cup panko bread crumbs

1 teaspoon dulse flakes

¼ teaspoon onion powder

¼ teaspoon garlic powder

¼ teaspoon paprika

Salt and ground black pepper

I like to serve these tender fillets topped with a lemony piccata sauce. They are also great to use in the fish and chips recipe on page 144.

1   Cut the tofu into ½-inch slices and press. (See page 13.)

2   Preheat the oven to 425°F. Lightly oil a baking sheet or line it with parchment paper.

3   In a shallow bowl, combine the oil, tamari, and lemon juice. In a separate shallow bowl, combine the panko crumbs, dulse flakes, onion powder, garlic powder, and paprika. Mix well.

4   Dip each tofu slice into the oil and lemon mixture, then season each slice with salt and pepper on both sides. Dredge the tofu slices in the crumb mixture, patting lightly to coat well. Arrange the coated tofu on the prepared baking sheet. Bake until nicely browned on both sides, turning once about halfway through, about 25 minutes total.

FISH-FREE STICKS

Sturdy tempeh is the ideal plant-based ingredient for making faux fish sticks. You can enjoy them as is with some cocktail sauce or use these to make the Veracruz-inspired tacos on page 142.

1 (8-ounce) package tempeh

½ cup chickpea flour

1 teaspoon baking powder

1 teaspoon Old Bay seasoning

1 tablespoon cider vinegar

⅓ cup seltzer

½ cup cornstarch

2 tablespoons dulse flakes

Sunflower oil, for frying

Salt

1   Cut the tempeh into 8 pieces to resemble the shape of fish sticks. Steam the tempeh for 15 minutes, then set aside to cool.

2   In a mixing bowl, combine the flour, baking powder, and Old Bay seasoning. Mix well. Add the vinegar and slowly mix in the seltzer to make a thick batter. If the batter is too thin, add a little more chickpea flour. If it's too thick, add a little more seltzer.

3   In a separate bowl, combine the cornstarch and dulse.

4   Heat a thin layer of oil in a large nonstick skillet. Dredge the tempeh pieces in the cornstarch mixture, then coat with the batter. When the oil in the pan is hot, carefully add the tempeh in batches, if needed, and cook, turning once, until golden brown, 3 to 4 minutes per side. Transfer to a plate and sprinkle with salt. Serve hot.

SEE SCALLOPS

1 (12- to 16-ounce) package extra-firm tofu, well drained

3 tablespoons tamari

1 teaspoon light miso paste

1 tablespoon water

¼ cup panko bread crumbs

2 teaspoons cornstarch

1 teaspoon ground dulse or other dried sea vegetable

½ teaspoon salt

1 tablespoon olive oil

When I was chef at a seafood restaurant in Charleston, South Carolina, scallops were always on the menu. Now I make See Scallops, which, as recipe tester Norine Dobiesz said when she came up with the name: "They're not from the sea but when you see them, they look like scallops." Although they don't share the unique taste or texture of scallops, they work well as a stand-in for scallops in recipes such as coquilles St. Jacques, bacon-wrapped scallops, or my favorite, the Creamy Sriracha See Scallops on page 153. Other plant-based ingredients that can be used to make "see scallops" are sliced rounds of hearts of palm and oyster mushroom stems, but I prefer to use tofu because it absorbs the marinade most readily and contains the most protein.

1 Cut the tofu into ½-inch slabs and press out any excess liquid (see page 13). Use a shot glass or a small (about 1½-inch-diameter) round cookie cutter to cut out rounds from the tofu slices, reserving the remaining tofu scraps for another use.

2 Combine the tamari and miso paste in a shallow bowl, stirring to blend well, then stir in the water. Arrange the scallops in the marinade in a single layer, turning to coat on both sides. Set aside for 1 hour.

3 In a shallow bowl, combine the panko crumbs, cornstarch, dulse, and salt, and mix well. Remove the scallops from the marinade and dredge them in the crumb mixture.

4 Heat the oil in a large nonstick skillet over medium-high heat. Add the scallops, in batches if needed, and cook for 2 to 3 minutes per side, or until lightly browned on the bottom. Once the scallops are browned on both sides, they can be enjoyed as is or used in recipes.

PALM-CRAB PO'BOYS

SERVES 3

Whenever I make the Hearts of Palm and Artichoke Cakes on page 150 for dinner, I always make a double batch so I have some handy to make these fantastic po'boy sandwiches later in the week.

1 recipe Hearts of Palm and Artichoke Cakes (page 150)

2 tablespoons olive oil

¼ cup vegan mayo, store-bought or homemade (page 35), or Remoulade Sauce (page 188)

1 French baguette, cut into 3 sections, or 3 small sub rolls, split

2 cups shredded lettuce

1 large ripe tomato, thinly sliced

Salt and ground black pepper

Tabasco or other hot sauce, for serving

1   Prepare the cakes according to the directions, dividing the mixture into 6 equal portions to make 6 small cakes. Heat the oil in a large skillet over medium heat. Add the cakes and cook until nicely browned, then flip over and cook the other side until browned, about 4 minutes per side.

2   To assemble the sandwiches, spread the mayonnaise on the inside top and bottom of the bread. Spread some lettuce onto the bottom of each sandwich, followed by tomato slices. Sprinkle with salt and pepper to taste. Top with the crab cakes (2 per sandwich). Serve at once with hot sauce to add as desired.

HEARTS OF PALM AND ARTICHOKE CAKES

MAKES
6 TO 8
CAKES

1 tablespoon olive oil, plus more for frying

½ cup minced onion

¼ cup minced celery

2 teaspoons minced garlic

1 (14-ounce) jar hearts of palm, well drained, patted dry, and roughly chopped

1 (6-ounce) jar marinated artichoke hearts, well drained, patted dry, and roughly chopped

2 teaspoons Old Bay seasoning

1 tablespoon cornstarch

1 teaspoon nori or dulse flakes

¼ cup vegan mayo, store-bought or homemade (page 35)

¾ cup panko bread crumbs

Lemon wedges, for serving

These delectable cakes are crisp on the outside and moist and flaky on the inside with a flavor that is remarkably similar to traditional crab cakes thanks to Old Bay seasoning and a dash of nori flakes. This recipe makes six to eight cakes (depending on how big you like them) that can be enjoyed as a main dish, in sandwiches (they're even good cold!), or as a component in the Seitan Oscar recipe on page 97.

1   Heat the oil in a large skillet over medium-high heat. Add the onion and celery and cook until softened, 5 minutes. Add the garlic and cook for 1 minute longer. Remove from the heat and set aside to cool.

2   In a large bowl, combine the hearts of palm, artichoke hearts, Old Bay seasoning, cornstarch, nori flakes, and mayo. Add the cooled onion mixture and ¼ cup of the panko, and mix well. Divide the mixture into 6 to 8 portions and shape into small patties.

3   Place the remaining ½ cup panko in a shallow bowl. Coat the patties with the bread crumbs and refrigerate or freeze for 20 minutes or longer.

4   Heat a thin layer of oil in a medium skillet over medium-high heat until hot and shimmering. Carefully place the patties in the skillet and cook until golden brown on each side, 3 to 4 minutes per side. Transfer the cooked patties to a plate. Serve hot with lemon wedges.

CREAMY SRIRACHA SEE SCALLOPS

SERVES
3 OR 4

The spicy, creamy, and delicious sauce is a fantastic topping for any variety of plant-based seafood. I like to serve the scallops over rice to catch every bit of the sauce.

1   In a small bowl, combine the mayo, chili sauce, sriracha, and lemon juice. Mix well.

2   Cook the scallops in a hot skillet as directed in the recipe. When they are browned on both sides, transfer them to serving plates and top with the sauce.

⅓ cup vegan mayo, store-bought or homemade (page 35), or Cashew Cream (page 32)

2 tablespoons Thai chili sauce

1 tablespoon sriracha

1 tablespoon fresh lemon juice

1 recipe See Scallops (page 148)

CHICKPEA AND ARTICHOKE TUNA SALAD

½ cup sunflower seeds, soaked in hot water for 1 hour, then drained

⅓ cup chopped celery

3 tablespoons chopped dill pickles

1 or 2 scallions, chopped

1½ cups cooked or 1 (15-ounce) can chickpeas, drained and rinsed

1 cup coarsely chopped marinated artichoke hearts

½ cup vegan mayo, store-bought or homemade (page 35)

2 teaspoons prepared yellow mustard

2 teaspoons fresh lemon juice

1 teaspoon dulse flakes (optional)

½ teaspoon salt

¼ teaspoon ground black pepper

I like this chickpea and artichoke salad better than I ever liked tuna salad. It's loaded with texture and flavor and can be enjoyed as a sandwich filling or scooped onto lettuce leaves.

1 In a food processor, combine the sunflower seeds, celery, pickles, and scallions and pulse until finely minced. Add the chickpeas and artichoke hearts and pulse until chopped, but leaving some texture.

2 Transfer the mixture to a bowl and stir in the mayo, mustard, lemon juice, dulse (if using), salt, and pepper. If not using right away, cover and refrigerate for up to 5 days.

PALM-CRAB IMPERIAL

SERVES 4

Another regular on seafood restaurant menus, crab imperial combines crabmeat with a white sauce, topped with bread crumbs, and baked. This vegan version uses hearts of palm and artichoke hearts instead of crab and a creamy vegan white sauce made with almond milk. The optional dulse flakes give it a more pronounced seafood flavor, but it's perfectly delicious without it.

3 tablespoons vegan butter, store-bought or homemade (page 36), melted

3 tablespoons all-purpose flour

2 cups unsweetened almond milk, store-bought or homemade (page 28)

1 (14-ounce) jar hearts of palm, drained and chopped

1 (6-ounce) jar marinated artichoke hearts, drained, patted dry, and chopped

¾ cup panko bread crumbs

¼ cup chopped pimiento, drained

¼ cup finely minced scallion

2 tablespoons minced fresh parsley

2 tablespoons dry sherry

1 tablespoon fresh lemon juice

1 teaspoon dulse or nori flakes (optional)

1 teaspoon Vegan Worcestershire Sauce, store-bought or homemade (page 186)

1 teaspoon dry mustard powder

1 teaspoon Old Bay seasoning

½ teaspoon paprika

Salt and ground black pepper

2 tablespoons olive oil

1   Preheat the oven to 400°F. Heat the butter in a saucepan over medium-high heat. Add the flour and cook, stirring, until smooth, about 2 minutes. Whisk in the almond milk and bring to a boil. Decrease the heat to medium and cook, stirring, until thickened, about 5 minutes. Remove from the heat and stir in the hearts of palm, artichoke hearts, half the bread crumbs, pimiento, scallion, half the parsley, sherry, lemon juice, dulse (if using), Worcestershire sauce, mustard, Old Bay seasoning, half the paprika, and salt and pepper to taste. Mix gently to combine, then taste and adjust the seasonings, if needed.

2   Divide the mixture evenly among 4 shallow oval baking dishes or a single 8-inch shallow baking dish. In a small bowl, combine the oil with the remaining bread crumbs and paprika, and mix well to coat the crumbs. Sprinkle the crumb mixture evenly over the baking dish(es). Bake until lightly browned and bubbling in the center, about 20 minutes. Sprinkle with the remaining parsley and serve hot.

VEGAN CRAB LOUIS

The crab Louis (pronounced "Louie") salad originated on the West Coast in the early 1900s and remained a fixture on restaurant menus throughout the mid-1900s. In this version, hearts of palm replace the crabmeat and vegan mayo is used to make the dressing. This will serve two for lunch, four as an appetizer.

4 ounces thin asparagus, cut into 1-inch pieces

1 teaspoon sweet paprika

1 teaspoon Old Bay seasoning

3 large hearts of palm (from a jar packed in water)

3 tablespoons vegan mayo, store-bought or homemade (page 35)

1 tablespoon fresh lemon juice

2 teaspoons chopped fresh dill

2 teaspoons capers, well drained

1 teaspoon sriracha sauce

Salt and freshly ground pepper

2 ripe Hass avocados

Lettuce leaves, for serving

1   Steam the asparagus until just tender, then rinse in cold water to stop the cooking process. Set aside.

2   In a medium bowl, combine the paprika and Old Bay, stirring to mix. Coarsely chop the hearts of palm and add to the spice mixture in the bowl, tossing gently to coat.

3   In a small bowl, combine the mayo, lemon juice, dill, capers, sriracha, and salt and pepper to taste. Mix well, then add the hearts of palm and reserved asparagus and mix gently to combine. If not serving right away, cover and refrigerate until needed.

4   When ready to serve, cut the avocados in half, then peel, pit, and cut lengthwise into slices. Arrange the slices fanned out on plates lined with lettuce leaves. Mound the hearts of palm mixture on top of the avocado slices. Serve immediately.

CHAPTER 6

VEGETABLE STEAK-OUT

From roasted asparagus to grilled zucchini,

vegetables are often best simply prepared, allowing their own great flavors and textures to shine brightly. Some vegetables, however, are also ideal for going above and beyond their traditional roles and can be employed as veganizers in some of our favorite animal-based dishes.

For example, the popular roasted slabs of cauliflower are often called "steaks," mainly because of the way they are sauced (I like them with béarnaise!) and served (you need a knife and fork!). No one is trying to say that roasted cauliflower tastes like a T-bone. Neither is anyone suggesting that the jackfruit in a BBQ sandwich tastes like pig meat. Because that is not the point.

What is the point, is that we can easily enjoy much of what it is people like about their favorite animal-based dishes—the sauce and the sizzle —without eating animals.

"Eat your vegetables" never tasted so good with recipes such as Baked Eggplant Italian Style, Vegetable Shepherd's Pie, Roasted Cauliflower Piccata, and Cheesy Steak-Out Sandwiches.

With these veganized recipes using vegetables as steaks and cutlets, there's no reason why eliminating animal products from your diet should mean giving up great taste or the familiar flavors you grew up with and enjoy.

BAKED EGGPLANT ITALIAN
STYLE 163

CORDON BLEU–STUFFED
PORTOBELLOS 164

JUMPIN'
JACKFRUIT CHILI 165

ROASTED
CAULIFLOWER PICCATA 166

VEGETABLE
SHEPHERD'S PIE 169

MUSHROOM STROGANOFF 170

MASHED POTATOES
WITH SOUR CREAM
AND CHIVES 171

PULLED JACKFRUIT
BBQ SANDWICHES 172

EGGPLANT PAPRIKASH 174

PAN-SEARED
PORTOBELLO STRIPS 175

CHEESY STEAK-OUT
SANDWICHES 177

BAKED EGGPLANT ITALIAN STYLE

In this veganized version of my family's baked eggplant recipe, the eggplant slices are baked (not fried) and layered with homemade tomato sauce (red gravy) and plant-based cheeses, resulting in a much healthier (but still delicious) dish.

1 large or 2 medium eggplants, cut lengthwise into 8 (⅓-inch-thick) slices (see Note)

Salt and freshly ground black pepper

3 cups Oven-Roasted Tomato Sauce (page 197) or store-bought marinara sauce

½ cup Nut-Parm (page 42)

2 cups Seasoned Tofu Ricotta (page 41)

1 cup Melty Vegan Cheese (page 43) or shredded vegan mozzarella

1   Preheat the oven to 375°F. Lightly oil a large baking sheet or line it with parchment paper. Ideally, you'll need 8 large slices of eggplant (cut lengthwise) that should be about 6 inches long by 3 inches wide and about ⅓ to ½ inch thick. Arrange the eggplant slices in a single layer on the prepared baking sheet. (You may need two baking sheets.) Spray with cooking spray and season with salt and pepper to taste. Bake until the eggplant is tender, 12 to 15 minutes, turning once. Remove from the oven and set aside. Leave the oven on.

2   Spread 1 cup of the tomato sauce in the bottom of a 9- x 12-inch baking dish. Arrange 4 of the cooked eggplant slices in the bottom of the pan. Sprinkle with a small amount of the Nut-Parm. Spread the ricotta evenly over the eggplant slices in the pan. Arrange the remaining 4 eggplant slices on top of the ricotta, pressing down gently to hold it all together. Spread the remaining 2 cups tomato sauce over the eggplant. Top with the melty cheese and sprinkle with the remaining Nut-Parm. Cover the baking dish with foil and bake for 30 minutes. Remove the foil and bake until the top is bubbly and lightly browned, about 10 minutes longer. Set aside for 5 to 10 minutes before serving.

Note: If your eggplants are small, cut them crosswise into rounds and, after baking the slices, arrange them into 4 equal groups, half of which can be used as the bottom layer for the 4 servings, with the ricotta in the middle, and then topped with the remaining eggplant slices.

CORDON BLEU–STUFFED PORTOBELLOS

SERVES 4

4 large portobello mushroom caps, stems and gills removed

1 tablespoon olive oil

¼ cup minced yellow onion

1 garlic clove, minced

2 tablespoons chopped fresh parsley

1 tablespoon tamari

1 teaspoon fresh lemon juice

1 cup chopped Hamish Loaf (page 112) or your favorite vegan ham

½ cup chopped Pretzel-Crusted Cheddary Log (page 52) or your favorite vegan cheese

¼ cup panko bread crumbs, or more if needed

Salt and freshly ground black pepper

Inspired by the classic "cordon bleu" dish of meat rollatini stuffed with ham and cheese, this veganized version stuffs meaty portobello mushrooms with a tasty hamish and cheesy filling. It makes a great main dish. For an appetizer version, use small white mushroom caps instead of the portobellos.

1 Preheat the oven to 400°F. Lightly oil a large baking dish. Arrange the mushroom caps, stemmed-side down, in the baking dish and bake for 10 minutes to soften.

2 While the mushrooms are baking, make the stuffing. Heat the oil in a medium skillet over medium heat. Add the onion and cook until softened, 5 minutes. Stir in the garlic and cook for 1 minute longer, then add the parsley, tamari, lemon juice, chopped ham, chopped cheese, panko crumbs, and salt and pepper to taste. Stir until the mixture is well combined and holds together when pressed. If the mixture doesn't hold together, add a little more cheese if too dry or a little more panko if too wet.

3 Flip over the baked mushrooms and spoon the stuffing mixture into the mushroom caps, sprinkling additional panko crumbs on top, if desired. Bake for about 20 minutes, or until the mushrooms are tender and the stuffing is lightly browned on top. Serve hot.

JUMPIN' JACKFRUIT CHILI

Jackfruit adds a meaty texture to chili and provides a nice contrast to the beans. It also makes great sloppy Joes and tacos. Look for canned jackfruit packed in water in Asian markets or online. For a less spicy chili, use fewer jalapeños and chipotles, or omit one or both of them altogether for a very mild chili.

Heat the oil in a large pot over medium heat. Add the onion and cook for 5 minutes to soften. Stir in the garlic and jalapeños and cook 1 to 2 minutes longer, then stir in the chili powder, cumin, oregano, salt, and pepper. Add the jackfruit, tomatoes and their juice, chipotles, pinto beans, and broth. Bring to a boil, then decrease the heat to low and cook until the vegetables are tender and the flavors are well blended, about 30 minutes. Taste and adjust the seasoning, if needed. Stir in the cilantro. Serve topped with the avocado.

1 tablespoon grapeseed oil

1 large onion, chopped

3 garlic cloves, minced

1 or 2 jalapeño chiles, seeded and minced

2 tablespoons chili powder

2 teaspoons ground cumin

1 teaspoon dried oregano

½ teaspoon salt

¼ teaspoon ground black pepper

1 (20-ounce) can jackfruit (packed in water), drained and chopped

1 (28-ounce) can petite diced tomatoes, undrained

1 or 2 canned chipotle chiles in adobo sauce, minced

3 cups cooked or 2 (15-ounce) cans pinto beans, drained and rinsed

2 cups vegetable broth, store-bought or homemade (page 182)

¼ cup coarsely chopped cilantro

1 ripe Hass avocado, peeled, pitted, and diced

ROASTED CAULIFLOWER PICCATA

1 head cauliflower, cored

Olive oil, for cooking

Salt and freshly ground black pepper

1 cup sliced mushrooms

2 scallions, minced

⅓ cup dry white wine or vegetable broth, store-bought or homemade (page 182)

3 tablespoons fresh lemon juice

1½ tablespoons capers, drained

¼ cup minced fresh parsley

2 teaspoons vegan butter, store-bought or homemade (page 36), chilled

1 recipe Mashed Potatoes with Sour Cream and Chives (page 171), for serving

When you cut a head of cauliflower like you would a loaf of bread, the resulting slabs can be roasted and served as delicious steaks. My favorite way to season them is with a luscious lemony piccata sauce and mushrooms atop a serving of creamy mashers.

1 Preheat the oven to 425°F. Lightly oil two large rimmed baking sheets or line them with parchment paper.

2 Place the cauliflower on a cutting board, cored-side down, and use a long serrated knife to cut it into ½-inch-thick slices, as if you were cutting a loaf of bread. Arrange the cauliflower slices in a single layer on the prepared baking sheets and brush with a little olive oil or spray with cooking spray and season with salt and pepper to taste. Roast the cauliflower until tender and nicely browned, 25 to 30 minutes, turning once with a large metal spatula about halfway through.

3 While the cauliflower is roasting, make the sauce. Heat 2 teaspoons oil in a skillet over medium heat. Add the mushrooms and scallions and sauté for about 3 minutes, or until softened. Add the wine, lemon juice, and capers and cook, stirring, until the liquid reduces slightly. Just before serving, add the parsley, then stir in the butter to melt it into the sauce.

4 To serve, spoon a serving of the mashed potatoes onto each plate and top with a cauliflower steak. Spoon the sauce on top.

VEGETABLE SHEPHERD'S PIE

I like to veganize this cozy casserole by using cooked lentils in place of the ground meat, but you can also use chopped seitan or tempeh if you prefer. This recipe easily doubles if you need to feed a crowd.

1 Preheat the oven to 375°F. Lightly oil a 2½-quart baking dish.

2 Heat the oil in a large skillet over medium heat. Add the onion and carrot and cook until tender, about 5 minutes. Add the mushrooms and cook, stirring occasionally, for 3 minutes. Season with salt and pepper to taste. Remove from the heat and stir in the cooked lentils, peas, and corn. Spoon the vegetable mixture into the prepared baking dish. Add the gravy, stirring to combine. Taste and adjust the seasonings, if needed. Spread the mashed potatoes over the top. Sprinkle with the paprika. Bake until the potatoes are hot and bubbly and the top is golden brown, about 45 minutes. Serve hot.

1 tablespoon olive oil

1 large onion, chopped

1 large carrot, chopped

8 ounces white mushrooms, chopped

Salt and freshly ground black pepper

2 cups cooked or canned lentils

¾ cup fresh or thawed frozen peas

¾ cup fresh or thawed frozen corn kernels

2 cups Great Brown Gravy (page 191)

3 cups Mashed Potatoes with Sour Cream and Chives (page 171)

¼ teaspoon sweet Hungarian paprika

MUSHROOM STROGANOFF

SERVES 4

2 tablespoons olive oil

1 large yellow onion, chopped

1 large green bell pepper, cored, seeded, and chopped

4 large portobello mushroom caps, gills scraped out, cut into ¾-inch dice

1½ cups sliced white mushrooms

2 tablespoons unbleached all-purpose flour

1 tablespoon sweet Hungarian paprika

2 tablespoons tomato paste

1 tablespoon tamari

2 cups vegetable broth, store-bought or homemade (page 182)

Salt and ground black pepper

½ cup vegan sour cream, store-bought or homemade (page 33), plus more for serving

No doubt about it, mushrooms make great stroganoff. I especially like using diced portobellos in combination with sliced white mushrooms to vary the flavor and texture. Serve over noodles topped with additional vegan sour cream.

1 Heat the oil in a large skillet over medium heat. Add the onion and bell pepper, cover, and cook until softened, about 5 minutes. Add the portobellos and brown on all sides, 7 to 8 minutes. Add the white mushrooms and cook until softened, about 3 minutes.

2 Sprinkle on the flour and paprika and cook, stirring, for about 1 minute to remove the raw taste from the flour.

3 In a small bowl, combine the tomato paste, tamari, and ½ cup of the broth, blending until smooth. Stir the tomato paste mixture into the mushroom mixture, stirring until smooth. Stir in the remaining 1½ cups broth and bring to a boil, then decrease the heat to low. Season to taste with salt and pepper and simmer until the flavors are blended and the sauce thickens somewhat, about 20 minutes. Slowly whisk in the vegan sour cream until well blended. Serve hot, topped with more sour cream, if desired.

VARIATION

Substitute seitan or reconstituted soy curls for the portobellos.

MASHED POTATOES WITH SOUR CREAM AND CHIVES

SERVES 4

You can make delicious veganized mashed potatoes by simply swapping out the dairy butter and milk for nondairy versions, or you can go all out and add some vegan sour cream and minced chives. Use as a topping for the Vegetable Shepherd's Pie on page 169.

Place the potatoes in a large pot with enough cold salted water to cover. Bring to a boil over medium-high heat and cook until the potatoes are tender when pierced with a fork, about 20 minutes. Drain the potatoes, return them to the pot, and mash with a potato masher. Mix in the milk, butter, and salt. Add the sour cream and chives and continue to mash until all of the ingredients are well mixed and the potatoes are smooth. Serve hot.

2 pounds Yukon Gold or russet potatoes, peeled and cut into 2-inch chunks

⅓ cup plain unsweetened nondairy milk, store-bought or homemade (page 28), heated

1 tablespoon vegan butter, store-bought or homemade (page 36), softened

½ teaspoon salt, or to taste

3 tablespoons vegan sour cream, store-bought or homemade (page 33)

1 tablespoon minced fresh chives

PULLED JACKFRUIT BBQ SANDWICHES

SERVES 4

1 tablespoon olive oil

1 yellow onion, minced

1 (16-ounce) can water-packed jackfruit, drained and shredded or thinly sliced

1 tablespoon tamari soy sauce

¼ teaspoon smoked paprika

Salt and ground black pepper

1½ cups barbecue sauce, store-bought or homemade (page 101)

4 sandwich rolls, split and toasted

Not only does jackfruit lend itself well to shredding for that pulled effect, but it's also great at soaking up the zesty barbecue sauce, making it an ideal candidate for these hearty sandwiches. Look for canned water-packed jackfruit in Asian markets or well-stocked supermarkets (be sure not to get the kind packed in syrup). If jackfruit is unavailable, substitute your choice of chopped seitan, steamed crumbled tempeh, or chopped or shredded mushrooms (portobellos or oyster mushrooms are especially good here).

Heat the oil in a large skillet over medium heat. Add the onion and cook until softened, about 5 minutes. Add the jackfruit and cook until softened, about 10 minutes. Stir in the soy sauce and season with the paprika and salt and pepper to taste. Add as much of the barbecue sauce as desired, stirring to mix well. Use a fork (or two) to break up the jackfruit. If hard pieces remain, remove them to a cutting board and finely chop, then return them to the skillet. Cook for about 10 minutes to heat through and blend the flavors. Pile the jackfruit mixture onto the toasted sandwich rolls. Serve hot.

EGGPLANT PAPRIKASH

2 tablespoons olive oil

1 large yellow onion, chopped

2 medium eggplants, peeled and cut into 1-inch dice

1 green bell pepper, diced

3 garlic cloves, minced

2 tablespoons sweet Hungarian paprika

2 teaspoons smoked paprika

2 tablespoons all-purpose flour

1 cup diced or crushed canned tomatoes

1 cup vegetable broth

½ cup dry white wine (or additional vegetable broth)

Salt and freshly ground black pepper

½ cup vegan sour cream, store-bought or homemade (page 33)

¼ teaspoon liquid smoke

Hearty and flavorful Hungarian paprikash gets veganized with meaty chunks of eggplant and vegan sour cream. If you're not a fan of eggplant, you can substitute diced portobello mushrooms, tempeh, or seitan. Serve over cooked noodles.

Heat the oil in a large saucepan over medium heat. Add the onion, cover, and cook until it begins to brown, 5 to 8 minutes. Stir in the eggplants, bell pepper, garlic, and both types of paprika. Cook, stirring, for 2 minutes. Sprinkle with the flour, then stir in the tomatoes, vegetable broth, and wine. Season with salt and pepper to taste. Cover and simmer until the eggplant is tender, about 30 minutes. Stir in the vegan sour cream and liquid smoke and cook for another minute, until heated through. Taste and adjust the seasonings, if needed.

PAN-SEARED PORTOBELLO STRIPS

SERVES 4

A robust pan sauce made with Dijon mustard, tomato paste, wine, and vegan Worcestershire sauce is the perfect complement to these meaty slices of pan-seared portobello. Serve over noodles, rice, or mashed potatoes and a green vegetable for a light and lovely meal.

1 Cut the portobello caps into ¼-inch-wide strips.

2 Heat the oil in a large skillet over medium-high heat. Add the portobellos and sauté until nicely seared on both sides, 2 to 3 minutes per side. Transfer to a plate.

3 To the same skillet, add the shallot and cook, stirring, until softened, about 2 minutes. Add the garlic and scallions and cook for 1 minute, then stir in the thyme, tomato paste, mustard, and Worcestershire sauce. Add the wine, then stir in the broth. Increase the heat to high, and bring to a boil. Decrease the heat to medium and simmer until the liquid is reduced by half, about 5 minutes. Return the portobellos to the skillet and season with salt and pepper to taste. Cook until heated through, 3 to 5 minutes. Serve hot, sprinkled with the parsley.

4 or 5 large portobello mushroom caps, gills scraped out

1 tablespoon olive oil

1 shallot, minced

1 garlic clove, minced

2 scallions, minced

1 teaspoon minced fresh thyme leaves or ½ teaspoon dried

2 teaspoons tomato paste

½ teaspoon Dijon mustard

1 tablespoon Vegan Worcestershire Sauce, store-bought or homemade (page 186), or tamari

½ cup dry red wine

½ cup vegetable broth, store-bought or homemade (page 182)

Salt and freshly ground black pepper

2 tablespoons chopped fresh parsley

CHEESY STEAK-OUT SANDWICHES

If ever there was a recipe in need of veganizing it's the Philadelphia cheesesteak sandwich. The good news is, it's easy to do and the result is fantastic. Made with thinly sliced portobello mushrooms, onions, and bell peppers, this hearty sandwich is then topped with some creamy, cheesy sauce and enveloped in a crusty baguette.

Heat the oil in a large skillet over medium-high heat. Add the onion and cook until softened, about 5 minutes. Add the bell pepper and mushroom slices and cook, stirring occasionally, until softened, about 5 minutes. Stir in the ketchup and Worcestershire sauce, and season with salt and pepper to taste. Continue to cook for 5 minutes longer, or until the vegetables are very soft. Spoon about half of the sauce onto the mushroom mixture and keep warm while you toast the bread. Divide the mushroom mixture among the baguette sections and top each with some of the remaining sauce. Serve hot.

1 tablespoon olive oil

1 yellow onion, thinly sliced

1 red bell pepper, cored, seeded, and thinly sliced

6 portobello mushroom caps, thinly sliced

⅓ cup ketchup

1 tablespoon Vegan Worcestershire Sauce, store-bought or homemade (page 186)

Salt and freshly ground black pepper

¾ cup Cheddary Sauce (page 44)

1 French baguette, cut into quarters, each quarter sliced lengthwise

VARIATION

Seitan Cheesy-Steaks Substitute thinly sliced seitan for the mushrooms.

GLOBAL
SAUCES, AN

CHAPTER 7

CONDIMENTS, DRESSINGS

From butter to anchovies, there's almost always something in traditional sauces that vegans can't eat. This chapter solves the problem with plant-based versions of favorite sauces and dressings, including pesto variations made without cheese and Mexican crema made without dairy. Featured recipes include the DIY sauces and other scratch ingredients to create dishes such as Seitan Gyros with Tzatziki Sauce and My Kinda Chef's Salad. Some sauces, such as the white sauce and the cheese sauces, can be found in chapter 2.

VEGETABLE BROTH 182

HOMEMADE
VEGETABLE BASE 183

RED WINE SAUCE WITH
MUSHROOMS 184

HOLLANDAISE SAUCE 185

VEGAN
WORCESTERSHIRE SAUCE 186

AVOCADO CREMA 187

REMOULADE SAUCE 188

FISH-FREE NUOC CHAM 189

BETTER BÉARNAISE SAUCE 190

GREAT BROWN GRAVY 191

TAPENADE 192

VEGAN AIOLI 193

BASIL PESTO 194

TZATZIKI SAUCE 195

CREAMY RANCH DRESSING 196

OVEN-ROASTED
TOMATO SAUCE 197

MUSHROOM OYSTER SAUCE 198

GODDESS DRESSING 199

HAIL CAESAR DRESSING 200

CREAMY PESTO PASTA
SALAD 201

SUMMER ROLLS WITH
FISH-FREE NUOC CHAM 203

SEITAN GYROS WITH
TZATZIKI SAUCE 205

BUFFALO CAULIFLOWER WITH
RANCH DRESSING 206

MY KINDA CHEF'S SALAD 208

EASY KIMCHI 209

NIÇOISE GODDESS SALAD 210

CREAMY COLESLAW 212

CALIFORNIA CAESAR SALAD 213

VEGETABLE BROTH

2 teaspoons olive oil

2 onions, coarsely chopped

8 garlic cloves, crushed

10 cups water

6 carrots, coarsely chopped

6 celery ribs, coarsely chopped

1 cup mushroom stems or 2 dried mushrooms

1 cup coarsely chopped fresh parsley stems

1 teaspoon fresh or dried thyme

1 teaspoon salt

½ teaspoon black pepper

2 bay leaves

Homemade broth is more economical than buying ready-made vegetable broth and requires very little effort. This is a low-sodium broth that is suitable for any of the recipes in this book. Mushroom and parsley stems add depth of flavor. Keep them on hand for making broth by saving the stems from mushrooms and parsley as you use them and keep them stored in airtight containers (I use zip-top freezer bags) in the freezer. That way, you'll always have some on hand to make broth.

Heat the oil in a large pot over medium-high heat. Add the onions and garlic, cover, and cook until golden, stirring occasionally, about 8 minutes. Add the water, carrots, celery, mushroom stems, parsley stems, thyme, salt, black pepper, and bay leaves. Bring to a boil and decrease the heat to medium. Cook until the vegetables are tender and the broth is well flavored, about 30 minutes. Strain the broth into a large bowl using a colander. Press on the vegetables in the colander to release as much liquid as possible. Discard or compost the vegetables. Strain the broth using a fine-mesh strainer. Store the broth in airtight 2-cup containers so they are easy to use in recipes. The broth will keep well for up to a week in the refrigerator or up to 6 months in the freezer.

Note: In addition to keeping homemade broth on hand, it's a good idea to make a jar of vegetable base to enrich soups and sauces or to use to make a quick broth when you don't have any on hand. Many different brands of vegetable base are available in both paste and granular form, or use the recipe on page 183 to make it yourself.

VARIATION

Slow-cooker method Place your vegetables and water in a slow cooker, put on the lid, and cook on Low for 8 hours.

HOMEMADE VEGETABLE BASE

MAKES
ABOUT
1 CUP

My favorite brand of vegetable base is Better Than Bouillon. It's a thick paste that can be used to make a flavorful broth or to give a flavor boost to sauces, stews, or soups. When my local supermarket stopped carrying the vegetable flavored base (they still carry the chicken and beef flavors!) I decided to make my own. This is the result. It may be more or less salty than the commercial brand you are used to, so you may need to experiment to get the flavor you want—I usually use about 2 teaspoons per 1 cup of boiling water. The paste freezes well, so you can arrange 2-teaspoon portions on a baking sheet lined with parchment paper and freeze until solid. Then, transfer the solid portions to a freezer bag and keep frozen, to use as needed. If storing in a jar in the refrigerator, it will need to be stirred before each use, as the solids may naturally settle to the bottom.

¼ cup water

¼ cup light-colored miso paste

2 tablespoons sunflower oil (or more water)

2 tablespoons tamari

⅔ cup nutritional yeast flakes

3 tablespoons dried mushroom powder (see Note)

2 tablespoons onion powder

1 tablespoon garlic powder

1 tablespoon salt

2 teaspoons sugar

1 teaspoon paprika

1 teaspoon ground dried thyme

1 teaspoon dried basil

½ teaspoon celery seeds

½ teaspoon turmeric

Combine all the ingredients in a food processor and process to a paste, scraping down the sides as needed. Transfer to a small jar with a tight-fitting lid. Store in the refrigerator for up to 3 months.

Note: To make mushroom powder, simply grind a few dried mushrooms in a spice grinder to a fine powder.

RED WINE SAUCE WITH MUSHROOMS

MAKES ABOUT 1½ CUPS

1 tablespoon olive oil

2 shallots, minced

1 garlic clove, minced

2 cups sliced mushrooms (any kind)

½ cup dry red wine (or port or Madeira)

1 cup vegetable broth, store-bought or homemade (page 182)

2 teaspoons tamari or Vegan Worcestershire Sauce, store-bought or homemade (page 186)

2 teaspoons tomato paste

1 teaspoon Dijon mustard

1 teaspoon minced fresh thyme leaves or ½ teaspoon dried

Salt and ground black pepper

No beef stock needed to make this full-flavored sauce that is a perfect match for sautéed seitan. It also adds a touch of class to vegan meatloaf and mashed potatoes. For a variation, substitute a fortified wine such as port or Madeira for the red wine. If you prefer a sauce without wine, opt for the Great Brown Gravy (page 191) instead. For a thicker sauce, stir in 1 tablespoon of cornstarch blended with 1½ tablespoons of water after the sauce has been reduced, stirring until thickened.

Heat the oil in a large skillet over medium-high heat. Add the shallots and garlic and cook, stirring, until softened, about 2 minutes. Stir in the mushrooms, then add the wine. Cook, stirring, to reduce the liquid slightly, about 2 minutes. Using a slotted spoon, transfer the mushrooms to a plate. Add the broth, tamari, tomato paste, mustard, and thyme to the skillet, stirring to blend. Increase the heat to high, and bring to a boil. Decrease the heat to medium and simmer until the liquid is reduced by half, about 5 minutes. Return the mushrooms to the skillet and season with salt and pepper to taste. Cook until heated through, 2 to 3 minutes. Serve hot.

HOLLANDAISE SAUCE

MAKES ABOUT 1¼ CUPS

This sauce is creamy-smooth and buttery and can be enjoyed in any way you would use traditional hollandaise.

Heat ¾ cup of the nondairy milk in a small saucepan until just about simmering. In a small bowl, combine the cornstarch with the remaining ¼ cup milk to make a slurry. Stir the cornstarch mixture into the milk. Add the salt and turmeric, stirring well to blend. Cook over medium-high heat, stirring constantly, until it is thick and translucent. Scrape the mixture into the blender. Add the melted butter and lemon juice. Blend the mixture until it is emulsified. Taste and adjust the seasonings, adding a little more lemon juice or salt if needed. Serve immediately or, if the sauce has cooled, reheat it gently until just warm.

1 cup plain unsweetened nondairy milk, store-bought or homemade (page 28)

2 tablespoons cornstarch

¾ teaspoon salt

Pinch of turmeric

3 tablespoons vegan butter, store-bought or homemade (page 36), melted

1½ tablespoons fresh lemon juice

SHORTCUT HOLLANDAISE

MAKES ABOUT 1 CUP

1 cup vegan mayo, store-bought or homemade (page 35)

2 tablespoons fresh lemon juice

Pinch of turmeric

Pinch of salt

1 tablespoon vegan butter, store-bought or homemade (page 36), melted

This quick and tasty hollandaise is especially great on roasted asparagus, cauliflower, broccoli, or anything named Benedict or Oscar.

In a small bowl, combine the mayo, lemon juice, turmeric, and salt. Mix well, then blend in the melted butter. Serve immediately.

VEGAN WORCESTERSHIRE SAUCE

MAKES ABOUT ½ CUP

⅓ cup tamari

¼ cup rice vinegar

3 tablespoons molasses

½ teaspoon ground ginger

½ teaspoon dry mustard powder

½ teaspoon onion powder

½ teaspoon salt

¼ teaspoon ground black pepper

¼ teaspoon garlic powder

Pinch of ground allspice

Regular Worcestershire sauce contains anchovies, so it is not vegan. Bottled vegan Worcestershire sauce is available, but it is expensive and can be difficult to find. Solution: Make your own with this easy and economical recipe.

Combine all the ingredients in a small saucepan, stirring to blend. Bring to a boil, then decrease the heat to a simmer and cook, stirring occasionally, until the liquid reduces slightly, about 8 minutes. Remove from the heat and set aside to cool. Once cooled, pour the liquid into a small jar with a tight-fitting lid and store in the refrigerator for up to 3 months.

AVOCADO CREMA

MAKES
ABOUT
1½ CUPS

This is best if served on the same day that it is made. In addition to using on the tacos (page 90), try this crema as a topping for chili, salads, and other dishes. It's also delicious spread on toast.

Cut the avocados in half and remove the pits, then scrape the flesh into a food processor. Add the cilantro, garlic, lime juice, oil, and salt, and blend until smooth. Transfer to a bowl. Taste and adjust the seasonings, adding more salt or lime juice if needed. Serve immediately or cover and refrigerate until needed.

2 ripe Hass avocados

⅓ cup cilantro leaves

1 garlic clove, chopped

¼ cup fresh lime juice

1½ tablespoons olive oil

¼ teaspoon salt

REMOULADE SAUCE

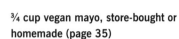

¾ cup vegan mayo, store-bought or homemade (page 35)

2 tablespoons spicy brown mustard

2 tablespoons minced scallion

2 tablespoons chopped fresh parsley

1 garlic clove, minced

1 tablespoon prepared horseradish

2 teaspoons rice vinegar

1 teaspoon fresh lemon juice

1 teaspoon Tabasco sauce

1 teaspoon paprika

½ teaspoon Creole or Cajun seasoning blend (optional)

¼ teaspoon cayenne pepper

This spicy mayo-based sauce is the perfect complement to the Palm-Crab Po'boys on page 149.

Combine all the ingredients in a small bowl. Mix well. Cover and refrigerate for at least 1 hour before using to blend the flavors.

FISH-FREE NUOC CHAM

Now you can have a flavorful alternative to Vietnamese fish sauce with this fish-free recipe.

¼ cup tamari

3 tablespoons rice vinegar

2 tablespoons water

1 tablespoon sugar

½ teaspoon garlic powder

¼ teaspoon red pepper flakes

1   Combine all of the ingredients in a small saucepan and bring to a boil. Decrease the heat to a simmer and cook, stirring, to dissolve the sugar and blend the flavors, about 5 minutes. Remove from the heat and set aside to cool.

2   Once cooled, pour the liquid into a small jar with a tight-fitting lid and store in the refrigerator for up to 3 months.

BETTER BÉARNAISE SAUCE

½ cup dry white wine

¼ cup minced shallot

1 tablespoon dried tarragon

⅔ cup vegan mayo, store-bought or homemade (page 35)

2 teaspoons fresh lemon juice

1 teaspoon Dijon mustard

Pinch of turmeric

Salt and ground black pepper

Béarnaise is an offshoot of hollandaise sauce, made with a tarragon and shallot white wine reduction and no eggs or butter. This easy better-made-vegan version is great over the vegan crab cakes on page 150 or on roasted vegetables. If you make this sauce ahead of when you need it, it rewarms well in the microwave.

Combine the wine, shallot, and tarragon in a small skillet over medium-high heat and simmer until the liquid reduces by half, 2 to 3 minutes. Place the reduced wine mixture in a food processor or blender along with the mayo, lemon juice, mustard, turmeric, and salt and pepper to taste and blend until smooth. Taste to adjust the seasonings, if needed. Serve warm.

GREAT BROWN GRAVY

MAKES ABOUT 2½ CUPS

Pureed onion, garlic, and mushrooms add a rich depth of flavor to this easy brown gravy you'll want to serve over veggie burgers, seitan, cooked grains, bean loaves, and mashed potatoes. For a flavor variation, use sage or rosemary in place of the thyme (or use a combination of all three to equal 1 teaspoon).

1 tablespoon olive oil

½ cup minced onion

2 garlic cloves, minced

1 cup chopped mushrooms (any kind)

2 tablespoons tamari

1 teaspoon dried thyme

¼ teaspoon salt

⅛ to ¼ teaspoon ground black pepper

1½ cups vegetable broth, store-bought or homemade (page 182)

¼ cup plain unsweetened nondairy milk, store-bought or homemade (page 28)

2 tablespoons nutritional yeast

2 tablespoons cornstarch

1 teaspoon gravy browner, such as Gravy Master or Kitchen Bouquet

1   Heat the oil in a saucepan over medium heat. Add the onion, cover, and cook until softened, about 5 minutes. Add the garlic and mushrooms and cook, stirring, until softened. Stir in the tamari, thyme, salt, and pepper.

2   Transfer the mushroom mixture to a high-speed blender. Add 1 cup of the broth and blend until smooth. Add the remaining ½ cup broth, milk, nutritional yeast, cornstarch, and browning sauce, and blend until smooth. Alternatively, use an immersion blender and blend everything right in the saucepan.

3   Pour the mixture into the same saucepan and bring to a boil, stirring constantly. Decrease the heat to low and continue stirring until the gravy is thickened, about 3 minutes. Taste and adjust the seasonings, if needed. Serve hot.

TAPENADE

1 teaspoon olive oil

2 garlic cloves, chopped

1½ cups pitted Kalamata olives

2 tablespoons capers, drained

2 tablespoons chopped fresh parsley

¼ teaspoon salt

Tapenade is a luxurious olive spread that feature capers (tapeno means "capers" in the Provençal dialect). When you buy it commercially, it may contain anchovies. Try this better-made-vegan recipe for a delicious spread without the fish.

Heat the oil in a small skillet over medium heat. Add the garlic and cook until soft and fragrant, about 1 minute. Transfer to a food processor. Add the olives, capers, parsley, and salt and pulse to blend, retaining some texture. The tapenade may be prepared ahead of time and refrigerated in a tightly sealed container. It will keep for 3 or 4 days. Bring it back to room temperature before using.

VEGAN AIOLI

MAKES
½ CUP

This garlicky aioli is a perfect complement to the crab cakes on page 150 or the Palm-Crab Po'boys on page 149. If you don't have dill or thyme on hand, you can add a little parsley or chives, or leave out the herbs and add a bit more garlic.

Combine the mayo and garlic in a small bowl. Add the lemon juice, dill (if using), and salt and pepper to taste. Mix well. If not using right away, cover and refrigerate until needed.

½ cup vegan mayo, store-bought or homemade (page 35)

1 teaspoon minced garlic

1 tablespoon fresh lemon juice

1 tablespoon chopped fresh dill or thyme (optional)

Salt and ground black pepper

BASIL PESTO

3 or 4 garlic cloves, crushed

½ cup walnut pieces

⅓ cup nutritional yeast

1½ cups packed fresh basil leaves

1 tablespoon light-colored miso paste

3 tablespoons olive oil, plus more to cover if needed

½ teaspoon salt

¼ teaspoon ground black pepper

Nothing beats homemade pesto made with fresh basil, especially since most commercial pesto sauces contain dairy. With this recipe you get fresh basil plus no dairy! Whether to use three or four cloves of garlic will depend on the size of the cloves and how pungent your garlic is (as well as if you "love" garlic or just "like" it).

1 In a food processor, combine the garlic and walnuts and process until finely ground. Add the remaining ingredients and process to a paste, leaving some texture. Taste and adjust the seasonings, if needed.

2 If not using right away, transfer to a container with a tight-fitting lid and pour a thin layer of olive oil on top of the pesto to keep it from turning brown. Refrigerate until needed.

TZATZIKI SAUCE

MAKES ABOUT 1½ CUPS

This tasty Greek sauce is traditionally served on gyros (page 205) or grilled vegetable kebabs. It also makes a great dip served with raw veggies and toasted pita chips. For best results, squeeze the liquid from the shredded cucumber before adding to the sauce.

1 Shred or grate the cucumber using the large holes on a box grater. Place the cucumber in a colander and sprinkle with salt. Set aside for 30 minutes over a bowl to allow the liquid to come out. Transfer the cucumber to a clean kitchen towel or a piece of cheesecloth. Bring up the sides of the cloth and twist to extract any remaining liquid from the cucumber.

2 Transfer the cucumber to a bowl. Add the garlic, yogurt, dill, lemon juice, and salt and pepper to taste. Mix well, then taste and adjust the seasonings, if needed. Cover and refrigerate until ready to use.

1 English cucumber, peeled and seeded

Salt and ground black pepper

2 garlic cloves, pressed or finely minced

1 cup plain unsweetened vegan yogurt, store-bought or homemade (page 34)

2 tablespoons chopped fresh dill

1 tablespoon fresh lemon juice

CREAMY RANCH DRESSING

MAKES ABOUT 1¼ CUPS

1 cup vegan mayo, store-bought or homemade (page 35)

1 tablespoon cider vinegar

1 tablespoon fresh lemon juice

1 teaspoon sugar

½ teaspoon onion powder

¼ teaspoon salt

¼ teaspoon black pepper

1 tablespoon minced fresh parsley

1 teaspoon chopped fresh dill

1 tablespoon minced scallion

Enjoy as a dressing on salads or a dip for vegetables.

Combine all the ingredients in a bowl and stir to mix well. Taste and adjust the seasonings, adding a little more vinegar or salt if needed. Cover and refrigerate for at least an hour before using to allow the flavors to develop.

OVEN-ROASTED TOMATO SAUCE

MAKES ABOUT 3 CUPS

Tomato-based pasta sauces can sometimes contain meat or butter for added richness. In this recipe, oven-roasting imparts a deep, rich flavor to the sauce. The recipe is easily doubled. If fresh plum tomatoes are unavailable, substitute canned whole plum tomatoes, preferably imported San Marzano tomatoes.

1 Preheat the oven to 350°F. Lightly oil a large glass baking dish or lasagna pan.

2 Cut the tomatoes in half lengthwise (remove the stem end if using fresh tomatoes) and place the tomatoes and their juice in the prepared baking dish. Add the garlic, onion, oil, sugar, dried basil, salt, oregano, and black pepper. Mix well to coat the tomatoes. Spread the tomatoes evenly in the baking dish and roast for 1 hour. The tomatoes should be slightly caramelized. Remove the tomatoes from the oven and stir in the tomato paste. Increase the oven temperature to 400°F and roast the tomatoes for 15 minutes longer, or until they are nicely caramelized, being careful not to let them burn. Remove from the oven and set aside to cool slightly.

3 Transfer the tomato mixture to a food processor, add the fresh basil, and pulse for a slightly chunky sauce or process until smooth, depending on your preference. If the sauce is too thin, simmer it in a saucepan on top of the stove until it reduces to the desired consistency. Taste and adjust the seasonings, if needed. If not using right away, the sauce will keep well in a covered container in the refrigerator for 1 week or in the freezer for 3 months.

20 to 24 ripe Roma tomatoes or 2 (28-ounce) cans San Marzano whole peeled tomatoes, undrained

3 or 4 garlic cloves, finely chopped

1 small onion, finely chopped

3 tablespoons olive oil

1 teaspoon sugar

1 teaspoon dried basil

1 teaspoon salt

½ teaspoon dried oregano or marjoram

¼ teaspoon ground black pepper

2 tablespoons tomato paste

⅓ cup fresh basil leaves

MUSHROOM OYSTER SAUCE

MAKES
ABOUT
1½ CUPS

5 dried shiitake mushrooms, or
more as needed

¼ cup tamari

3 tablespoons brown sugar

2 tablespoons dark miso paste
mixed with 3 tablespoons water

1 cup hot water

2 teaspoons cornstarch dissolved in
1 tablespoon cold water

Asian recipes sometimes call for oyster sauce, and although you
can find vegan versions made with mushrooms in Asian markets
or online, I prefer to make this sauce at home to avoid the MSG
in the commercial brands.

Note: If you do shop for vegan oyster sauce, it may be labeled
"vegetarian stir-fry sauce" or "mushroom soy sauce."

1 Remove and discard the stems of the mushrooms and break up
the mushroom caps. Place the pieces of mushroom caps in a dry
blender or spice grinder and grind to a powder. Grind enough to equal
¼ cup.

2 In a blender, combine the tamari, mushroom powder, sugar, miso,
and hot water and blend until smooth. Pour the mixture into a small
saucepan and heat to a boil. Add the cornstarch mixture, stirring until
the sauce is thickened. Remove from the heat and set aside to cool.
Once the sauce is cool, transfer it to a bottle or jar with a tight-fitting
lid and store in the refrigerator, where it will keep for a month or
longer.

Note: Depending on how finely ground your mushrooms are, you may
notice some small "dots" of mushrooms in the finished sauce. If you
find this objectionable, simply pour the sauce through a fine-mesh
sieve.

GODDESS DRESSING

MAKES
ABOUT
1½ CUPS

The original Green Goddess dressing, created in the early 1920s, was made with mayonnaise, sour cream, and anchovies. Try this rich and delicious plant-based version on the salad on page 210 or as a dip for raw vegetables. It also makes a great dressing for potato salad. Since this dressing tastes best when allowed to sit overnight, I usually make it a day ahead or early in the morning on the day that I am serving it. Cover tightly and store in the refrigerator for up to a week. If you don't have a high-speed blender, you can use a food processor, but the dressing won't be as smooth.

2 garlic cloves, crushed

2 scallions (green and white parts), chopped

3 tablespoons chopped fresh parsley

½ cup vegan mayo, store-bought or homemade (page 35)

¼ cup plain unsweetened almond milk, store-bought or homemade (page 28)

3 tablespoons fresh lemon juice or rice vinegar

2 tablespoons nutritional yeast

2 tablespoons olive oil

2 teaspoons tamari

1 teaspoon dried tarragon

½ teaspoon dried basil

½ teaspoon prepared mustard

½ teaspoon salt

¼ teaspoon ground black pepper

1   In a food processor, combine the garlic, scallions, and parsley, and pulse until minced. Add the mayo, almond milk, lemon juice, nutritional yeast, oil, tamari, tarragon, basil, mustard, salt, and pepper, and blend until smooth. Taste and adjust the seasonings, if needed.

2   Transfer to a jar or other container with a tight-fitting lid and refrigerate for several hours or overnight for best flavor.

HAIL CAESAR DRESSING

MAKES ABOUT ¾ CUP

3 garlic cloves, crushed

¼ cup olive oil

2 tablespoons water

2 tablespoons fresh lemon juice

2 tablespoons nutritional yeast

1 tablespoon white miso paste

1 tablespoon tahini (sesame paste)

1½ teaspoons tamari

Salt and ground black pepper

Enjoy the same garlicky goodness in this Caesar dressing, but without the raw eggs and anchovies of the original. This fresh interpretation gets its punch from miso paste and nutritional yeast, and its creaminess from tahini. Hail Caesar!

In a blender, combine the garlic and oil and blend until smooth. Add the water, lemon juice, nutritional yeast, miso, tahini, tamari, and salt and pepper to taste. Blend until smooth. Taste and adjust the seasonings, if needed.

CREAMY PESTO PASTA SALAD

Serve this salad as a side dish or enjoy it as a main dish on a bed of baby spinach. For best results, serve this salad on the same day that you make it.

1 Cook the rotini in a large pot of salted boiling water, stirring occasionally, until just tender. Drain the cooked pasta and rinse with cold water. Return the cooled pasta to the pot.

2 In a small bowl, combine the pesto, mayo, and almond milk, stirring to blend well. Stir half of the pesto mixture into the pot with the pasta and toss gently to combine. Transfer to a large bowl. Add the beans, bell pepper, artichokes, tomatoes, olives, and the remaining pesto mixture. Season with salt and pepper to taste. Mix gently to combine. Serve immediately or cover tightly and refrigerate until needed.

8 ounces rotini, cut fusilli, or other bite-size pasta

½ cup **Basil Pesto** (page 194)

½ cup vegan mayo, store-bought or homemade (page 35)

¼ cup plain unsweetened almond milk, store-bought or homemade (page 28)

1½ cups cooked or 1 (15-ounce) can cannellini beans, drained and rinsed

1 roasted red bell pepper (jarred or homemade), cut into 1-inch pieces

1 (6-ounce) jar marinated artichoke hearts, drained and quartered

1 cup grape or cherry tomatoes, halved

¼ cup pitted Kalamata olives, halved

Salt and ground black pepper

SUMMER ROLLS WITH FISH-FREE NUOC CHAM

SERVES 4

Fresh summer rolls are delicious, but many restaurants offer only versions made with shrimp or chicken, and then there's the matter of the fish sauce. Solution: Make them at home using marinated baked tofu and vegan nuoc cham.

Pour warm water into a wide shallow bowl or pie plate and set a clean dish towel next to it. Dip a rice paper wrapper into the water for a few seconds to soften, then remove it from the water and place it on a flat work surface. Arrange a row of cilantro leaves on the rice paper, near the end closest to you. On top of the cilantro, arrange a row of tofu strips, then top with noodles, shredded carrot, and cucumber strips. Do not overfill. Fold the edge of the rice paper closest to you over the filling, then fold in the sides and roll it up, away from you, to form a neat roll. Repeat with the remaining ingredients. Serve immediately, 2 rolls per serving, with small bowls of nuoc cham for dipping.

8 rice paper wrappers

1½ cups fresh cilantro, mint, or Thai basil leaves

8 ounces marinated baked tofu, store-bought or homemade (page 74), cut into thin strips

Cooked thin rice noodles

1 large carrot, coarsely shredded

½ English cucumber, peeled and cut into thin strips

Fish-Free Nuoc Cham (page 189)

SEITAN GYROS WITH TZATZIKI SAUCE

This plant-based version of the hearty Greek gyro sandwich features thinly sliced seitan wrapped in pita bread with a garlicky tzatziki sauce and sliced tomatoes, onions, and cucumbers.

1   Heat the oil in a skillet over medium heat. Add the seitan and cook until browned, about 5 minutes. Add the oregano and lemon juice and season with salt and pepper to taste, tossing to coat.

2   To assemble, spread the tzatziki sauce onto the pitas, divide the seitan mixture among them, and top with the lettuce, tomato, cucumber, and onion. Serve immediately.

1 tablespoon olive oil

12 ounces seitan, very thinly sliced

1 teaspoon dried oregano

1 tablespoon fresh lemon juice

Salt and ground black pepper

Tzatziki Sauce (page 195)

4 pitas or other flatbreads, warmed

2 cups shredded lettuce

1 large ripe tomato, halved and thinly sliced

½ English cucumber, peeled and chopped

½ red onion, thinly sliced

BUFFALO CAULIFLOWER WITH RANCH DRESSING

¾ cup chickpea flour or all-purpose flour

¾ cup water or nondairy milk, store-bought or homemade (page 28)

1 teaspoon garlic powder

½ teaspoon salt

1 head cauliflower, broken into small florets

¾ cup hot sauce

1 tablespoon vegan butter, store-bought or homemade (page 36), melted

Creamy Ranch Dressing (page 196)

This popular plant-based alternative to wings is hard to resist. Even people who think they don't like cauliflower have been known to devour these tasty bites.

1 Preheat the oven to 450°F. Lightly oil a large baking sheet.

2 In a bowl, combine the flour, water, garlic powder, and salt. Whisk together until smooth. Add the cauliflower pieces to the batter, turning to coat completely. Transfer the battered cauliflower to the prepared baking sheet. Bake for 15 minutes, or until just tender and golden brown, turning halfway through.

3 While the cauliflower bakes, make the sauce. In a bowl, combine the hot sauce and melted butter, stirring to blend.

4 Remove the cauliflower from the oven and carefully transfer the cauliflower pieces to the bowl with the hot sauce. Gently toss the cauliflower in the hot sauce mixture to coat, then return to the baking sheet. Bake the sauced cauliflower for an additional 15 minutes, or until it becomes crispy. Serve with a bowl of the ranch dressing for dipping.

VARIATION

For a delicious version without the heat, instead of the buffalo hot sauce, combine ¾ cup mild barbecue sauce, store-bought or homemade (page 101), with 1 tablespoon melted butter and 2 tablespoons water. Toss the cauliflower in this sauce and proceed with the recipe.

MY KINDA CHEF'S SALAD

6 cups chopped romaine lettuce

1 (15-ounce) can chickpeas, drained and rinsed

1 carrot, shredded

1 cup diced marinated baked tofu, store-bought or homemade (page 74)

1 cup chopped Hamish Loaf (page 112) or store-bought vegan ham

1 ripe Hass avocado, peeled, pitted, and diced

1 cup grape tomatoes, halved

¼ cup sunflower seeds

Goddess Dressing (page 199) or your favorite salad dressing

On the menu of the first restaurant I worked in was a standard chef's salad, complete with iceberg lettuce, sliced turkey, cheese, and hard-boiled eggs, topped with a thick Thousand Island dressing—boring and loaded with cholesterol. This retooled version features healthy plant-based ingredients, including avocado for creamy richness and sunflower seeds for crunch. The Goddess Dressing is especially good on this, but you can use any dressing you prefer.

In a large bowl, combine the lettuce, chickpeas, carrot, tofu, vegan ham, avocado, tomatoes, and sunflower seeds. Add as much dressing as desired and toss to combine. Serve immediately.

EASY KIMCHI

Because commercial kimchi often contains shrimp paste or other non-vegan ingredients, I've included a recipe here for this zesty Korean condiment made with Napa cabbage, garlic, and ginger. For a mild kimchi, omit or cut back on the red pepper flakes. For a hotter kimchi, add more red pepper flakes or some cayenne pepper. Enjoy as a salad or as a condiment, or add to fried rice.

1   In a large bowl, combine the cabbage and carrot. In a small bowl, combine the scallion, garlic, vinegar, tamari, nuoc cham, sesame oil, ginger, red pepper flakes, sugar, salt, and pepper. Add the water and mix well. Pour the sauce over the vegetables and stir to combine and coat the cabbage well.

2   Cover and set aside at room temperature for 1 hour or longer before serving. Taste and adjust the seasonings, if needed. If not using right away, cover tightly and refrigerate until needed. It will keep well for several weeks. Serve at room temperature.

4 cups coarsely chopped Napa cabbage (Chinese cabbage)

1 carrot, thinly sliced

¼ cup minced scallion

3 garlic cloves, minced

3 tablespoons rice vinegar

1 tablespoon tamari

1 tablespoon Fish-Free Nuoc Cham (page 189) or more tamari

1 tablespoon dark (toasted) sesame oil

2 teaspoons grated fresh ginger

1 teaspoon red pepper flakes or 1 tablespoon kochijan paste combined with 2 tablespoons hot water

1 teaspoon sugar

½ teaspoon salt

¼ teaspoon ground black pepper

¼ cup water

NIÇOISE GODDESS SALAD

1 pound small new potatoes, halved or cut into ½-inch pieces

Salt and ground pepper

8 ounces green beans, trimmed and cut into 2-inch pieces

1½ cups cooked or 1 (15-ounce) can cannellini beans, drained and rinsed

1 cup cherry or grape tomatoes, halved lengthwise

⅓ cup pitted Kalamata olives, halved

5 cups torn butter lettuce leaves

Goddess Dressing (page 199)

VARIATION

Substitute diced and cooled marinated baked tofu, store-bought or homemade (page 74), for the cannellini beans.

This recipe combines two of my favorites: Niçoise salad ingredients tossed with creamy Goddess Dressing. I roast the potatoes and green beans for extra flavor, but you can steam them, if you prefer.

1   Preheat the oven to 425°F. Arrange the potatoes on a lightly oiled baking pan and spray with a little cooking spray. Season to taste with salt and pepper and roast until just softened and lightly browned, turning once, about 30 minutes.

2   While the potatoes are roasting, steam the green beans until just tender, 5 to 7 minutes. After you turn the potatoes, before returning them to the oven, add the green beans to the pan and spray with a little cooking spray. Season with salt and pepper to taste. Return the pan to the oven and bake until the potatoes and green beans are tender, about 15 minutes. Remove from the oven and set the vegetables aside to cool to room temperature.

3   In a large bowl, combine the cannellini beans, tomatoes, olives, and lettuce. Add the cooled potatoes and green beans. Pour on as much dressing as desired and toss to combine. Serve immediately.

CREAMY COLESLAW

SERVES 4

1 small head green cabbage, finely shredded

1 large carrot, grated

¾ cup vegan mayo, store-bought or homemade (page 35)

3 tablespoons plain unsweetened nondairy milk, store-bought or homemade (page 28)

2 tablespoons cider vinegar

1 teaspoon sugar

½ teaspoon dry mustard

¼ teaspoon celery seeds

½ teaspoon salt

Freshly ground black pepper

Classic creamy coleslaw is easy to veganize when you replace the dairy mayo and milk with their nondairy counterparts.

Place the cabbage and carrot in a large bowl. In a small bowl, combine the mayonnaise, milk, vinegar, sugar, mustard, celery seeds, salt, and pepper to taste. Mix until smooth and well blended. Add the dressing to the slaw, and mix well to coat the vegetables. Taste and adjust the seasonings, if needed.

VARIATIONS

Pasta Slaw Add 2 to 3 cups cooked, cut fusilli or other small pasta shape and 1 minced scallion, and toss to combine.

Potato Slaw Add 2 to 3 cups diced, cooked white potatoes and 2 to 3 tablespoons sweet pickle relish, and toss to combine.

CALIFORNIA CAESAR SALAD

If you enjoy the crunchy goodness of romaine lettuce tossed with fresh croutons and a garlicky dressing but want to avoid the raw eggs, Parmesan, and anchovies found in a traditional Caesar, this salad is for you. My California twist on the classic includes creamy diced avocado and briny black olives.

4 thick slices Italian bread

1 head romaine lettuce

Hail Caesar Dressing (page 200)

1 ripe Hass avocado, peeled, pitted, and diced

⅓ cup pitted and halved Kalamata olives

1 Preheat the oven to 325°F. Cut the bread into 1-inch cubes and spread on a baking sheet. Bake, turning occasionally, until lightly toasted on all sides, about 20 minutes. Set aside to cool.

2 Cut or tear the lettuce leaves into bite-size pieces and place in a large serving bowl. Pour the dressing over the lettuce and toss until evenly coated. Add the croutons, avocado, and olives. Toss again, and serve immediately.

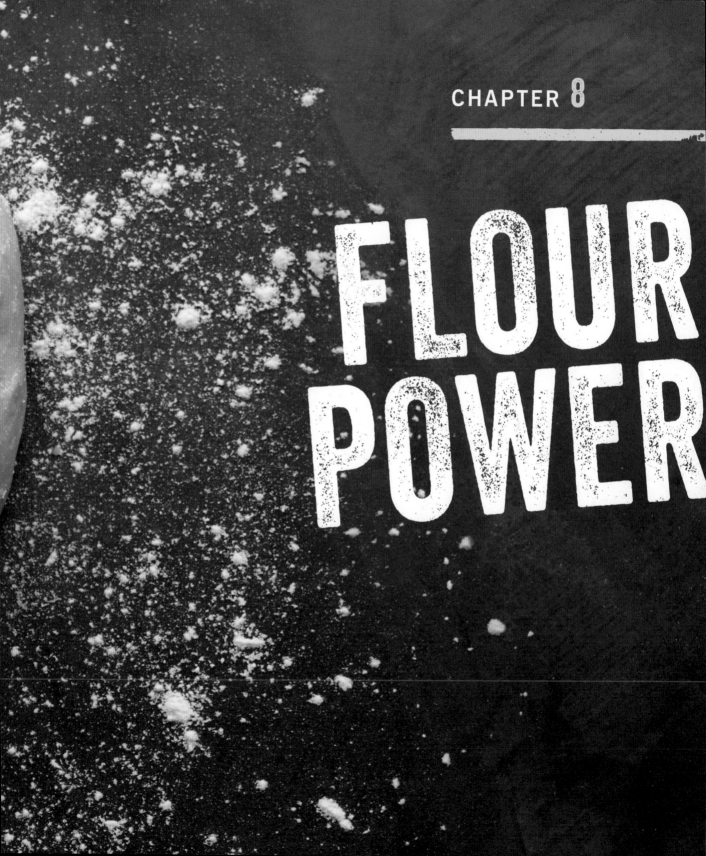

CHAPTER 8

FLOUR POWER

In this chapter, you'll find foods powered by

flour, from pie dough, which figures prominently in the quiche and pie recipes in this book (as well as in a delicious pot pie recipe), to pizza dough and homemade pasta (and recipes that use them).

Easy to prepare, infinitely versatile, and consistently delicious, pasta can be the basis for convenient, economical, and satisfying vegan meals. While many traditional Italian pasta dishes are naturally vegan, others are not. Fortunately, this chapter has you covered with recipes for a delectable Handcrafted Lasagna, Fettuccine Bolognese, Spaghetti Carbonara, Orecchiette with Pistachio Pesto, and rotini with a creamy and flavorful roasted garlic Alfredo sauce.

There are also recipes for bread, biscuits, homemade granola, and cheesy crackers. Purchasing ready-made bread can involve a lot of label reading for vegans because it often includes dairy, eggs, and other animal products. In this chapter, you will find recipes for a variety of quick breads, biscuits, and scones, all of which can satisfy the baking urge when time is limited. And when you have time to enjoy the satisfaction of making yeast bread from scratch, you can try my recipe for Easy Artisan Bread.

DIY GRANOLA   218

HOMEMADE PASTA   219

HANDCRAFTED LASAGNA   221

FETTUCCINE BOLOGNESE   222

SPAGHETTI CARBONARA   223

ORECCHIETTE WITH PISTACHIO
PESTO   224

ROTINI WITH ROASTED GARLIC
ALFREDO SAUCE   226

PIE DOUGH   228

EASY ARTISAN BREAD   229

PERFECT POT PIE   230

CHEESY SAUSAGE
BISCUITS   233

CHEESY CRACKERS   234

SCRATCH BISCUITS   236

ALL-IN-ONE CAULIFLOWER
PIZZA   237

PIZZA DOUGH   238

BENEDICT PIZZA   239

MEATY-CHEESY PIZZA   240

LOADED POLENTA PIZZA   242

CRANBERRY-WALNUT
SCONES   243

DIY GRANOLA

3 cups old-fashioned rolled oats

1 cup sliced or slivered almonds

¾ cup unsweetened shredded coconut

½ cup coarsely chopped pecans

½ cup pure maple syrup

¼ cup sunflower oil

2 tablespoons brown sugar

¾ teaspoon ground cinnamon

¼ teaspoon salt

1 cup dried cranberries

¾ cup dried blueberries or other dried fruit

When you make granola at home you can leave out the honey found in most commercial brands and customize it to include your favorite ingredients. As a bonus, DIY granola is less expensive than the ready-made kind you buy at the store. I like to mix some granola into my morning oatmeal. It's also great for dessert—sprinkled on ice cream or baked apples.

1 Preheat the oven to 325°F. Line a 9- x 12-inch baking dish with parchment paper.

2 In a large bowl, combine the oats, almonds, coconut, pecans, maple syrup, oil, brown sugar, cinnamon, and salt. Stir well until the oats and nuts are coated. Spread the mixture on the prepared sheet. Bake, stirring every 10 to 15 minutes, until the mixture turns golden brown, 35 to 40 minutes. Remove the granola from the oven and allow to cool, stirring occasionally. Once the granola is cool, add the cranberries and blueberries. Store the completely cooled granola in an airtight container.

VARIATIONS

You can customize the granola by swapping in different ingredients for all or part of the nuts or fruit, such as raisins, chopped pitted dates, chopped dried apricots or apples, walnuts, cashews, or vegan chocolate or butterscotch chips. Try a pumpkin spice version with toasted pumpkin seeds, pumpkin pie spice, and walnuts, or a tropical version with dried mango and pineapple, large flake coconut, and macadamia nuts.

HOMEMADE PASTA

Fresh pasta usually contains eggs. The good news is that it's easy to prepare it yourself. Made from durum wheat, semolina flour is sturdier than all-purpose flour and tastes better, too. If it is unavailable, you can use all-purpose flour, but it will be less sturdy with a slightly doughier flavor, so it's really worth getting the semolina flour.

2 cups fine semolina flour or unbleached all-purpose flour

½ cup white whole wheat flour or unbleached all-purpose flour

⅛ teaspoon salt

1 tablespoon olive oil

½ to ¾ cup warm water, or more

1   Combine the two kinds of flour and the salt in a food processor and pulse to mix. With the machine running, add the oil and then slowly drizzle in ½ cup of the water, processing until the dough begins to hold together. If the dough is too dry, add more of the remaining water, 1 tablespoon at a time. Transfer the dough to a lightly floured work surface and knead briefly until smooth. Cover with a clean dry towel and set aside for 15 minutes to rest. Knead again until the dough is smooth and silky, and just slightly sticky.

2   Shape the pasta by hand or with a rolling pin or pass the dough through a pasta machine according to its instructions. Dust with flour as needed, rolling the pasta until very thin. To make lasagna noodles, cut long rectangles with a pizza cutter. To make linguini, use a pizza cutter or knife to cut the pasta into thin strips. Place on a lightly floured surface and dust with more flour so they don't stick.

3   To cook, prepare a large pot of boiling water, salt liberally, and add the fresh pasta. Fresh pasta takes less time to cook, so watch it closely. It should be ready in 3 minutes, more or less, depending on the thickness of the pasta and how al dente you like it.

HANDCRAFTED LASAGNA

You can assemble the lasagna up to 2 days ahead of baking it. Tightly wrap the baking dish in plastic and refrigerate. Let the lasagna come to room temperature before baking. Since the pasta will absorb much of the tomato sauce, you may want to heat some extra sauce to serve on the side. If using boxed lasagna noodles, you will need 9 to 12 lasagna noodles from a 16-ounce box. Do not use "no-boil" noodles as they usually contain eggs.

1 recipe Homemade Pasta (page 219), rolled and cut into lasagna noodles, or about ½ (16-ounce) box lasagna noodles (regular, NOT "no-boil")

2 recipes Seasoned Tofu Ricotta (page 41)

1 cup squeezed-dry, thawed frozen chopped spinach

½ cup Nut-Parm (page 42)

3 cups Oven-Roasted Tomato Sauce (page 197) or store-bought marinara sauce

1½ cups Melty Vegan Cheese (page 43)

1   Arrange a layer of noodles in the bottom of a 9- x 12-inch baking dish. Carefully pour boiling water over the noodles to soften, then remove the noodles from the water and arrange them next to each other (without touching) on a sheet of plastic wrap or parchment paper. Repeat until all the noodles are softened. Wipe out the baking dish.

2   In a bowl, combine the ricotta, spinach, and ¼ cup of the Nut-Parm. Preheat the oven to 375°F.

3   Spread ½ cup of the tomato sauce in the bottom of the baking dish. Cover the sauce with a layer of the noodles. It's okay if they overlap slightly. Spread about half of the ricotta mixture over the noodles. Arrange another layer of noodles, and spread a layer of tomato sauce over the noodles. Repeat the layers with more noodles, the ricotta mixture, and more tomato sauce, ending with the sauce. Spoon the melty cheese on top of the tomato sauce and sprinkle with the remaining ¼ cup Nut-Parm. Cover the baking dish with foil and bake for 40 minutes. Remove the foil and bake until the top is bubbly and lightly browned, 10 to 15 minutes. Let the lasagna cool for 10 minutes before serving. Top with any remaining tomato sauce.

FETTUCCINE BOLOGNESE

2 tablespoons olive oil

1 onion, chopped

1 cup minced chopped celery

1 carrot, minced

5 garlic cloves, minced

2 to 3 cups ground or finely chopped seitan or tempeh

2 tablespoons tomato paste

1 tablespoon light-colored miso paste

½ cup dry white wine

½ cup chopped vegan bacon, store-bought or homemade (pages 106–107)

1 (28-ounce) can crushed tomatoes

Salt and ground black pepper

¼ cup nutritional yeast

1 teaspoon dried thyme

1 cup Cashew Cream (page 32)

½ teaspoon liquid smoke

⅛ teaspoon ground nutmeg

1 cup vegetable broth, store-bought or homemade (page 182)

12 to 16 ounces fettuccine, store-bought or homemade (page 219)

2 tablespoons minced fresh parsley

In Bologna, this hearty sauce is usually served over tagliatelle, a flat pasta that is a little wider than fettuccine. Since fettucine is easier to find, that's what I call for in the recipe, but if you make your own pasta, I recommend making the tagliatelle. The sauce, traditionally made with ground meat and heavy cream, features cashew cream, vegan bacon, and your choice of seitan or tempeh. Chopped mushrooms or reconstituted Soy Curls may be used in place of the seitan or tempeh, if desired.

1 Heat the oil in a large saucepan or Dutch oven over medium heat. Add the onion, celery, carrot, and garlic and cook until softened, 7 to 8 minutes. Add the seitan and cook, stirring, for 5 minutes. Stir in the tomato paste, miso paste, wine, and bacon. Cook for 2 minutes, then add the tomatoes and salt and pepper to taste. Simmer over medium-low heat for about 30 minutes to blend the flavors. Near the end of the cooking time, stir in the nutritional yeast, thyme, cream, liquid smoke, nutmeg, and broth. Taste and adjust the seasonings, if needed. Keep warm while you cook the pasta.

2 Bring a large pot of salted water to a boil over high heat, add the pasta, and cook until the pasta is just tender. Drain it well and return to the pot or transfer to a large serving bowl. Add the sauce and toss well. Serve hot, sprinkled with parsley.

SPAGHETTI CARBONARA

Classic spaghetti carbonara made with cured pork, eggs, and Parmesan cheese is about as non-vegan as you can get. Some versions add a little cream. This recipe combines the requisite spaghetti with plant-based bacon and a creamy, cheesy sauce for a nontraditional interpretation that is still delicious.

8 to 12 ounces spaghetti, store-bought or homemade (page 219)

2 tablespoons olive oil

3 scallions, minced

1 garlic clove, minced

1 cup chopped Mushroom Bacon (page 110) or your favorite plant-based bacon

1 teaspoon smoked paprika

1 tablespoon light-colored miso paste

1 cup Cashew Cream (page 32)

¼ cup nutritional yeast

Salt and freshly cracked black pepper

2 tablespoons minced fresh parsley

1 Bring a large pot of salted water to boil over high heat. Add the spaghetti and cook until al dente, 8 to 10 minutes. Drain the pasta, reserving ½ cup of the cooking water. Return the drained spaghetti to the pot, add 1 tablespoon of the olive oil, and toss to coat. Set aside.

2 Heat the remaining 1 tablespoon olive oil in a skillet over medium heat. Add the scallions, garlic, and chopped bacon and cook for 2 to 3 minutes, or until the bacon is nicely browned. Turn off the heat and stir in the paprika, miso, and ¼ cup of the reserved cooking water. Keep warm.

3 In a bowl, combine the cashew cream, nutritional yeast, and the remaining ¼ cup pasta water. Add the cashew mixture to the pot with the spaghetti, then add the reserved bacon mixture and toss gently over medium heat to combine well and heat through. Season with salt and pepper to taste. Serve in shallow bowls, sprinkled with the parsley.

ORECCHIETTE WITH PISTACHIO PESTO

SERVES
4 TO 6

2 garlic cloves, crushed

½ teaspoon salt

1½ cups shelled unsalted pistachios

1 cup mint leaves

½ cup olive oil

Ground black pepper

1 pound orecchiette, store-bought or homemade (page 225), or other small bite-size pasta

In Sicily, local pistachios are used to make a fragrant green pesto. It is sometimes made with mint or basil, or some of both, but I prefer to use mint alone to help keep it distinctively different from basil pesto. If not using right away, store the pesto in a tightly sealed jar in the refrigerator, where it will keep for up to a week. The dramatic flavors of the pistachios and mint stand up to any pasta, so no cheese is required.

1   In a food processor, combine the garlic and salt and process to a paste. Add the pistachios and mint and process until finely chopped. With the machine running, slowly add the oil. Add pepper to taste and process to a smooth paste. Taste and adjust the seasonings, if needed.

2   Bring a large pot of salted water to a boil over high heat, add the pasta, and cook until al dente. Drain the pasta and return it to the pot, reserving ½ cup of the pasta water. Add the reserved pasta water to the pesto and process until smooth. Add the pesto to the pasta and toss gently to coat the pasta with the pesto. Serve hot.

MAKE-YOUR-OWN ORECCHIETTE

SERVES 4

A specialty of the Puglia region of Italy, orecchiette, or "little ears," is traditionally made with a combination of semolina and all-purpose flour. It is "handmade" without the use of a pasta machine or special tools.

1 cup semolina flour

1½ cups all-purpose flour

1 cup warm water

1 Combine the semolina and all-purpose flours in a large bowl. Make a well in the center and pour half the water into the center. With a fork, stir the flour into the water to form a paste. Continue adding the rest of the water as you stir in the flour, to make a soft but not sticky dough. Once a dough ball has formed, knead it for 5 to 7 minutes.

2 Divide the dough into 4 pieces; reserve 3 and cover them with a clean dish towel or plastic wrap. Take the remaining piece of dough and roll it into a ½-inch cylindrical shape, then cut into ⅛-inch disks. One at a time, place a disk in the palm of your hand, and press an indentation into the center of the disk with the thumb of your other hand, moving your thumb to thin out the center of the disk and stretch it to about 1 inch wide. Place on a clean dish towel or sheet of parchment paper. Repeat the process with the remaining disks, flouring your thumb if it sticks to the dough.

3 When finished, sprinkle flour over the pasta and repeat with the remaining 3 pieces of dough. When finished shaping the orecchiette, you can cook them right away or air-dry them. They may take up to 24 hours to air-dry. If the center is still damp, leave them out. You will know they are dry when they are too hard to cut with a knife. Dried orecchiette will keep at room temperature for several months. If preparing fresh, they will cook in about 7 minutes, whereas the dried may take up to 15 minutes to cook.

ROTINI WITH ROASTED GARLIC ALFREDO SAUCE

SERVES
4 TO 6

1 head roasted garlic (recipe follows)

8 ounces asparagus, cut into 1-inch pieces

1½ cups grape tomatoes

1 tablespoon olive oil

Salt and ground black pepper

8 to 12 ounces rotini, store-bought or homemade (page 219)

1 tablespoon vegan butter, store-bought or homemade (page 36)

2 cups Cashew Cream (page 32)

3 tablespoons nutritional yeast

2 teaspoons fresh lemon juice

1 teaspoon Dijon mustard

¼ teaspoon paprika

Pinch of nutmeg

Nut-Parm (page 42), for serving (optional)

Roasted veggies, chewy pasta, and a creamy, rich garlicky sauce combine to make a sensational meal that is deceptively quick and easy to prepare.

1   Roast the garlic according to the instructions. About halfway through the roasting, arrange the asparagus and tomatoes on a lightly oiled rimmed baking sheet. Drizzle with the oil and season with salt and pepper to taste. Roast the asparagus and tomatoes for 15 to 20 minutes, or until tender. Keep warm.

2   Bring a large pot of salted water to a boil over high heat, add the pasta, and cook until it is al dente.

3   While the pasta is cooking, melt the butter in a small saucepan over medium-low heat. Add the mashed roasted garlic, then stir in the cashew cream and heat until very warm. Do not boil. Stir in the nutritional yeast, lemon juice, mustard, paprika, nutmeg, and salt and pepper to taste. Transfer the sauce to a blender and blend until smooth.

4   When the pasta is done cooking, drain it and return it to the pot. Add the sauce and roasted vegetables and cook over medium heat, tossing gently to heat through and coat with the sauce. Serve hot, sprinkled with the Nut-Parm, if using.

ROASTED GARLIC

MAKES
ABOUT
¼ CUP

When you roast garlic it gives it a mellow, nutty flavor that is delicious in the pasta sauce on page 226. It's also great spread on toasted bread as crostini.

1 head garlic

Olive oil

1 Preheat the oven to 400°F. Peel some of the outer skin off the head of garlic, leaving the skin on the individual cloves. Use a sharp knife to cut about ½ inch off the top off of the garlic head so that you can see the individual cloves. Place the head of garlic on a small sheet of aluminum foil. Drizzle the top of the garlic with olive oil. Wrap up the garlic head in the foil. Bake for 30 minutes, or until the garlic cloves are tender when lightly squeezed. Set aside until cool enough to handle.

2 Remove the individual cloves and squeeze each clove at the bottom to remove the garlic from the skin — it should pop right out. Transfer the roasted garlic cloves to a small bowl and mash them with a fork.

3 To store, cover the mashed garlic cloves with olive oil, then cover with a tight-fitting lid and refrigerate for up to a week.

PIE DOUGH

3 cups all-purpose flour

⅔ cup vegan butter, store-bought or homemade (page 36)

2 teaspoons sugar

1 teaspoon salt

½ cup cold water, plus more if needed

This recipe makes enough dough for a two-crust pie. If you only need a single crust, wrap the second dough tightly in plastic wrap and freeze for up to 2 months, then thaw in the refrigerator overnight before using.

1   In a food processor, combine the flour, butter, sugar, and salt and pulse until crumbly. With the machine running, add the water and process to form a dough ball, adding an extra 1 to 2 tablespoons of water if the dough seems too dry. Divide the dough in half, flatten the dough into disks, and wrap them in plastic wrap. Refrigerate for 20 minutes.

2   To use in recipes: Roll one of the dough pieces into a circle on a lightly floured surface. Arrange the dough in a pie plate, pressing evenly with your fingers to fit it into the pan, trimming and fluting the edges. Roll out the second crust. Fill the pie with the filling and top with the second crust. Crimp the edges and trim the crust, then bake as directed.

3   To prebake a single crust: Prick the bottom of the crust with the tines of a fork. Cover the edges of the crust with aluminum foil to protect from browning and bake the crust at 425°F for 15 minutes.

EASY ARTISAN BREAD

Although many breads you can buy contain no animal products, there are many others that include milk, honey, and other animal ingredients. This easy artisan loaf removes the guesswork. With only four ingredients (plus water), this no-knead loaf is moist, dense, and especially delicious served warm slathered with vegan butter.

3 cups bread flour

2¼ teaspoons instant yeast

1¼ teaspoons salt

2 teaspoons sugar

1¼ cups warm water, or more as needed

1 In a large bowl, combine the flour, yeast, salt, and sugar, and mix well. Add enough of the water until a smooth dough is achieved, adding a little more water, if needed. Cover the bowl with a clean kitchen towel or plastic wrap and set aside at room temperature for 12 hours.

2 Preheat the oven to 400°F. Place a 9- x 5-inch bread pan or 9-inch round baking dish in the oven for 30 minutes. While the pan is heating, transfer the dough to a floured work surface and let it rest.

3 Carefully grease the insides of the hot bread pan. Place the dough inside the bread pan and cover with aluminum foil. Bake the bread for 25 minutes, then remove the foil and bake for 20 to 25 minutes longer, or until golden brown. Cool on a wire rack for 30 minutes before slicing.

Note: If you don't have bread flour, you can instead use all-purpose flour plus 3 teaspoons vital wheat gluten.

VARIATION

Add bits of pureed roasted garlic and minced pitted Kalamata olives to the dough just before letting it rest.

PERFECT POT PIE

1 cup diced peeled potatoes

1 cup sliced carrots

¾ cup frozen corn kernels

¾ cup frozen peas

¼ cup olive oil

½ cup chopped onion

2 cups chopped cooked seitan, tempeh, or reconstituted Soy Curls

½ cup all-purpose flour

1 teaspoon salt

¾ teaspoon dried thyme

½ teaspoon dried basil

¼ teaspoon ground black pepper

1½ cups vegetable broth, store-bought or homemade (page 182)

¾ cup plain unsweetened almond milk, store-bought or homemade (page 28)

½ teaspoon gravy browner, such as Gravy Master or Kitchen Bouquet (optional)

2 pie crusts, store-bought or homemade (page 228)

VARIATION

Customize the filling to suit your own taste, using mixed frozen vegetables, frozen lima beans, or cooked cannellini beans for all or part of the vegetables or seitan.

Sometimes pot pie is topped with biscuits or dumplings, but I find that to be too "bready." Other versions have only a top crust, which isn't quite comforting enough in my book. To me, the perfect pot pie is a hearty blend of vegetables and meaty plant protein, such as seitan in a creamy gravy, all surrounded by a flaky top and bottom crust. Serve with a green salad tossed with a light balsamic vinaigrette.

1 Cook the potatoes and carrots in a steamer basket in a covered saucepan over simmering water until just tender, about 10 minutes. Add the corn and peas, then drain and set aside. (The hot water will thaw the frozen vegetables.)

2 In a skillet, heat the oil over medium-high heat. Add the onion and cook, stirring, until tender, about 5 minutes. Add the seitan and cook for 5 minutes longer to brown slightly. Add the flour, salt, thyme, basil, and pepper and stir to combine. Gradually stir in the broth, milk, and gravy browner, if using. Bring to a boil, stirring constantly; cook and stir for 2 minutes, or until thickened. Stir in the reserved vegetables. Remove from the heat. Preheat the oven to 425°F.

3 Roll out one of the doughs and place it inside a 9-inch pie plate, lightly pressing the dough to conform to the plate. Add the filling mixture. Roll out the remaining dough and carefully place over the filling. Trim the dough, then seal and crimp or flute the edges. Cut a few slits in the top crust. Bake for about 40 minutes, or until the crust is lightly browned. If the edges start to brown before the rest of the crust, loosely wrap aluminum foil around the edges and bake until done. Let the pot pie stand for about 10 minutes before cutting.

CHEESY SAUSAGE BISCUITS

MAKES 9 TO 12 BISCUITS

These biscuits are nicely browned on the outside, tender on the inside, with a rich, cheesy flavor and tasty bites of sausage throughout.

1 Preheat the oven to 425°F. Lightly oil a large baking sheet or line it with parchment paper.

2 In a small bowl, combine the chopped sausage and olive oil and mix to coat the sausage with oil.

3 In a medium bowl, combine the flour, nutritional yeast, baking powder, and salt. Add the butter, working it into the mixture until it is crumbly. Add the sour cream, milk, and sausage. Mix until combined and the dough comes together. If the mixture is too dry, add a little more milk, 1 teaspoon at a time.

4 Place the dough on a sheet of parchment paper or a lightly floured work surface. Roll the dough into a 6-inch square about ¾ inch thick. Use a 2-inch biscuit cutter to cut the dough into 12 rounds or use a knife to cut it into nine 2-inch squares. Arrange the biscuits on the prepared baking sheet, about 1 inch apart. Bake the biscuits for 15 to 20 minutes, or until deep golden brown. Serve warm.

1 cup chopped Maple Breakfast Sausage (page 123) or store-bought vegan sausage

2 teaspoons olive oil

1½ cups unbleached all-purpose flour

3 tablespoons nutritional yeast

2 teaspoons baking powder

½ teaspoon salt

⅓ cup vegan butter, store-bought or homemade (page 36), chopped into pieces

¾ cup vegan sour cream, store-bought or homemade (page 33)

2 tablespoons plain unsweetened nondairy milk, or more if needed, store-bought or homemade (page 28)

CHEESY CRACKERS

1 cup all-purpose flour

2 tablespoons nutritional yeast

½ teaspoon baking powder

½ teaspoon salt

½ teaspoon garlic powder

¼ teaspoon smoked paprika

⅛ teaspoon turmeric

1 tablespoon olive oil

1 tablespoon vegan butter, store-bought or homemade (page 36)

1 teaspoon fresh lemon juice

5 to 6 tablespoons cold water, or more as needed

It's easy to find crackers without animal ingredients, unless of course, your favorite crackers happen to be the cheesy ones. Now you can make them at home, complete with the delicious crunch and cheesy color and flavor you love but without the animal ingredients and additives.

1　Preheat the oven to 350°F. In a medium bowl, combine the flour, nutritional yeast, baking powder, salt, garlic powder, smoked paprika, and turmeric. Mix well. Add the olive oil, butter, and lemon juice, mixing with a fork until the dough is fine and crumbly. Add the water a tablespoon at a time until the dough becomes cohesive.

2　Transfer the dough to a piece of parchment paper large enough to fit a large rimmed baking pan. (You can use a Silpat instead, if you have one.) Top the dough with another sheet of parchment paper and roll out the dough until thin, measuring about 11 x 13 inches. Transfer the parchment paper and rolled-out dough to a large rimmed baking sheet. Remove the top sheet of parchment paper and cut the rolled dough into 2-inch squares. If desired, remove any uneven pieces of dough from around the edges and press together into a small disk and roll it out to get more crackers that are a uniform size. (Otherwise, you'll have a few partial crackers from around the end to nibble on!)

3　Bake for 15 to 17 minutes, or until the crackers are baked but not browned. The color should be golden. Cool completely on the baking sheet. These crackers keep well for a week in a sealed container at room temperature.

SCRATCH BISCUITS

1⅔ cups all-purpose flour

3 teaspoons baking powder

1 teaspoon salt

⅔ cup unsweetened nondairy milk,
store-bought or homemade
(page 28)

⅓ cup sunflower oil or other neutral
vegetable oil

Fresh biscuits are easy to prepare and make a great addition to
a cozy cold-weather meal, such as a stew or chili. With only five
ingredients, this basic recipe couldn't be easier.

1   Preheat the oven to 475°F. Line a large baking sheet with parchment paper.

2   In a large mixing bowl, combine the flour, baking powder, and salt.
Mix well. Form a well in the center of the mixture, and add the milk
and oil. Mix well until the dough comes together.

3   Divide the dough into biscuit-shaped balls and arrange them on
the prepared baking sheet, about 1 inch apart. Alternatively, you can
flatten the dough on a work surface to about 1 inch thick and use a
2-inch biscuit cutter to cut the biscuits into rounds and arrange on the
baking sheet.

4   Bake for 10 minutes, or until the biscuits are golden and slightly
brown on the bottom. Serve warm.

VARIATIONS

Customize these biscuits by
adding minced fresh chives or
your favorite herbs to the mixture,
or add shredded vegan cheese or
nutritional yeast to give it a cheesy
flavor.

ALL-IN-ONE CAULIFLOWER PIZZA

SERVES 2 TO 4

Cauliflower as a pizza crust has been making the rounds on the Internet. Trouble is, many of the recipes use eggs and cheese, negating the otherwise healthy benefits. In this recipe, flaxseeds blended with water help hold the crust together, and flavorful toppings are baked right into the crust for a self-contained pizza that is great for a snack on its own or a meal when served with a salad. You'll need a knife and fork to eat this!

1   In a small bowl, combine the flaxseed and water and set aside for 10 minutes. Preheat the oven to 400°F. Line a pizza pan with parchment paper.

2   Place the cauliflower in a food processor and process into tiny pieces resembling rice. Measure out 2 cups of the riced cauliflower and place in a mixing bowl. Save the remaining cauliflower for another use.

3   In the same food processor (no need to clean it out), add the sunflower seeds and process until finely ground. Add the 2 cups riced cauliflower, chickpea flour, nutritional yeast, oregano, basil, garlic powder, ground fennel, salt, and red pepper flakes. Process to mix. Add the flax mixture, sun-dried tomatoes, olives, and capers and pulse to combine well. If the mixture is too wet, add a little more chickpea flour; if it's too dry, add a little water.

4   Spread the mixture onto the prepared pan and press it evenly. It should be thin—about ¼-inch thick. Bake for 25 minutes, or until golden brown. Remove the crust from the oven and top with a thin layer of pizza sauce and shredded vegan cheese, if using, then return to the oven for 5 to 10 minutes. Serve hot.

1 tablespoon ground flaxseed

2 tablespoons warm water

½ small head cauliflower, cored and broken into florets

¼ cup sunflower seeds

¼ cup chickpea flour

¼ cup nutritional yeast

½ teaspoon dried oregano

½ teaspoon dried basil

½ teaspoon garlic powder

½ teaspoon ground fennel

1 teaspoon salt

¼ teaspoon red pepper flakes

2 tablespoons chopped reconstituted or oil-packed sun-dried tomatoes

2 tablespoons chopped pitted Kalamata olives

2 teaspoons capers (chopped if large)

1 cup pizza sauce or Oven-Roasted Tomato Sauce (page 197)

Vegan shredded cheese or Melty Vegan Cheese (page 43, optional)

PIZZA DOUGH

3 cups unbleached all-purpose flour

2¼ teaspoons instant-rise yeast

2 teaspoons sugar

1 teaspoon salt

2 tablespoons olive oil

1¼ cups warm water

Okay, so pizza dough doesn't usually contain animal products (unless you count the "cheese-stuffed" crusts featured by some pizza chains). Still, since pizza is often synonymous with cheese and meat toppings, I've included a few plant-based options in the book and, for your convenience, I'm also including this recipe for pizza dough. I like to make enough dough for two pizzas at a time (even when I only need one). That way I can stash the extra one in the freezer for a future meal. I find it quicker to make the dough in a food processor, but you can make it in a bowl by hand, if you prefer. If not using right away, the dough can be tightly wrapped and frozen for 2 to 3 months, then thawed in the refrigerator and brought to room temperature before shaping into a crust and baking. Use this dough to make the Meaty-Cheesy Pizza on page 240 and the Benedict Pizza on page 239.

1 In a large bowl, combine the flour, yeast, sugar, and salt. Add the oil, then slowly mix in the water as needed until it is well mixed and forms a soft dough ball, adding a little more water if needed to make a smooth dough.

2 Shape the dough into a smooth ball and leave it in the bowl. Cover the bowl tightly with plastic wrap and let the dough rise in a warm place for 1 to 2 hours.

3 Punch down the dough and divide it into 2 pieces. Shape each piece into a round ball. The dough is now ready to use in your favorite pizza recipes.

BENEDICT PIZZA

SERVES
4 TO 8

I originally created this recipe as a brunch dish for a crowd. Much easier than making individual vegan eggs Benedict or Florentine with English muffins, this "pizza" is easy to prepare ahead of time for last-minute baking when ready to serve. Use the homemade pizza dough on page 238 or save time by using ready-made dough such as Trader Joe's brand. I keep a few in the freezer and one in the fridge. Be sure to plan ahead so you can bring the dough to room temperature before using. Serve alone or with a side of hash browns.

1 pizza dough, store-bought or homemade (page 238), at room temperature

1 tablespoon olive oil

10 ounces fresh or frozen chopped spinach

Salt and ground black pepper

Hollandaise Sauce (page 185)

8 slices Mushroom Bacon (page 110) or Hamish Loaf (page 112) or your favorite vegan bacon or ham

8 thin slices marinated baked tofu, store-bought or homemade (page 74)

3 plum tomatoes, thinly sliced

1 Place the oven rack in the bottom position in the oven. Preheat the oven to 450°F.

2 Stretch the dough onto a 9- x 13-inch rimmed baking sheet. Use your fingertips to form a rim around the perimeter of the crust. Bake the crust for 5 minutes, then remove from the oven.

3 Heat the oil in a skillet over medium heat. Add the spinach and season with salt and pepper to taste. Cook, stirring, until wilted (if fresh) or cooked (if frozen). Set aside to cool.

4 Spread a layer of hollandaise on the crust, then top with a layer of bacon. Top each bacon slice with a slice of tofu. Drain any remaining liquid from the spinach and place a spoonful of the spinach on top of each tofu slice. Arrange the plum tomato slices on top. The pizza can be made ahead to this point.

5 When ready to serve, return the pizza to the oven for 10 minutes, or until the toppings are hot and the crust is golden brown. Cut into slices and drizzle with more hollandaise sauce. Serve hot.

MEATY-CHEESY PIZZA

MAKES
1 (12-INCH)
PIZZA

1 pizza dough, store-bought or homemade (page 238), at room temperature

1 tablespoon olive oil

1 cup thinly sliced pepperoni, store-bought or homemade (page 116)

½ cup Oven-Roasted Tomato Sauce (page 197) or store-bought pizza sauce or marinara sauce

½ teaspoon dried oregano

1 cup Crispy Crumbles (page 78) or store-bought vegan burger crumbles

Salt and ground black pepper

⅔ cup Melty Vegan Cheese (page 43) or store-bought shredded vegan mozzarella

Basil or arugula leaves (optional garnish)

A plant-based meaty, cheesy pizza is not a pipe dream. It's right here for the making. I like to keep a supply of pizza dough in the freezer so I always have some on hand.

1 Place the oven rack in the bottom position in the oven. Preheat the oven to 450°F.

2 Stretch the dough onto a baking sheet or pizza stone. Use your fingertips to form a rim around the perimeter of the crust.

3 Heat the oil in a skillet over medium heat. Add the pepperoni and sauté until warm and coated with oil.

4 Spread the tomato sauce thinly on the pizza crust, to within ½ inch of the edge. Arrange the pepperoni slices on top of the tomato sauce. Sprinkle with the oregano and the crumbles. Season to taste with salt and pepper. Top the pizza with the cheese and bake for 12 to 15 minutes, or until the pizza is hot and the crust is nicely browned. Serve hot, topped with a few basil or arugula leaves, if using.

LOADED POLENTA PIZZA

3 cups vegetable broth, store-bought or homemade (page 182)

Salt

2 tablespoons olive oil

1 cup cornmeal

2 cups thinly sliced mushrooms, any kind

2 garlic cloves, minced

½ teaspoon dried oregano

Ground black pepper

1 cup Oven-Roasted Tomato Sauce (page 197) or your favorite pizza sauce

1 cup thinly sliced marinated artichoke hearts

1 cup Smoky Chickpeas (page 111)

Polenta is a delicious alternative to traditional pizza crust and is wonderful with a variety of toppings. My favorite is this iteration topped with chickpeas, sautéed spinach, mushrooms, and artichoke hearts. Note that the polenta crust isn't easy to eat out of hand like regular pizza, so serve it with a knife and fork.

1 In a large saucepan, combine the broth, salt to taste (depending on the saltiness of your broth), and 1 tablespoon of the oil, and bring to a boil. Add the cornmeal, stirring constantly with a wire whisk. Decrease the heat to medium and cook, stirring frequently, until thickened, 12 to 15 minutes. Preheat the oven to 375°F. Lightly oil a pizza pan or shallow rectangular baking dish. As soon as the polenta is cooked, spread it quickly onto the prepared pan, using the back of a large spoon to spread it evenly to the ends of the pan. It should be about ¼ inch thick. Bake for 12 minutes, then set it aside.

2 Heat the remaining 1 tablespoon oil in a skillet over medium heat. Add the mushrooms, garlic, and oregano. Season with salt and pepper to taste and cook until the mushrooms are tender and have released their liquid, 5 to 7 minutes. Transfer the mushrooms to a plate.

3 Spread the sauce evenly over the partially baked polenta, to within ¼ inch of the edge. Arrange the artichoke hearts and mushrooms on top. Sprinkle with the chickpeas. Bake for 10 to 12 minutes longer, or until hot. Serve hot.

CRANBERRY-WALNUT SCONES

Enjoy these scones for breakfast or as a snack with a cup of tea or coffee. The variations on this treat are many—you can swap out the cranberries for another type of fruit or chocolate chips and replace the walnuts with different kinds of nuts.

2 cups all-purpose flour

½ cup sugar

2 teaspoons baking powder

1 teaspoon baking soda

½ teaspoon salt

½ teaspoon ground cinnamon

½ cup vegan butter, softened, store-bought or homemade (page 36)

⅓ cup sweetened dried cranberries

⅓ cup chopped walnuts

⅓ cup nondairy milk

1   Preheat the oven to 400°F. In a large bowl, combine the flour, sugar, baking powder, baking soda, salt, and cinnamon. Cut the butter into the flour mixture until it is crumbly. Mix in the cranberries, walnuts, and milk, stirring until just blended. Do not overmix.

2   Transfer the dough to a lightly floured surface, and pat the dough into a 1-inch-thick circle. Cut the dough into 12 wedges, and place them on a lightly greased baking sheet. Bake until golden brown, 18 to 20 minutes. Serve warm.

CHAPTER 9

SWEETS
OM SCRATCH

Unless you have a vegan bakery around the corner, finding vegan sweets can be a challenge. The solution is to "veganize it" using plant-based ingredients to replace dairy and eggs in your favorite desserts, from Lemon Meringue Pie and Tiramisu to Strawberry Shortcake and Chocolate–Chocolate Chip Brownies. This chapter begins with the basics, including dairy-free whipped cream, caramel sauce, and ganache. There are even recipes for vegan ice cream (without an ice cream maker), vegan meringue, and a delicious scratch cake that is the basis for several decadent desserts.

WHIPPED COCONUT CREAM 248

CASHEW CHANTILLY
CREAM 249

DATE-CARAMEL SAUCE 250

FUDGY CHOCOLATE SAUCE 251

BUTTERCREAM FROSTING 252

VEGAN MASCARPONE 253

GANACHE 254

VEGANIZED MARSHMALLOW
FLUFF 255

MERINGUE 256

LEMON MERINGUE PIE 259

SCRATCH CAKE 260

TIRAMISU 261

STRAWBERRY SHORTCAKE 262

MANGO FRO-YO 264

BELLINI TRIFLE 265

CRANBERRY
OATMEAL COOKIES 266

CHOCOLATE TRUFFLES 267

LUSCIOUS LAVA CAKES 269

CHOCOLATE–CHOCOLATE CHIP
BROWNIES 271

NO-BAKE CHOCOLATE
CHEESECAKE 273

NO-BAKE NUT LOVER'S
CHEESECAKE 274

CHOCOLATE-COVERED ELVIS
ICE CREAM 275

CHOCOLATE–PEANUT BUTTER
MILKSHAKE 276

ICE CREAM
SUNDAE CAKE 278

BANANA SPLIT SOFT-SERVE
SUNDAES 280

WHIPPED COCONUT CREAM

2 (13.5-ounce) cans full-fat coconut milk

1 tablespoon pure vanilla extract

½ cup confectioners' sugar

Be sure to use full-fat coconut in this recipe so that the coconut cream will solidify when chilled. If you only need a small amount of whipped cream you can use just one can of the coconut milk and reduce the amount of vanilla to 1½ teaspoons and the confectioners' sugar to 3 tablespoons.

1 Refrigerate the coconut milk in their cans overnight to allow the coconut cream to solidify. Chill a metal mixing bowl for about an hour before making the whipped cream.

2 Remove the chilled cans from the refrigerator without shaking the cans or turning them upside down. With the pointy part of a bottle opener, puncture the bottom of the cans (without turning it upside down) and let the liquid drain out (save the liquid for another use). Once the liquid is drained, open the can tops to reveal the solid coconut cream. Use a spatula to transfer the coconut cream to the chilled bowl.

3 Use a stand mixer or a hand mixer to beat the coconut cream until it is thick and fluffy. Add the vanilla and beat it into the coconut cream. Add the confectioners' sugar and beat it into the coconut cream, scraping down the sides of the bowl as needed, until the desired consistency is reached. Chill for 1 to 2 hours before serving. Refrigerate leftovers in an airtight container for up to 5 days.

CASHEW CHANTILLY CREAM

MAKES ABOUT 2½ CUPS

Chantilly cream is a fancy name for whipped cream (in this case, thick Cashew Cream) sweetened with confectioners' sugar. Works for me! Use it to top cakes, pies, ice cream, or fresh fruit.

1½ cups Cashew Cream (page 32)

1¼ cups confectioners' sugar

1 teaspoon pure vanilla extract

½ cup melted refined coconut oil

1 In a food processor or blender, combine the cashew cream, confectioners' sugar, and vanilla and blend until smooth. With the machine running, add the melted coconut oil, blending well.

2 Transfer the cream to a bowl, cover tightly, and refrigerate for at least 4 hours or overnight before using.

DATE-CARAMEL SAUCE

1 cup pitted dates (about 10 large Medjool dates)

½ cup hot water

½ cup almond milk, store-bought or homemade (page 28), warmed

1 teaspoon pure vanilla extract

Pinch of salt

Dates have a natural caramel flavor that when pureed with a few ingredients makes a seriously delicious caramel sauce. If you prefer a thinner sauce, add a little more water or nondairy milk. Serve over vegan ice cream or cake or swirl into vegan vanilla yogurt.

1   Use a wet knife to chop the dates, then transfer them to a high-speed blender or food processor. Add the hot water and warm nondairy milk and let the dates soak for 20 minutes to soften. Add the vanilla and salt and blend until smooth and creamy, adding a little more milk if a thinner sauce is desired.

2   If not using right away, transfer to a glass jar or bowl with a tight-fitting lid and store in the refrigerator for up to a week.

FUDGY CHOCOLATE SAUCE

MAKES
ABOUT
1 CUP

If you want a pourable syruplike sauce, you'll need to add about 3 extra tablespoons of nondairy milk.

1   In a blender, combine the maple syrup, nondairy milk, melted coconut oil, vanilla, and salt and blend to mix well. Add the cocoa powder and blend until smooth. Use immediately or transfer to a glass jar or bowl. Cover and keep at room temperature until ready to use. The sauce will thicken as it sits.

2   For a thinner sauce, stir in about 3 tablespoons additional nondairy milk, 1 tablespoon at a time. If not using right away, store it in the refrigerator for up to 2 weeks. If refrigerated, it will need to come to room temperature before using or warmed over a saucepan of simmering water.

⅓ cup pure maple syrup

¼ cup nondairy milk, store-bought or homemade (page 28), plus more as needed

¼ cup melted coconut oil

1 teaspoon pure vanilla extract

Pinch of salt

½ cup cocoa powder

BUTTERCREAM FROSTING

MAKES
ABOUT
2 CUPS

1 cup vegan butter, store-bought or homemade (page 36), chilled

2 cups confectioners' sugar, or more as needed

2 tablespoons vegan sour cream, store-bought or homemade (page 33)

¾ teaspoon cider vinegar

1 teaspoon pure vanilla extract

⅛ teaspoon salt

Plant-based butter and sour cream combine to make a luxurious dairy-free frosting for cakes and cupcakes.

1   Place the vegan butter in a mixing bowl (if using a hand mixer) or in the bowl of a standing mixer and beat until smooth and fluffy, 1 to 2 minutes. (It may take longer using a hand mixer.) Turn the mixer speed to low, and add 1 cup of the confectioners' sugar, a little at a time. Add the sour cream, vinegar, vanilla, and salt, then add the remaining 1 cup confectioners' sugar. Slowly increase the mixer speed to high, and continue to beat until the mixture is smooth and creamy, about 2 minutes longer.

2   If not using right away, cover and refrigerate until needed. Once refrigerated, let the frosting come to room temperature for about 10 minutes before using.

VEGAN MASCARPONE

This plant-based version of mascarpone cheese is ideal for making the Tiramisu on page 261. You can also use it to make cheesecakes or in a pasta sauce to make it thick and creamy.

¾ cup raw cashews, soaked in hot water for 30 minutes, then drained

1 tablespoon fresh lemon juice

Pinch of salt

1 (12-ounce) box extra-firm silken tofu, drained

1   In a high-speed blender or food processor, combine the drained cashews, lemon juice, and salt and blend to a paste. Add the tofu and blend until very smooth and creamy, stopping the machine as needed to scrape the mixture from the bottom and sides so that everything blends smoothly.

2   If not using right away, transfer to a container, cover with a tight-fitting lid, and refrigerate until needed.

GANACHE

8 ounces vegan semisweet
chocolate chips

¾ cup cashew milk, store-bought
or homemade (page 28)

The classic blend of chocolate and heavy cream is easily made vegan by using a thick nondairy milk such as cashew milk. This ganache makes a delectable frosting for cakes and cupcakes. If you want a firmer ganache, refrigerate before using, then stir it to lighten it up for spreading or piping. For a thinner ganache, use up to ¼ cup additional cashew milk.

Place the chocolate in a heatproof bowl. In a saucepan, bring the cashew milk just to a boil over medium-high heat. Pour the milk over the chocolate, and let stand for 10 minutes to melt the chocolate without stirring so it doesn't get grainy. After about 10 minutes, stir the chocolate mixture with a whisk until smooth and shiny, scraping any chocolate from the bottom or sides of the bowl to incorporate. Cool to room temperature to thicken before using.

VEGANIZED MARSHMALLOW FLUFF

MAKES ABOUT 3 CUPS

Thanks to the magic of aquafaba (page 257) it is possible to make an easy veganized version of marshmallow fluff. Use it to top ice cream, make s'mores, and, of course, fluffernutter sandwiches.

Pour the aquafaba into a stand mixer or a large mixing bowl. Add the remaining ingredients and beat with an electric mixer or in a stand mixer for about 15 minutes. (It should begin to thicken after about 10 minutes.) Use immediately or cover and refrigerate until needed. If the fluff begins to separate, beat again to re-fluff.

½ cup aquafaba (liquid from one 15-ounce can white beans or chickpeas)

½ cup sugar

¼ teaspoon pure vanilla extract

Pinch of cream of tartar

MERINGUE

½ cup aquafaba (liquid from one 15-ounce can white beans or chickpeas)

¼ teaspoon cream of tartar or ½ teaspoon guar gum or xanthan gum

1 teaspoon pure vanilla extract

¾ cup superfine sugar (see Note)

When vegans discovered via the Internet that bean liquid, when combined with a few ingredients and beaten, makes a plant-based meringue, you could almost hear the collective sigh of joy. I'm not sure who originally discovered the magical "aquafaba" but I'm glad they did. I prefer to use cream of tartar to help stabilize the meringue because it's easy to find at regular supermarkets. If you have either guar gum or xanthan gum on hand, you can use either one of them, if you like. I prefer to use white bean liquid for this recipe (not chickpeas or other beans) to keep the flavor mild. If you don't have cannellini beans, use Great Northern or navy beans for best results.

1   Pour the aquafaba into a mixing bowl or the bowl of a stand mixer.

2   To the aquafaba, add the cream of tartar and mix on high speed using a hand mixer or the whisk attachment of a stand mixer. Continue to mix until the liquid starts to thicken like thick whipped cream. Add the vanilla and then slowly add the sugar, a little at a time. Continue mixing on high speed until the meringue forms stiff peaks, 5 to 10 minutes. The meringue is now ready to use in recipes.

Note: If you don't have superfine sugar, grind regular sugar in a blender or food processor until finely powdered.

EGG EXCHANGE

Eggs are used in baking to add moisture, emulsification, structure, and leavening. Here is a list of the most popular ways to replace eggs in baking. For each egg that the recipe calls for, use one of the following:

Applesauce Blend 3 tablespoons apple-sauce and ½ teaspoon baking powder.

Aquafaba (Bean Liquid) 3 tablespoons liquid from canned or cooked chickpeas or white beans.

Arrowroot Blend 2 tablespoons arrowroot in a blender with 3 tablespoons water.

Baking Powder Blend 2 tablespoons water with 1 tablespoon oil and 1 teaspoon baking powder.

Banana Puree ½ ripe banana with ½ teaspoon baking powder.

Chia Seeds Combine 1 tablespoon chia seeds with ¼ cup water in a bowl and set aside until thickened.

Chickpea Flour Blend 3 tablespoons chickpea flour with 3 tablespoons water.

Ener-G Egg Replacer Blend 1½ teaspoons powder with 2 tablespoons water. (Available in health food stores and online.)

Flaxseed Mixture Blend 1 tablespoon ground golden flaxseed with 2 to 3 table-spoons warm water until viscous and slightly thickened.

Mashed Potato Blend 3 tablespoons mashed potato with ½ teaspoon baking powder.

Nut Butter Use 3 tablespoons creamy nut butter (at room temperature).

Tofu Blend 3 tablespoons silken or soft tofu with ½ teaspoon baking powder.

Vegan Yogurt Blend 3 tablespoons vegan yogurt, store-bought or homemade (page 34), with ½ teaspoon baking powder.

LEMON MERINGUE PIE

My mom was a great baker and her lemon meringue pies were especially wonderful. For years I've enjoyed her lemon pie recipe with just a few tweaks, but a good plant-based meringue topping had eluded me until recently. Kudos to the geniuses who first discovered aquafaba (page 257), the magic bean liquid that makes meringue possible again.

1 (9-inch) vegan pie dough, store-bought or homemade (page 228)

1½ cups sugar

⅓ cup cornstarch

⅛ teaspoon salt

1 cup nondairy milk, store-bought or homemade (page 28)

½ cup water

1 cup fresh lemon juice

1 recipe Meringue (page 256)

1   Preheat the oven to 400°F. Roll out the dough on a floured surface and transfer to a pie plate. Crimp the edges, then use a fork to pierce a few holes in the bottom of the pan. Bake for about 15 minutes, or until the crust is a light golden brown. Remove from the oven and set aside to cool.

2   In a saucepan, combine the sugar, cornstarch, and salt. Stir in the nondairy milk and water and bring to a boil over medium-high heat. Cook, stirring constantly, until the mixture thickens, about 5 minutes. Stir in the lemon juice, then remove from the heat. Let the filling cool to room temperature, then pour the filling evenly into the prepared crust. Refrigerate uncovered for at least 1 hour to set the filling. Preheat the oven to 300°F while preparing the meringue.

3   Spoon the meringue evenly onto the pie filling, spreading to the edge of the crust. Use the back of a spoon to make peaks in the meringue. Bake for 30 minutes, or until the meringue is lightly browned. Remove from the oven and cool to room temperature, then refrigerate, uncovered, to chill completely before serving. Store the pie in the refrigerator but do not cover it or the meringue will start to weep.

SCRATCH CAKE

¼ cup vegan sour cream, store-bought or homemade (page 33)

2 tablespoons sunflower oil or other neutral vegetable oil

1 teaspoon cider vinegar

1½ cups nondairy milk, store-bought or homemade (page 28)

2 teaspoons pure vanilla extract

2½ cups all-purpose flour

1 cup sugar

3 tablespoons tapioca starch

2 teaspoons baking powder

¾ teaspoon baking soda

½ teaspoon salt

This is a basic white cake that I use as a base for the Strawberry Shortcake on page 262 and the Tiramisu on page 261. Its structure is slightly dense (as opposed to light and fluffy), making it ideal to absorb all the syrupy goodness in those desserts. It makes eight generous servings (or ten to twelve smaller servings). It also freezes well, so for those desserts where you only need one cake layer, you can freeze the second one for future use.

1 Preheat the oven to 350°F. Grease two 8-inch round or square cake pans or one 9- x 13-inch rectangular cake pan with vegan butter, then dust lightly with flour.

2 In a large mixing bowl, combine the sour cream, oil, vinegar, milk, and vanilla and beat with a whisk or an electric mixer until blended. Add the flour, sugar, starch, baking powder, baking soda, and salt and beat until just combined.

3 Divide the batter equally between the prepared pans. Bake for about 30 minutes, or until a toothpick inserted into the center of the cake comes out clean. Cool on racks for 10 minutes, then loosen the cakes and remove from the pans to cool completely. When completely cool, the cakes are ready to use in recipes.

Note: If you're making this cake as a component for Tiramisu (page 261), use square or rectangular cake pans.

TIRAMISU

Now you can enjoy the famous Italian "pick-me-up" dessert at home with this delicious dairy-free recipe. This is a great "make ahead" dessert because the tiramisu (as well as its various components) can all be made well in advance of when you need them.

1 Scratch Cake (page 260), baked in two 8-inch square pans

1 recipe Vegan Mascarpone (page 253)

1 recipe Cashew Chantilly Cream (page 249)

1 teaspoon pure vanilla extract

⅓ cup sugar

⅓ cup brewed coffee, cooled to room temperature

3 tablespoons Kahlúa or other coffee liqueur or brandy (optional but recommended)

1 tablespoon cocoa powder

1   Bake the cake and set aside to cool. Leave one cake layer in the baking pan; remove the second cake layer from the pan and set aside. Make the mascarpone and refrigerate until needed. Make the cream and refrigerate until needed.

2   In a mixing bowl, combine the mascarpone, vanilla, and all but 1 tablespoon of the sugar, mixing well. In a small bowl, combine the coffee, the remaining 1 tablespoon sugar, and the coffee liqueur, if using.

3   Brush the cake layer in the pan with the coffee mixture, allowing it to soak into the cake. Spread the mascarpone mixture evenly on top of the cake. Top with the second layer of cake, pressing down gently. Spread the cream on top and sprinkle with the cocoa. Chill for at least 1 hour before serving.

STRAWBERRY SHORTCAKE

SERVES 9

1 recipe Cashew Chantilly Cream
(page 249)

1 Scratch Cake (page 260), baked
in a 9- x 13-inch rectangular pan

6 cups strawberries, hulled and
sliced

⅔ cup sugar

¾ teaspoon pure vanilla extract

My favorite summertime dessert is easy to make vegan. Just
prepare the components ahead of time so you can assemble it
whenever you're ready.

1   Prepare the cream several hours or up to a day ahead of when you
need it. Keep refrigerated.

2   Bake the cake a few hours or a day ahead of when you need it.
Cool to room temperature.

3   At least an hour before serving time, combine the strawberries,
sugar, and vanilla in a bowl, stirring to coat the berries with sugar.
Cover and set aside for at least an hour. If making well ahead of time,
refrigerate until needed.

4   To assemble, cut the cake into serving-size pieces and arrange on
dessert plates. Spoon a dollop of cream on top of the cake, followed
by a large spoonful of strawberries. Serve immediately.

MANGO FRO-YO

2 cups frozen diced mango

½ cup vegan yogurt or vegan sour cream, store-bought or homemade (page 34 or 33)

3 tablespoons agave nectar

2 teaspoons fresh lime juice

I especially enjoy mango frozen yogurt as a refreshing finish to an Indian meal because it tastes like a mango lassi.

In a high-speed blender or food processor, combine all the ingredients and blend until smooth. Scrape the mixture into a bowl and freeze for 3 to 4 hours. Serve as is or let stand for a few minutes to soften before serving.

Note: Homemade ice cream is best served the day it's made, but it still tastes delicious for up to a month in the freezer in an airtight plastic container. If you freeze for more than a day, be sure to thaw the ice cream for 15 minutes prior to serving.

VARIATIONS

Change up the flavor by using different fruit (such as strawberries or raspberries) to replace the mango and fresh lemon juice to replace the lime juice.

BELLINI TRIFLE

The only thing I enjoy more than a Bellini is a Bellini made into a dessert, in this case a delicious trifle complete with the requisite peaches and Prosecco, combined with cake and vegan whipped cream.

8 fresh ripe peaches, pitted and sliced

1½ cups Prosecco

½ cup sugar

1 Scratch Cake (page 260), baked and cooled

1 recipe Cashew Chantilly Cream (page 249), chilled

1 In a large bowl, combine the peaches with the Prosecco and sugar and toss to coat. Cover and refrigerate until well chilled, 5 hours to overnight.

2 Cut the cooled cake into 1- to 2-inch cubes. Arrange a layer of cake cubes in a clear glass serving bowl, spoon a layer of whipped cream on top of the cake, and top with a layer of the peaches. Repeat with the remaining ingredients. Serve at once or refrigerate until needed.

CRANBERRY OATMEAL COOKIES

MAKES ABOUT 24 COOKIES

3 cups old-fashioned rolled oats

1 cup all-purpose flour

1 teaspoon baking soda

½ teaspoon salt

½ teaspoon cinnamon

½ cup packed brown sugar

½ cup pure maple syrup

½ cup almond milk, store-bought or homemade (page 28)

3 tablespoons coconut oil, melted

1 teaspoon pure vanilla extract

¾ cup sweetened dried cranberries

VARIATION

Swap out the cranberries for raisins and/or add ½ cup walnut pieces to the cookie dough.

I always sprinkle some dried cranberries on my morning oatmeal, so it was a natural extension to add them to oatmeal cookies for a chewy burst of flavor in every bite.

1 Preheat the oven to 350°F. Lightly grease a baking sheet or line it with parchment paper.

2 Add 1 cup of the oats to a food processor and process until finely ground. Add the flour, baking soda, salt, cinnamon, and brown sugar and process until well combined. Add the maple syrup, almond milk, coconut oil, and vanilla and process until thoroughly combined.

3 Transfer the mixture in the food processor to a large bowl. Add the remaining 2 cups oats and the cranberries and stir to incorporate.

4 Scoop about 2 tablespoons of cookie dough onto the prepared baking sheet. Repeat with the remaining dough. Bake for 12 to 15 minutes, or until golden brown on the bottom.

CHOCOLATE TRUFFLES

MAKES ABOUT 16 CANDIES

This is my go-to truffle recipe. Dates provide the sweetness and richness, so they're sugar free, and with only 1 tablespoon of coconut oil, they're also low in fat, and, of course, dairy-free.

2 cups soft dates, pitted (see Note)

3 tablespoons cocoa powder, plus more to coat

1 tablespoon coconut oil, melted

1 teaspoon pure vanilla extract

Pinch of salt

1   In a food processor, combine the dates, cocoa, melted coconut oil, vanilla, and salt, and process until smooth and well mixed, scraping down the sides as needed. Line a baking sheet with parchment paper.

2   Roll the mixture into 1-inch balls and arrange on the prepared baking sheet. Place about ¼ cup cocoa powder in a shallow bowl and roll the truffles in it, moving around to coat, adding more cocoa if needed. Arrange the truffles on a plate and refrigerate until firm, about 1 hour. Store in the refrigerator in a covered container.

Note: If your dates are not soft, soak them in warm water for 1 hour, then drain well and blot dry before using.

LUSCIOUS LAVA CAKES

MAKES
4 CAKES

The darling of '90s restaurant menus is still around—and for good reason. This warm, gooey chocolatey dessert is a chocolate lover's dream. And now it's vegan, too. Win-win. Top with a spoonful of Cashew Chantilly Cream (page 249) or a dusting of confectioners' sugar and some berries.

4 Lava Balls (recipe follows)

1 tablespoon ground flaxseed

3 tablespoons hot water

¾ cup almond milk, store-bought or homemade (page 28)

¾ cup sugar

3 tablespoons coconut oil, melted

1 teaspoon pure vanilla extract

1 cup unbleached all-purpose flour

⅓ cup unsweetened cocoa powder

1 teaspoon baking powder

⅛ teaspoon salt

½ cup vegan semisweet chocolate chips, melted

1   Make the Lava Balls ahead of time and place in the freezer to firm up while you assemble the cakes.

2   In a cup or small bowl, stir together the flaxseed and water. Set aside for 5 minutes. Grease the inside of four 1-cup ramekins. Sprinkle the insides with sugar or cocoa and tap out the excess. Preheat the oven to 375°F.

(continued)

LAVA BALLS

MAKES
4 LAVA
BALLS

⅓ cup vegan semisweet chocolate chips

1½ tablespoons almond milk, store-bought or homemade (page 28)

1 teaspoon vegan butter, store-bought or homemade (page 36)

Place the chocolate chips in a heatproof bowl. Heat the milk, pour over the chocolate, and whisk until smooth. Add the butter and whisk until incorporated. Place the bowl in the refrigerator to cool and thicken the chocolate mixture—do not allow it to get too firm. Spoon out portions of the chocolate mixture and shape into 4 balls. Arrange the chocolate balls on a plate lined with parchment paper and place in the freezer until ready to use.

3 In a bowl, combine the almond milk, sugar, coconut oil, vanilla, and flax mixture. Mix until well blended. Add the flour, cocoa, baking powder, and salt. Mix until no large lumps remain. Add the melted semisweet chocolate and mix again.

4 Divide the batter evenly among the ramekins. Press a Lava Ball into the center of each cake. Use a spoon to cover the ball with cake batter. Bake for about 20 minutes, or until the edges pull away slightly.

5 Serve directly in the ramekins, or if you prefer, unmold them from the ramekins as follows: Let the cakes rest in the ramekins for about 10 minutes before removing. Then gently loosen the edges with a knife, top with a plate, and invert. Gently transfer to serving plates and serve warm. If you need to reheat, microwave each cake for 30 seconds.

BETTER THAN BUTTER

When butter is called for in baking, you can use the vegan butter recipe on page 36 or a store-bought brand such as Earth Balance butter spread. There's also a third option: coconut oil. To substitute coconut oil in a baking recipe, use three parts coconut oil and one part water. For example, in a recipe calling for 1 cup of dairy butter, use ¾ cup coconut oil combined with ¼ cup water.

CHOCOLATE–CHOCOLATE CHIP BROWNIES

MAKES 16
BROWNIES

In this brownie recipe, chocolate gets a little help from its friends, coffee and black beans. The result is fudgy, chocolatey brownies with a decadently rich flavor and an extra infusion of chocolate from the chocolate chips.

1   Preheat the oven to 350°F. Grease an 8-inch square baking pan (or an 8-inch round cake pan or springform pan if making the Ice Cream Sundae Cake on page 278).

2   In a food processor, combine the black beans, sugar, and oil, and blend until smooth. Add the applesauce, coffee, and vanilla, and blend until smooth.

3   Scrape the mixture into a mixing bowl. Add the flour, cocoa, baking powder, and salt and mix until smooth. Stir in the chocolate chips.

4   Scrape the batter into the prepared pan. Bake for 25 to 30 minutes, or until a toothpick inserted into the center comes out clean. Let cool in the pan completely, then refrigerate for several hours before cutting into squares.

1 cup cooked or canned black beans, drained and rinsed

½ cup sugar

3 tablespoons sunflower or grapeseed oil

½ cup applesauce

1 tablespoon instant coffee

2 teaspoons pure vanilla extract

½ cup all-purpose flour

¼ cup unsweetened cocoa powder

2 teaspoons baking powder

⅛ teaspoon salt

¾ cup vegan semisweet chocolate chips

NO-BAKE CHOCOLATE CHEESECAKE

Easy to make and decadently delicious, this cheesecake can satisfy anyone's chocolate craving. Best of all, there's no need to heat the oven.

1 Lightly oil an 8-inch springform pan or spray it with cooking spray.

2 **Crust:** In a food processor, combine the cookie crumbs and melted butter and pulse to combine. The mixture should hold together when pressed between two fingers. If it's too dry, add another tablespoon of melted butter; if it's too wet, add another tablespoon of crumbs. Transfer the crumb mixture to the prepared pan and spread evenly. Press the mixture into the springform pan using your fingers to make a firm, even crust. Refrigerate or freeze while you make the filling.

3 **Filling:** Place the chocolate chips in a heatproof bowl and melt in the microwave or over a saucepan of simmering water. Keep warm.

4 In a high-speed blender, combine the drained cashews, coconut milk, maple syrup, and coconut oil and process until smooth. Add the melted chocolate and process until smooth and creamy, scraping down the sides as needed. Scrape the filling into the prepared crust. Tap on the counter a few times to release any air bubbles, then refrigerate until set, at least 4 hours or overnight. Once set, run a butter knife along the edge and gently remove the sides of the pan. Top with your choice of berries, whipped cream, or chocolate curls. Store leftovers tightly covered in the refrigerator for up to a week.

Crust

1¾ cups vegan chocolate cookie crumbs

¼ cup vegan butter, store-bought or homemade (page 36), or coconut oil, melted

Filling

7 ounces vegan semisweet chocolate chips, melted

1½ cups raw cashews, soaked in hot water for 30 minutes, then drained

1 (14-ounce) can full-fat coconut milk

¼ cup pure maple syrup or agave nectar

¼ cup coconut oil, melted

Garnish options: Your choice of fresh raspberries, Cashew Chantilly Cream (page 249), chocolate curls, or cacao nibs

VARIATIONS

Top the cheesecake with Fudgy Chocolate Sauce (page 251) or Date-Caramel Sauce (page 250).

NO-BAKE NUT LOVER'S CHEESECAKE

Crust

1 cup pitted dates

1 cup walnut or pecan pieces

Filling

2 cups raw cashews, soaked in hot water for 30 minutes, then drained

½ cup agave nectar or pure maple syrup

⅓ cup almond milk, store-bought or homemade (page 28)

⅓ cup coconut oil, melted

1 tablespoon fresh lemon juice

1 teaspoon pure vanilla extract

2 tablespoons almond butter, store-bought or homemade (page 36)

Chopped nuts of choice, for garnish

Fudgy Chocolate Sauce (page 251), for garnish (optional)

If you love nuts, you'll love this no-bake cheesecake made with walnuts, cashews, and almonds. Top it with a drizzle of chocolate sauce for added decadence.

1   Lightly oil an 8-inch springform pan or spray it with cooking spray.

2   **Crust:** In a food processor, combine the dates and walnuts. Blend until finely ground. Transfer the date-walnut mixture to the springform pan and press it evenly into the bottom and sides of the pan.

3   **Filling:** In a high-speed blender, combine the drained cashews with the agave, almond milk, coconut oil, lemon juice, and vanilla. Add the almond butter and blend on high until the mixture is very smooth, scraping down the sides as needed. Scrape the filling mixture into the crust and smooth the surface. Cover with foil and place in the freezer until solid, about 4 hours.

4   Remove from the freezer about 10 minutes prior to serving and remove the outer ring of the springform pan. Garnish with chopped nuts and chocolate sauce, if using. Store leftovers tightly covered in the freezer for up to 2 weeks.

CHOCOLATE-COVERED ELVIS ICE CREAM

SERVES 4

Inspired by the sandwich made famous by Elvis, these iconic ingredients join forces again to make the easiest ice cream on the planet.

4 large ripe bananas, peeled, sliced, and frozen (see Note)

⅓ cup peanut butter, store-bought or homemade

Fudgy Chocolate Sauce (page 251)

Place the frozen banana slices in a food processor or high-speed blender and process until smooth, scraping down the sides as needed. Add the peanut butter and process to combine. Transfer to a bowl or other container. For soft-serve ice cream, place in the freezer for 15 to 20 minutes. For a firmer ice cream, freeze for 2 to 3 hours before serving. If frozen for longer than 4 hours, the ice cream will become hard and should be removed from the freezer for 10 to 15 minutes before serving to soften it slightly. To serve, scoop the ice cream into dessert dishes and spoon the chocolate sauce over the top.

Note: To freeze banana slices, line a rimmed baking sheet with parchment paper and spread the banana slices on it in a single layer. Place in the freezer for 2 hours. If not using right away, transfer the frozen banana slices to a zip-top freezer bag and store in the freezer until needed.

CHOCOLATE–PEANUT BUTTER MILKSHAKE

½ cup **Cashew Cream (page 32)** or nondairy creamer, chilled

½ cup **nondairy milk, store-bought or homemade (page 28), chilled, plus more if needed**

2 tablespoons **peanut butter, store-bought or homemade**

½ cup **Elvis Soft Serve (page 275)** or store-bought vegan vanilla or chocolate ice cream

1 tablespoon **Fudgy Chocolate Sauce (page 251), plus more if needed**

½ **banana, sliced and frozen (optional)**

Cashew Chantilly Cream (page 249, optional)

No need to miss milkshakes when you can easily whip up some creamy decadence in a glass using plant-based ingredients. To save time, you can use store-bought vegan ice cream in place of the homemade.

In a blender, combine the cashew cream, nondairy milk, and peanut butter. Blend until smooth. Add the ice cream and chocolate sauce and blend until thick and smooth. For a thicker shake, add the frozen banana slices and blend again. For a thinner shake, add more nondairy milk and blend again. Serve in a chilled tall glass, topped with whipped cream, if using, and/or drizzled with a little of the chocolate sauce.

VARIATIONS

Vanilla Shake Omit the peanut butter and chocolate sauce; use vegan vanilla ice cream and add 1 teaspoon pure vanilla extract.

Strawberry Shake Omit the peanut butter, chocolate sauce, and optional banana; use vegan vanilla ice cream and add ½ cup fresh or frozen strawberries.

ICE CREAM SUNDAE CAKE

1 recipe Chocolate–Chocolate Chip Brownies (page 271), baked in an 8-inch round cake pan or springform pan

4 cups Banana Soft Serve (page 280) or store-bought vegan vanilla ice cream, softened

1½ cups Whipped Coconut Cream (page 248), chilled for 1 hour

1½ cups chopped strawberries

½ cup Fudgy Chocolate Sauce (page 251)

¼ cup shredded coconut, toasted

2 tablespoons chopped or crushed roasted peanuts

8 whole pitted cherries or hulled strawberries

This decadent showpiece dessert may be time-consuming to prepare, but the results are worth it. The trick to making it with the minimum amount of fuss is to prepare the various components separately over the course of a few days. You can even make the brownies a week or so in advance and freeze them. Be sure to carefully read the recipe all the way through before beginning and make room in the freezer for the cake to sit undisturbed.

1 Several hours or a day ahead of when you want to assemble this dessert, bake the brownies and make the ice cream and whipped cream. Cool the brownies in the pan, then cool completely on a wire rack. If you baked the brownies in a cake pan, place the cooled brownies in the bottom of an 8-inch springform pan and set aside. If you baked them in a springform pan, run a thin knife along the edge of the cooled brownies to loosen them from the sides of the pan but leave them in the springform pan.

2 In a bowl, combine 2 cups of the ice cream with the strawberries and stir to mix. Spread the strawberry mixture evenly over the brownies in the pan. Freeze for 60 minutes.

3 Soften the remaining 2 cups ice cream in a bowl and combine it with the whipped cream, stirring to mix well. This will be your "frosting." If the consistency is too soft to use as a frosting, place the bowl in the freezer for about an hour to firm it up somewhat.

4 Remove the cake from the freezer. Remove the sides from the springform pan and place the cake on a serving plate. Frost the top and sides of the cake with the ice cream/whipped cream mixture. Return the cake to the freezer for 3 hours to firm up.

5 When ready to serve, drizzle the chocolate sauce on top of the cake and sprinkle with the coconut and peanuts. Top with the cherries and let the cake stand at room temperature for about 15 minutes, more or less, depending on how hard your ice cream is, to soften slightly before slicing and serving. Store any remaining cake covered in the freezer.

VARIATION

If you want all the flavor of this dessert without all the fuss, just put out all of the components—the brownies, ice cream, whipped cream, and the various toppings—and let diners build their own sundaes.

BANANA SPLIT SOFT-SERVE SUNDAES

3 large ripe bananas, peeled, sliced, and frozen

1 cup miniature vegan marshmallows

1 cup canned crushed pineapple, well drained (see Note) and blotted dry

1 cup sliced strawberries

¼ cup sugar

Fudgy Chocolate Sauce (page 251)

1 cup Cashew Chantilly Cream (page 249)

Crushed roasted peanuts

4 hulled strawberries

This luscious dessert combines an easy soft-serve ice cream made with bananas, vegan marshmallows, and pineapple and topped with strawberries, vegan whipped cream, chocolate, and nuts.

1   Place the banana slices in a food processor or high-speed blender and process until smooth and creamy, scraping down the sides as needed. Transfer to a bowl and fold in the marshmallows and pineapple. Cover and freeze for 2 hours to firm up.

2   Place the sliced strawberries in a bowl. Sprinkle with the sugar and stir to combine. Set aside at room temperature for at least an hour to allow the strawberries to macerate and become saucy.

3   When ready to serve, scoop the banana and marshmallow mixture into bowls and top with the chocolate sauce, macerated strawberries, cream, and peanuts. Top each serving with a strawberry.

Note: It's important to remove all the excess liquid from the pineapple. For best results, drain it in a fine-mesh sieve, and then use your hands to press out the liquid.

ACKNOWLEDGMENTS

As with any book-length project, this cookbook was a team effort—and what a great team it was!

I must begin by expressing my gratitude to an amazing group of recipe testers: Eve-Marie Williams, Daneen Agecoutay, Kim Logan, Kelly Cavalier, Lyndsay Orwig, Danielle Deskins, Norine Dobiesz, Anna Holt, and Chris and Darlene Bruce—thanks for all your hard work and helpful feedback. I could not have fine-tuned these recipes without you!

Many thanks to the team at Houghton Mifflin Harcourt, especially my fabulous editor Anne Ficklen and Editorial Associate, Molly Aronica. I'd also like to thank Helen Seachrist, Production Editor; Kevin Watt, Lead Manufacture; and Melissa Lotfy, Art Director for their excellent work. A special thanks to Adam Kowit, who got this project off the ground.

I also want to thank "cookbook whisperer" Suzanne Lenzer and her team, who guided the setups, props, and food styling, as well as the gorgeous photography by William Brinson and his wife, Susan, that truly brought my recipes to life.

To my longtime agent, Stacey Glick of Dystel Goderich Literary Management: Thanks for all that you do!

And to my husband, Jon Robertson, thank you for asking me to veganize all of your favorite foods over the years—who knew all those requests would one day turn into a cookbook!

INDEX

A

Agar-agar, 48
Agave nectar, 17
Aioli, Vegan, 193
All-in-One Cauliflower Pizza, 237
Almond butter
  Almost-Instant Nut Milk, 29
  BBQ Seitan Ribs, 99
  No-Bake Nut Lover's Cheesecake, 274
Almond(s)
  DIY Granola, 218
  Nut Butter, 38
  Nut Milk, 28
  Nut-Parm, 42
Almost-Instant Nut Milk, 29
Andouille Sausage
  basic recipe, 118
  Jambalaya, 120, *121*
Animal ingredients in processed foods, 13
Appetizers
  Buffalo Cauliflower with Ranch Dressing, 206, *207*
  Cheesy Crackers, 234, *235*
  Country-Style Pâté, 119
  Htipiti (Feta Spread), 49
  Spinach-Artichoke Dip, *50,* 51
  Spinach-Feta Quesadillas, 62
  Summer Rolls with Fish-Free Nuoc Cham, *202,* 203
Apples
  DIY Granola, 218
Applesauce
  Chocolate–Chocolate Chip Brownies, 271
  as egg substitute in baking, 257
Apricot(s)
  DIY Granola, 218
Aquafaba, 37
  Butter, 37
  as egg substitute in baking, 257
  Lemon Meringue Pie, *258,* 259
  Meringue, 256
  Veganized Marshmallow Fluff, 255
  Vive la French Toast, 67

Arrowroot
  as egg substitute in baking, 257
  powder, 48
Artichoke(s)
  -Hummus Potatoes, 58
  Cakes, Hearts of Palm and, 150, *151*
  Creamy Pesto Pasta Salad, 201
  Dip, Spinach-, *50,* 51
  Loaded Polenta Pizza, 242
  Palm-Crab Imperial, 155
  Tuna Salad, Chickpea and, 154
Artisan Bread, Easy, 229
Arugula
  Meaty-Cheesy Pizza, 240, *241*
Asparagus
  and Ham Quiche, 61
  Omelet, French-Style, 65
  Piccata Meatballs with Penne and, *88,* 89
  Rotini with Roasted Garlic Alfredo Sauce, 226
  Seitan Oscar with Béarnaise Sauce, *96,* 97
  Vegan Crab Louis, *156,* 157
Avocado Crema
  basic recipe, 187
  Tuesday Tacos with, 90, *91*
Avocado(s)
  Beyond BLT, 127
  Breakfast Nachos, *68,* 69
  California Caesar Salad, 213
  Crema, 187
  Fish-Free Tacos, 142, *143*
  Guacamole and Salsa Potato Topper, 58
  Join the Club Sandwich, *132,* 133
  Jumpin' Jackfruit Chili, 165
  My Kinda Chef's Salad, 208
  Vegan Crab Louis, *156,* 157

B

Bacon
  Benedict Pizza, 239
  Beyond BLT, 127
  Bits, Coconut, 108
  Fettuccine Bolognese, 222
  Join the Club Sandwich, *132,* 133

  Mushroom, 110
  Strips, Eggplant, 109
  Tempeh, 106
  Tofu, 107
  -Topped Mac Uncheese, 54, *55*
Baked Eggplant Italian Style, *162,* 163
Baked Seitan Roast
  basic recipe, 92–93
  slow cooker directions, 93
  Wellington, The, 98
Baking powder as egg substitute in baking, 257
Banana(s)
  Chocolate-Covered Elvis Ice Cream, 275
  Chocolate–Peanut Butter Milkshake, 276, *277*
  as egg substitute in baking, 257
  Split Soft-Serve Sundaes, 280, *281*
  Vanilla Shake, 276, *277*
Banh Mi, *114,* 115
Barbecue Sauce
  basic recipe, 101
  BBQ Seitan Ribs, 99, *100*
  DIY Jerky, 113
  Iron Kettle Chili, 83
  Pulled Jackfruit BBQ Sandwiches, 172, *173*
Basic White Sauce, 39
Basil
  All-in-One Cauliflower Pizza, 237
  Garlicky Mustard Marinade, 75
  Goddess Dressing, 199
  Home-Style Marinade, 75
  Homemade Vegetable Base, 183
  Mama's Meatballs, 86
  Meaty-Cheesy Pizza, 240, *241*
  Oven-Roasted Tomato Sauce, 197
  Perfect Pot Pie, 230, *231*
  Pesto, 194
  Seasoned Tofu Ricotta, 41
  Spinach-Feta Quesadillas, 62
  Summer Rolls with Fish-Free Nuoc Cham, *202,* 203
Basil Pesto
  basic recipe, 194
  Creamy Pesto Pasta Salad, 201

Bay leaves
  Beans from Scratch, 80–81
  Clam-Free Chowder, *138,* 139
  Vegetable Broth, 182
  BBQ Seitan Ribs, 99, *100*
Bean curd, 12
Bean(s). *See also* Black Beans;
      Cannellini Beans; Kidney
      Beans; Pinto Beans
  Aquafaba Butter, 37
  Burgers, Best, 84, *85*
  canned *versus* home-cooked, 80
  cooking dried, 15
  Cutlets, White, 87
  Glazed Hamish Loaf, 112
  Hamish Loaf, 112
  pressure cooker, cooking in, 81
  from Scratch, 80–81
  slow cooker, cooking in, 81
  soaking dried, 15
  types of, 15
  White Bean Cutlets, 87
Béarnaise Sauce, Better, 190
Beer
  Cheddary Sauce, 44
Bellini Trifle, 265
Benedict Pizza, 239
Best Bean Burgers, 84, 85
Better Béarnaise Sauce
  basic recipe, 190
  Seitan Oscar with, *96,* 97
Beyond BLT, 127
Biscuits
  Cheesy Sausage, *232,* 233
  Scratch, 236
Black bean(s)
  Best Bean Burgers, 84, *85*
  Breakfast Nachos, *68,* 69
  Chocolate–Chocolate Chip
      Brownies, 271
  Iron Kettle Chili, 83
  Soup, Smoky, 82
Black-eyed peas
  Andouille Sausage, 118
Blenders, 20
BLT, Beyond, 127
Blueberries
  DIY Granola, 218
Brandy
  Country-Style Pâté, 119
  Lobster Mushroom Bisque, 140–
      141
  Tiramisu, 261

Bread(s)
  Cheesy Sausage Biscuits, *232,* 233
  Cranberry-Walnut Scones, 243
  Easy Artisan, 229
  Scratch Biscuits, 236
  Vive la French Toast, 67
Breakfast dishes
  Asparagus and Ham Quiche, 61
  Breakfast Nachos, *68,* 69
  Broccoli and Sausage Quiche, 61
  Cheesy Mushroom Scramble, 66
  Chickpea Flour Omelets, 63
  DIY Granola, 218
  French-Style Asparagus Omelet, 65
  Loaded Frittata, *64,* 65
  Mediterranean Quiche, 61
  Spinach and Mushroom-Bacon
      Quiche, 60–61
  Vive la French Toast, 67
Breakfast Nachos, *68,* 69
Broccoli
  and Sausage Quiche, 61
  Soup, Cheesy, 56
Broth
  bouillon cubes, 16
  homemade *versus* purchased, 16
  soup base powder, 16
  Vegetable, 182
Brown Gravy, Great, 191
Brownies, Chocolate–Chocolate Chip,
      271
Buffalo Cauliflower with Ranch
      Dressing, 206, *207*
Burgers, Best Bean, 84, *85*
Burmese Tofu, 76
Butter
  Aquafaba, 37
  Easy Vegan, 36
  Nut, 38
  vegan alternatives for, 270
Buttercream Frosting, 252
Buttermilk, nondairy substitute for, 30

C
Cabbage
  Creamy Coleslaw, 212
  Easy Kimchi, 209
  Fish-Free Tacos, 142, *143*
  Pasta Slaw, 212
  Potato Slaw, 212
  Tuesday Tacos with Avocado
      Crema, 90, *91*
Caesar Dressing, Hail, 200

Caesar Salad, California, 213
Cake(s)
  Ice Cream Sundae, 278–279
  Luscious Lava, *268,* 269–270
  Scratch, 260
  Strawberry Shortcake, 262, *263*
Calcium, plant sources of, 10
California Caesar Salad, 213
Cannellini beans
  Cassoulet, *124,* 125
  Creamy Pesto Pasta Salad, 201
  Mama's Meatballs, 86
  Niçoise Goddess Salad, 210, *211*
  Oven-Baked Seitan Cutlets, 94–95
  Perfect Pot Pie, 230, *231*
  Spinach-Feta Quesadillas, 62
Capers
  Piccata Meatballs with Penne and
      Asparagus, *88,* 89
  Roasted Cauliflower Piccata, 166, *167*
  Tapenade, 192
  Vegan Crab Louis, *156,* 157
Caramel-Date Sauce, 250
Carrots
  Banh Mi, *114,* 115
  Cassoulet, *124,* 125
  Creamy Coleslaw, 212
  Easy Kimchi, 209
  Pasta Slaw, 212
  Perfect Pot Pie, 230, *231*
  Potato Slaw, 212
  Smoky Black Bean Soup, 82
  Summer Rolls with Fish-Free Nuoc
      Cham, *202,* 203
  Vegetable Broth, 182
  Vegetable Shepherd's Pie, *168,* 169
Cashew butter
  Almost-Instant Nut Milk, 29
Cashew Chantilly Cream
  Banana Split Soft-Serve Sundaes,
      280, *281*
  basic recipe, 249
  Bellini Trifle, 265
  Chocolate–Peanut Butter
      Milkshake, 276, *277*
  No-Bake Chocolate Cheesecake,
      272, 273
  Strawberry Shake, 276, *277*
  Strawberry Shortcake, 262, *263*
  Tiramisu, 261
  Vanilla Shake, 276, *277*
Cashew Cream
  basic recipe, 32

Cashew Chantilly Cream, 249
Chocolate–Peanut Butter
   Milkshake, 276, *277*
Creamy Sriracha See Scallops, *152*,
   153
Fettuccine Bolognese, 222
Lobster Mushroom Bisque, 140–141
Rotini with Roasted Garlic Alfredo
   Sauce, 226
Spaghetti Carbonara, 223
Spinach and Mushroom-Bacon
   Quiche, 60–61
Strawberry Shake, 276, *277*
Vanilla Shake, 276, *277*
Cashew Cream Cheese
   basic recipe, 40
   Spinach-Artichoke Dip, *50*, 51
Cashew Sour Cream
   basic recipe, 33
   Eggplant Paprikash, 174
   Mashed Potatoes with Sour Cream
      and Chives, 171
   Mushroom Stroganoff, 170
   Scratch Cake, 260
   Spinach and Mushroom-Bacon
      Quiche, 60–61
Cashew(s)
   Bacon-Topped Mac Uncheese, 54, *55*
   Basic White Sauce, 39
   Chantilly Cream, 249
   Cheddary Sauce, 44
   Clam-Free Chowder, *138*, 139
   Cream, 32
   Cream Cheese, 40
   DIY Granola, 218
   Easy Vegan Yogurt, 34
   Mayo, Creamy, 35
   Melty Cheddary Cheese, 43
   Melty Vegan Cheese, 43
   No-Bake Chocolate Cheesecake,
      272, 273
   No-Bake Nut Lover's Cheesecake,
      274
   Nut Butter, 38
   Nut Milk, 28
   Pretzel-Crusted Cheddary Log,
      52, *53*
   Say (Veganized) Cheese!, 46–47
   Sour Cream, 33
   Vegan Mascarpone, 253
Casseroles
   Baked Eggplant Italian Style, *162*, 163
   Cassoulet, *124*, 125

Handcrafted Lasagna, *220*, 221
Palm-Crab Imperial, 155
Perfect Pot Pie, 230
Vegetable Shepherd's Pie, *168*, 169
Cassoulet, *124*, 125
Cauliflower
   Piccata, Roasted, 166, *167*
   Pizza, All-in-One, 237
   with Ranch Dressing, Buffalo, 206,
      207
Charcuterie alternatives
   Andouille Sausage, 118
   Coconut Bacon Bits, 108
   Country-Style Pâté, 119
   DIY Jerky, 113
   Eggplant Bacon Strips, 109
   Glazed Hamish Loaf, 112
   Hamish Loaf, 112
   Handcrafted Pepperoni, 116
   Haute Dogs, 128, *129*
   Maple Breakfast Sausage, 123
   Mushroom Bacon, 110
   No-Meat Loaf, 126
   Smoky Chickpeas, 111
   Spicy Italian Sausage, 117
   Tempeh Bacon, 106
   Tofu Bacon, 107
   Veganized Scrapple, 122
Cheddary Sauce
   basic recipe, 44
   Cheesy Broccoli Soup, 56
   Cheesy Mushroom Scramble, 66
   Cheesy Steak-Out Sandwiches,
      176, 177
   Loaded Baked Potatoes, 57–58, *59*
Cheese
   Ball, 47
   Cashew Cream, 40
   Cheesy Christmas Tree, 47
   Creamy Chive, 47
   Holiday, 47
   Log, 47
   Melty Cheddary, 43
   Melty Vegan, 43
   Nut-Parm, 42
   Porcini, 47
   Pretzel-Crusted Cheddary Log,
      52, *53*
   Say (Veganized), 46–47
   Seasoned Tofu Ricotta, 41
   Tofu Feta, 48
   Two-for-One Cheesy Wheels, 47
   Vegan Mascarpone, 253

Cheesecake
   No-Bake Chocolate, *272*, 273
   No-Bake Nut Lover's, 274
Cheesy Broccoli Soup, 56
Cheesy Crackers, 234, *235*
Cheesy-Meaty Pizza, 240, *241*
Cheesy Mushroom Scramble, 66
Cheesy Sausage Biscuits, *232*, 233
Cheesy Steak-Out Sandwiches, *176*,
   177
Cheesy White Sauce, 39
Chef's Salad, My Kinda, 208
Cherries
   Ice Cream Sundae Cake, 278–279
Chia seeds as egg substitute in
   baking, 257
Chickpea flour as egg substitute in
   baking, 257
Chickpea Flour Omelets, 63
Chickpea(s)
   and Artichoke Tuna Salad, 154
   My Kinda Chef's Salad, 208
   Smoky, 111
   Smoky Black Bean Soup, 82
   Veganized Scrapple, 122
Chile(s)
   Banh Mi, *114*, 115
   Barbecue Sauce, 101
   Breakfast Nachos, *68*, 69
   Fish-Free Tacos, 142, *143*
   Guacamole and Salsa Potato
      Topper, 58
   Hot and Spicy White Sauce, 39
   Jumpin' Jackfruit Chili, 165
   Smoky Queso Sauce, 45
Chili
   Iron Kettle, 83
   Jumpin' Jackfruit, 165
Chili-Cheesy Potato Topper, 58
Chive(s)
   Cheese, Creamy, 47
   Loaded Baked Potatoes, 57–58, *59*
   Lobster Mushroom Bisque, 140–141
   Mashed Potatoes with Sour Cream
      and, 171
   Scratch Biscuits, 236
Chocolate
   Cheesecake, No-Bake, *272*, 273
   –Chocolate Chip Brownies, 271
   -Covered Elvis Ice Cream, 275
   Ganache, 254
   Ice Cream Sundae Cake, 278–279
   Lava Balls, 270

Chocolate (*cont*)
    Luscious Lava Cakes, *268*, 269–270
    –Peanut Butter Milkshake, 276, *277*
    Sauce, Fudgy, 251
    Tiramisu, 261
    Truffles, 267
Chowder, Clam-Free, *138*, 139
Cilantro
    Avocado Crema, 187
    Banh Mi, *114*, 115
    Breakfast Nachos, *68*, 69
    Fish-Free Tacos, 142, *143*
    Guacamole and Salsa Potato
        Topper, 58
    Indian Samosa, 58
    Jumpin' Jackfruit Chili, 165
    Summer Rolls with Fish-Free Nuoc
        Cham, *202*, 203
    Tuesday Tacos with Avocado
        Crema, 90, *91*
Clam-Free Chowder, *138*, 139
Club Sandwich, Join the, *132*, 133
Coconut
    Bacon Bits, 108
    DIY Granola, 218
    Ice Cream Sundae Cake, 278–279
    Milk, 30
Coconut Bacon Bits
    basic recipe, 108
    Loaded Baked Potatoes, 57–58, *59*
Coconut oil as butter substitute in
    baking, 270
Coconut oil, buying, 17
Coffee
    Chocolate–Chocolate Chip
        Brownies, 271
    Tiramisu, 261
Coleslaw, Creamy, 212
Condiments
    Avocado Crema, 187
    Creamy Cashew Mayo, 35
    Easy Kimchi, 209
    Fish-Free Nuoc Cham, 189
    Mushroom Oyster Sauce, 198
    Tapenade, 192
    Vegan Aioli, 193
    Vegan Worcestershire Sauce, 186
Cookies, Cranberry Oatmeal, 266
Cordon Bleu–Stuffed Portobellos, 164
Corn
    Iron Kettle Chili, 83
    Perfect Pot Pie, 230, *231*
    Vegetable Shepherd's Pie, *168*, 169

Cornmeal
    Loaded Polenta Pizza, 242
    Veganized Scrapple, 122
Country-Style Pâté, 119
Crab Louis, Vegan, *156*, 157
Crab-Palm Imperial, 155
Crackers, Cheesy, 234, *235*
Cranberry(ies)
    -Walnut Scones, 243
    DIY Granola, 218
    Oatmeal Cookies, 266
Cream
    Cashew, 32
    Cashew Chantilly, 249
    Cashew Sour, 33
    Whipped Coconut, 248
Cream Cheese, Cashew, 40
Creamy Cashew Mayo
    Banh Mi, 115
    basic recipe, 35
    Spinach and Mushroom-Bacon
        Quiche, 60
Creamy Chive Cheese, 47
Creamy Coleslaw, 212
Creamy Pesto Pasta Salad, 201
Creamy Ranch Dressing
    basic recipe, 196, *207*
    Buffalo Cauliflower with Ranch
        Dressing, 206, *207*
Creamy Spinach Potatoes, 58
Creamy Sriracha See Scallops, *152*,
    153
Crispy Crumbles
    basic recipe, 78
    Meaty-Cheesy Pizza, 240, *241*
    Tuesday Tacos with Avocado
        Crema, 90, *91*
Crispy Tofu, 77
Crispy Tofu Bacon, 107
Cucumber(s)
    Banh Mi, *114*, 115
    Seitan Gyros with Tzatziki Sauce,
        204, 205
    Summer Rolls with Fish-Free Nuoc
        Cham, *202*, 203
    Tzatziki Sauce, 195
Curry White Sauce, 39
Cutlets, White Bean, 87

D

Dairy alternatives
    Almost-Instant Nut Milk, 29
    Aquafaba Butter, 37

    benefits of, 9–10
    Cashew Cream, 32
    Cashew Cream Cheese, 40
    Cashew Sour Cream, 33
    Cheddary Sauce, 44
    Cheese Ball, 47
    Cheese Log, 47
    Cheesy Christmas Trees, 47
    Coconut Milk, 30
    Creamy Chive Cheese, 47
    Easy Vegan Butter, 36
    Easy Vegan Yogurt, 34
    Holiday Cheese, 47
    Htipiti (Feta Spread), 49
    Melty Cheddary Cheese, 43
    Melty Vegan Cheese, 43
    Nut Butter, 38
    Nut Milk, 28
    Nut-Parm, 42
    Oat Milk, 31
    Porcini Cheese, 47
    Pretzel-Crusted Cheddary Log, 52, *53*
    Say (Veganized) Cheese!, 46
    Seasoned Tofu Ricotta, 41
    Smoky Queso Sauce, 45
    Tofu Feta, 48
    Two-for-One Cheesy Wheels, 47
Date sugar, 17
Date syrup, 17
Date-Caramel Sauce
    basic recipe, 250
    No-Bake Chocolate Cheesecake,
        272, 273
Date(s)
    -Caramel Sauce, 250
    Chocolate Truffles, 267
    DIY Granola, 218
    No-Bake Nut Lover's Cheesecake,
        274
Dessert sauce(s)
    Cashew Chantilly Cream, 249
    Date-Caramel, 250
    Fudgy Chocolate, 251
    Veganized Marshmallow Fluff, 255
    Whipped Coconut Cream, 248
Desserts
    Banana Split Soft-Serve Sundaes,
        280, *281*
    Bellini Trifle, 265
    Chocolate–Chocolate Chip
        Brownies, 271
    Chocolate-Covered Elvis Ice
        Cream, 275

Chocolate Truffles, 267
Cranberry Oatmeal Cookies, 266
Ice Cream Sundae Cake, 278–279
Lava Balls, 270
Lemon Meringue Pie, *258*, 259
Luscious Lava Cakes, *268*, 269–270
Mango Fro-Yo, 264
No-Bake Chocolate Cheesecake, *272*, 273
No-Bake Nut Lover's Cheesecake, 274
Scratch Cake, 260
Strawberry Shortcake, 262, *263*
Tiramisu, 261
Deviled Hamish Salad, 131
Dill
　Creamy Ranch Dressing, 196, *207*
　Tzatziki Sauce, 195
　Vegan Aioli, 193
　Vegan Crab Louis, *156*, 157
Dip(s)
　Creamy Ranch Dressing, 196, *207*
　Htipiti (Feta Spread), 49
　Spinach-Artichoke, *50*, 51
DIY Granola, 218
DIY Jerky, 113
Drinks
　Chocolate–Peanut Butter Milkshake, 276, *277*
　Strawberry Shake, 276, *277*
　Vanilla Shake, 276, *277*
　Dutch oven, 20

E

Easy Artisan Bread, 229
Easy Kimchi, 209
Easy Vegan Butter, 36
Easy Vegan Yogurt
　basic recipe, 34
　Tzatziki Sauce, 195
Egg-free dishes
　Asparagus and Ham Quiche, 61
　Breakfast Nachos, *68*, 69
　Broccoli and Sausage Quiche, 61
　Cheesy Mushroom Scramble, 66
　Chickpea Flour Omelets, 63
　French-Style Asparagus Omelet, 65
　Loaded Frittata, *64*, 65
　Mediterranean Quiche, 61
　Spinach and Mushroom-Bacon Quiche, 60–61

Eggplant
　Bacon Strips, 109
　Italian Style, Baked, *162*, 163
　Paprikash, 174
Eggplant Bacon Strips, 109
Eggs
　alternatives to egg dishes, 28
　substitutes in baking, 257
Ener-G Egg Replacer, 257
Equipment, 19–21
　blender, 20
　food processor, 19
　knives, 20
　pots and saucepans, 20
　skillets, 21

F

Feta
　and Pecans Potato Topper, Greens with, 58
　Quesadillas, Spinach-, 62
　Spread (Htipiti), 49
　Tofu, 48
Fettuccine Bolognese, 222
Fish and Chips with Tartar Sauce, Vegan, 144, *145*
Fish-Free Fillets
　basic recipe, 146
　Vegan Fish and Chips with Tartar Sauce, 144, *145*
Fish-Free Nuoc Cham
　basic recipe, 189
　Easy Kimchi, 209
　Summer Rolls with, *202*, 203
Fish-Free Sticks
　basic recipe, 147
Fish-Free Tacos, 142, *143*
Flaxseed
　All-in-One Cauliflower Pizza, 237
　Best Bean Burgers, 84, *85*
　buying, 17
　Country-Style Pâté, 119
　as egg substitute in baking, 257
　flax egg, 84
　Luscious Lava Cakes, *268*, 269–270
　Mama's Meatballs, 86
Food processor, 19
French-Style Asparagus Omelet, 65
French Toast, Vive la, 67
Frittata, Loaded, *64*, 65
Frosting(s)
　Buttercream, 252
　Ganache, 254

Fudgy Chocolate Sauce
　Banana Split Soft-Serve Sundaes, 280, *281*
　basic recipe, 251
　Chocolate-Covered Elvis Ice Cream, 275
　Chocolate–Peanut Butter Milkshake, 276, *277*
　Ice Cream Sundae Cake, 278–279
　No-Bake Chocolate Cheesecake, *272*, 273
　No-Bake Nut Lover's Cheesecake, 274

G

Ganache, 254
Garlic
　Basil Pesto, 194
　Cassoulet, *124*, 125
　Cordon Bleu–Stuffed Portobellos, 164
　Easy Artisan Bread, 229
　Easy Kimchi, 209
　Eggplant Paprikash, 174
　Garlicky Mustard Marinade, 75
　Goddess Dressing, 199
　Hail Caesar Dressing, 200
　Hearts of Palm and Artichoke Crab Cakes, 150, *151*
　Jambalaya, 120
　Jumpin' Jackfruit Chili, 165
　Loaded Polenta Pizza, 242
　Mama's Meatballs, 86
　No-Meat Loaf, 126
　Orecchiette with Pistachio Pesto, 224
　Oven-Baked Seitan Cutlets, 94–95
　Oven-Roasted Tomato Sauce, 197
　Red Wine Sauce with Mushrooms, 184
　Roasted, 227
　Roasted, Alfredo Sauce, Rotini with, 226
　Smoky Black Bean Soup, 82
　Spaghetti Carbonara, 223
　Spinach-Artichoke Dip, *50*, 51
　Tapenade, 192
　Totally Tempting Tempeh, 79
　Tzatziki Sauce, 195
　Vegan Aioli, 193
　Vegetable Broth, 182
Ginger
　Easy Kimchi, 209
　Indian Samosa Potatoes, 58

Ginger (cont)
    Vegan Worcestershire Sauce, 186
Glazed Hamish Loaf, 112
Gluten-free vegan cooking, 20
Goddess Dressing
    basic recipe, 199
    My Kinda Chef's Salad, 208
    Niçoise Goddess Salad, 210, 211
Granola, DIY, 218
Gravy, Great Brown, 191
Great Brown Gravy
    basic recipe, 191
    Vegetable Shepherd's Pie, 168, 169
    Wellington, The, 98
Greek-style recipes
    Htipiti (Feta Spread), 49
    Seitan Gyros with Tzatziki Sauce,
        204, 205
    Tofu Feta, 48
    Tzatziki Sauce, 195
Green beans
    Niçoise Goddess Salad, 210, 211
Greens with Feta and Pecans Potato
    Topper, 58
Guacamole and Salsa Potato Topper, 58
Gyros with Tzatziki Sauce, Seitan,
    204, 205

H

Hail Caesar Dressing
    basic recipe, 200
    California Caesar Salad, 213
Hamish Loaf
    Asparagus and Ham Quiche, 61
    Banh Mi, 114, 115
    basic recipe, 112
    Benedict Pizza, 239
    Cordon Bleu–Stuffed Portobellos, 164
    Deviled Hamish Salad, 131
    Glazed, 112
    Join the Club Sandwich, 132, 133
    My Kinda Chef's Salad, 208
Handcrafted Lasagna, 220, 221
Handcrafted Pepperoni
    basic recipe, 116
    Meaty-Cheesy Pizza, 240, 241
    Mediterranean Quiche, 61
Haute Dogs
    basic recipe, 128, 129
    Cassoulet, 124, 125
    Wellington, 130
Hearts of palm
    and Artichoke Cakes, 150, 151

Palm-Crab Imperial, 155
    Vegan Crab Louis, 156, 157
Hearts of Palm and Artichoke Cakes
    basic recipe, 150, 151
    Palm-Crab Po'boys, 149
    Seitan Oscar with Béarnaise
        Sauce, 96, 97
Herb(s). See also Basil; Mint;
        Oregano; Parsley; Sage;
        Tarragon; Thyme
    Cheese Ball, 47
    Cheese Log, 47
    Chickpea Flour Omelets, 63
    Say (Veganized) Cheese!, 46
    Scratch Biscuits, 236
Holiday Cheese, 47
Hollandaise Sauce
    basic recipe, 185
    Benedict Pizza, 239
    Shortcut, 185
Home-Style Marinade, 75
Homemade foods, benefits of, 7–8
Homemade Pasta
    basic recipe, 219
    Fettuccine Bolognese, 222
    Handcrafted Lasagna, 220, 221
    Spaghetti Carbonara, 223
Homemade Vegetable Base, 183
Honey, 17
Hot and Spicy White Sauce, 39
Htipiti (Feta Spread)
    basic recipe, 49
    Spinach-Feta Quesadillas, 62
Hummus, Potatoes, Artichoke-, 58

I

Ice cream
    Banana Split Soft-Serve Sundaes,
        280, 281
    Chocolate-Covered Elvis, 275
    Chocolate–Peanut Butter
        Milkshake, 276, 277
    Strawberry Shake, 276, 277
    Sundae Cake, 278–279
    Vanilla Shake, 276, 277
Indian Samosa Potatoes, 58
Iron Kettle Chili, 83
Italian-style recipes
    All-in-One Cauliflower Pizza, 237
    Baked Eggplant Italian Style, 162,
        163
    Basil Pesto, 194
    Benedict Pizza, 239

Fettuccine Bolognese, 222
    Handcrafted Lasagna, 220, 221
    Handcrafted Pepperoni, 116
    Homemade Pasta, 219
    Loaded Frittata, 64, 65
    Loaded Polenta Pizza, 242
    Make-Your-Own Orecchiette, 225
    Meaty-Cheesy Pizza, 240, 241
    Nut-Parm, 42
    Orecchiette with Pistachio Pesto,
        224
    Piccata Meatballs with Penne and
        Asparagus, 88, 89
    Pizza Dough, 238
    Roasted Cauliflower Piccata, 166,
        167
    Rotini with Roasted Garlic Alfredo
        Sauce, 226
    Seasoned Tofu Ricotta, 41
    Spaghetti Carbonara, 223
    Spicy Italian Sausage, 117
    Tiramisu, 261
    Vegan Mascarpone, 253

J

Jackfruit
    BBQ Sandwiches, Pulled, 172, 173
    Chili, Jumpin', 165
Jambalaya, 120, 121
Jerky, DIY, 113
Join the Club Sandwich, 132, 133
Jumpin' Jackfruit Chili, 165

K

Kale
    Greens with Feta and Pecans
        Potato Topper, 58
Kidney beans
    Iron Kettle Chili, 83
    Jambalaya, 120, 121
    No-Meat Loaf, 126
    Spicy Italian Sausage, 117
Kimchi, Easy, 209
Knives, 20
Kuzu root starch, 48

L

Lasagna, Handcrafted, 220, 221
Lava Balls, 270
Lava Cakes, Luscious, 268, 269–270
Lemon(s)
    Meringue Pie, 258, 259

Piccata Meatballs with Penne and
Asparagus, *88*, 89
Lentils
No-Meat Loaf, 126
Vegetable Shepherd's Pie, *168*, 169
Lima beans
Perfect Pot Pie, 230, *231*
Liquid smoke, 18
Loaded Baked Potatoes, 57–58, *59*
Loaded Frittata, *64*, 65
Loaded Polenta Pizza, 242
Lobster Mushroom Bisque, 140–141
Luscious Lava Cakes, *268*, 269–270

M

Mac Uncheese, Bacon-Topped, 54,
55
Make-Your-Own Orecchiette
basic recipe, 225
Orecchiette with Pistachio Pesto,
224
Mama's Meatballs
basic recipe, 86
Piccata Meatballs with Penne and
Asparagus, 89
Mango(es)
DIY Granola, 218
Fro-Yo, 264
Maple Breakfast Sausage
basic recipe, 123
Cheesy Sausage Biscuits, *232*, 233
Maple syrup, 17
Marinade(s)
Garlicky Mustard, 75
Home-Style, 75
Marinated Baked Tofu, 74–75
Marshmallow Fluff, Veganized, 255
Marshmallows
Banana Split Soft-Serve Sundaes,
280, *281*
Mascarpone, Vegan, 253
Mashed Potatoes with Sour Cream
and Chives
basic recipe, 171
Roasted Cauliflower Piccata, 166,
167
Vegetable Shepherd's Pie, *168*, 169
Mayo, Creamy Cashew, 35
Meat alternatives
Baked Seitan Roast, 92–93
Best Bean Burgers, 84, *85*
Burmese Tofu, 76
Crispy Crumbles, 78

Crispy Tofu, 77
Mama's Meatballs, 86
Marinated Baked Tofu, 74
Oven-Baked Seitan Cutlets, 94–95
Oven-Fried Crispy Tofu, 77
Totally Tempting Tempeh, 79
White Bean Cutlets, 87
Meat Loaf, No-, 126
Meat, defined for vegan diet, 16
Meatball(s)
Mama's, 86
Piccata, with Penne and
Asparagus, *88*, 89
Meaty-Cheesy Pizza, 240, *241*
Mediterranean Quiche, 61
Melty Cheddary Cheese, 43
Melty Vegan Cheese, 43
Baked Eggplant Italian Style, *162*,
163
basic recipe, 43
Handcrafted Lasagna, *220*, 221
Meaty-Cheesy Pizza, 240, *241*
Meringue, 256
basic recipe, 256
Pie, Lemon, *258*, 259
Mexican-style recipes
Avocado Crema, 187
Breakfast Nachos, *68*, 69
Fish-Free Tacos, 142, *143*
Smoky Queso Sauce, 45
Spinach-Feta Quesadillas, 62
Tuesday Tacos with Avocado
Crema, 90, *91*
Milk, dairy, health risks, 10
Milk, dairy, role in American diet, 10
Milk, nondairy
Almost-Instant Nut, 29
buying, 15
Coconut, 30
homemade *versus* purchased, 15
Nut, 28
Oat, 31
substitutes for dairy, 30
types of, 15–16
Milkshake
Chocolate–Peanut Butter, 276, *277*
Strawberry Shake, 276, *277*
Vanilla Shake, 276, *277*
Mint
Orecchiette with Pistachio Pesto,
224
Summer Rolls with Fish-Free Nuoc
Cham, *202*, 203

Mise-en-place, 19
Mushroom Bacon
basic recipe, 110
Benedict Pizza, 239
Quiche, Spinach and, 60–61
Spaghetti Carbonara, 223
Mushroom(s)
Bacon, 110
-Bacon Quiche, Spinach and,
60–61
Bisque, Lobster, 140–141
Cheesy Steak-Out Sandwiches,
176, 177
Clam-Free Chowder, *138*, 139
Cordon Bleu–Stuffed Portobellos,
164
Country-Style Pâté, 119
Great Brown Gravy, 191
Loaded Polenta Pizza, 242
Mama's Meatballs, 86
No-Meat Loaf, 126
Oyster Sauce, 198
Pan-Seared Portobello Strips, 175
powder, 183
Pulled Jackfruit BBQ Sandwiches,
172, *173*
Red Wine Sauce with, 184
Roasted Cauliflower Piccata, 166,
167
Scramble, Cheesy, 66
Stroganoff, 170
Vegetable Broth, 182
Vegetable Shepherd's Pie, *168*, 169
Wellington, The, 98
My Kinda Chef's Salad, 208

N

Nachos, Breakfast, *68*, 69
Niçoise Goddess Salad, 210, *211*
No-Bake Chocolate Cheesecake, *272*,
273
No-Bake Nut Lover's Cheesecake,
274
No-Meat Loaf, 126
Noodles
Summer Rolls with Fish-Free Nuoc
Cham, *202*, 203
Nuoc Cham, Fish-Free, 189
Nut butter as egg substitute in
baking, 257
Nut-Parm
Baked Eggplant Italian Style, *162*,
163

Nut-Parm (cont)
  basic recipe, 42
  Handcrafted Lasagna, *220*, 221
  Rotini with Roasted Garlic Alfredo
    Sauce, 226
Nut(s)
  -Parm, 42
  Butter, 38
  Milk, 28
Nutritional yeast
  All-in-One Cauliflower Pizza, 237
  Bacon-Topped Mac Uncheese, 54,
    55
  Basil Pesto, 194
  BBQ Seitan Ribs, 99, *100*
  Breakfast Nachos, *68*, 69
  Cheddary Sauce, 44
  Cheesy Crackers, 234, *235*
  Cheesy Sausage Biscuits, *232*, 233
  Cheesy White Sauce, 39
  Chickpea Flour Omelets, 63
  Country-Style Pâté, 119
  Glazed Hamish Loaf, 112
  Goddess Dressing, 199
  Great Brown Gravy, 191
  Hail Caesar Dressing, 200
  Hamish Loaf, 112
  Handcrafted Pepperoni, 116
  Homemade Vegetable Base, 183
  Melty Cheddary Cheese, 43
  Melty Vegan Cheese, 43
  Nut-Parm, 42
  Oven-Baked Seitan Cutlets, 94–95
  Pretzel-Crusted Cheddary Log,
    52, *53*
  role in recipes, 18
  Rotini with Roasted Garlic Alfredo
    Sauce, 226
  Say (Veganized) Cheese!, 46–47
  Seasoned Tofu Ricotta, 41
  Smoky Queso Sauce, 45
  Spaghetti Carbonara, 223
  Tofu Bacon, 107
  White Bean Cutlets, 87

O

Oat(s)
  Best Bean Burgers, 84, *85*
  Cranberry Oatmeal Cookies, 266
  DIY Granola, 218
  Milk, 31
  No-Meat Loaf, 126
  Veganized Scrapple, 122

Olives
  All-in-One Cauliflower Pizza, 237
  California Caesar Salad, 213
  Creamy Pesto Pasta Salad, 201
  Easy Artisan Bread, 229
  Loaded Frittata, *64*, 65
  Niçoise Goddess Salad, 210, *211*
  Tapenade, 192
  Tapenade–Sour Cream Potato
    Topper, 58
Omelet(s)
  Chickpea Flour, 63
  French-Style Asparagus, 65
Orecchiette with Pistachio Pesto,
    224
Oregano
  All-in-One Cauliflower Pizza, 237
  Andouille Sausage, 118
  Fish-Free Tacos, 142, *143*
  Htipiti (Feta Spread), 49
  Iron Kettle Chili, 83
  Jumpin' Jackfruit Chili, 165
  Mama's Meatballs, 86
  Meaty-Cheesy Pizza, 240, *241*
  Oven-Roasted Tomato Sauce, 197
  Seasoned Tofu Ricotta, 41
  Seitan Gyros with Tzatziki Sauce,
    204, 205
  Smoky Black Bean Soup, 82
  Spinach-Feta Quesadillas, 62
  Tofu Feta, 48
Oven-Baked Seitan Cutlets
  basic recipe, 94–95
  Seitan Oscar with Béarnaise
    Sauce, *96*, 97
Oven-Fried Crispy Tofu, 77
Oven-Roasted Tomato Sauce
  All-in-One Cauliflower Pizza, 237
  Baked Eggplant Italian Style, *162*,
    163
  basic recipe, 197
  Handcrafted Lasagna, *220*, 221
  Loaded Polenta Pizza, 242
  Meaty-Cheesy Pizza, 240, *241*
Oyster Sauce, Mushroom, 198

P

Palm-Crab Imperial, 155
Palm-Crab Po'boys, 149
Pan-Seared Portobello Strips, 175
Pantry stocking the, 9–11
Paprikash, Eggplant, 174
Parm, Nut-, 42

Parsley
  Cassoulet, 125
  Chickpea Flour Omelets, 63
  Cordon Bleu–Stuffed Portobellos, 164
  Country-Style Pâté, 119
  Creamy Ranch Dressing, 196, *207*
  Goddess Dressing, 199
  Mama's Meatballs, 86
  No-Meat Loaf, 126
  Palm-Crab Imperial, 155
  Pan-Seared Portobello Strips, 175
  Piccata Meatballs with Penne and
    Asparagus, *88*, 89
  Remoulade Sauce, 188
  Roasted Cauliflower Piccata, 166,
    167
  Seasoned Tofu Ricotta, 41
  Spaghetti Carbonara, 223
  Tapenade, 192
  Vegetable Broth, 182
Pasta
  Bacon-Topped Mac Uncheese, 54,
    55
  Fettuccine Bolognese, 222
  Handcrafted Lasagna, *220*, 221
  Homemade, 219
  Make-Your-Own Orecchiette, 225
  Orecchiette with Pistachio Pesto, 224
  Piccata Meatballs with Penne and
    Asparagus, *88*, 89
  Rotini with Roasted Garlic Alfredo
    Sauce, 226
  Salad, Creamy Pesto, 201
  Slaw, 212
  Spaghetti Carbonara, 223
Pâté, Country-Style, 119
Pea(s)
  Indian Samosa Potatoes, 58
  Perfect Pot Pie, 230, *231*
  Vegetable Shepherd's Pie, *168*, 169
Peaches
  Bellini Trifle, 265
Peanut butter
  Chocolate-Covered Elvis Ice
    Cream, 275
  Milkshake, Chocolate–, 276, *277*
Peanuts
  Ice Cream Sundae Cake, 278–279
Pecan(s)
  Country-Style Pâté, 119
  DIY Granola, 218
  No-Bake Nut Lover's Cheesecake,
    274

Potato Topper, Greens with Feta and, 58
Pepper(s). *See also* Chile(s); Pimientos
   Cheddary Sauce, 44
   Cheesy Mushroom Scramble, 66
   Cheesy Steak-Out Sandwiches, *176*, 177
   Creamy Pesto Pasta Salad, 201
   Eggplant Paprikash, 174
   Htipiti (Feta Spread), 49
   Iron Kettle Chili, 83
   Jambalaya, 120, *121*
   Mediterranean Quiche, 61
   Mushroom Stroganoff, 170
   Pretzel-Crusted Cheddary Log, 52, *53*
Pepperoni, Handcrafted, 116
Perfect Pot Pie, 230, *231*
Pesto, Pistachio, Orecchiette with, 224
Piccata Meatballs with Penne and Asparagus, *88*, 89
Piccata, Roasted Cauliflower, 166, *167*
Pie Dough
   basic recipe, 228
   Lemon Meringue Pie, *258*, 259
   Perfect Pot Pie, 230, *231*
Pie, Lemon Meringue, *258*, 259
Pimientos
   Cheddary Sauce, 44
   Palm-Crab Imperial, 155
   Pretzel-Crusted Cheddary Log, 52, *53*
   Smoky Queso Sauce, 45
Pineapple
   Banana Split Soft-Serve Sundaes, 280, *281*
   DIY Granola, 218
Pinto beans
   Jumpin' Jackfruit Chili, 165
   Maple Breakfast Sausage, 123
Pistachio Pesto, Orecchiette with, 224
Pizza
   All-in-One Cauliflower, 237
   Benedict, 239
   Dough, 238
   Loaded Polenta, 242
   Meaty-Cheesy, 240, *241*
Polenta Pizza, Loaded, 242
Porcini Cheese, 47

Pot Pie, Perfect, 230, *231*
Potato(es)
   Artichoke-Hummus, 58
   Cheesy Broccoli Soup, 56
   Cheesy Mushroom Scramble, 66
   Chili-Cheesy Topper, 58
   Clam-Free Chowder, *138*, 139
   Creamy Spinach, 58
   Greens with Feta and Pecans Topper, 58
   Guacamole and Salsa Topper, 58
   Indian Samosa, 58
   Loaded Baked, 57–58, *59*
   mashed, as egg substitute in baking, 257
   Mashed, with Sour Cream and Chives, 171
   Niçoise Goddess Salad, 210, *211*
   Perfect Pot Pie, 230, *231*
   Potato, 212
   Slaw, 212
   Tapenade–Sour Cream Topper, 58
   Vegan Fish and Chips with Tartar Sauce, 144, *145*
Pots and saucepans, 20
Pretzel-Crusted Cheddary Log
   basic recipe, 52, *53*
   Cordon Bleu–Stuffed Portobellos, 164
Proteins, plant-based, 12–14
Pulled Jackfruit BBQ Sandwiches, 172, *173*
Pumpkin seeds
   DIY Granola, 218
Pumpkin-y White Sauce, 39

Q

Quesadillas, Spinach-Feta, 62
Quiche
   Asparagus and Ham, 61
   Broccoli and Sausage, 61
   Mediterranean, 61
   Spinach and Mushroom-Bacon, 60–61
Quinoa
   No-Meat Loaf, 126
   Smoky Black Bean Soup, 82

R

Raisins
   Cranberry Oatmeal Cookies, 266
   DIY Granola, 218

Raspberry(ies)
   Mango Fro-Yo, 264
   No-Bake Chocolate Cheesecake, *272*, 273
Red Wine Sauce with Mushrooms
   basic recipe, 184
   Wellington, The, 98
Remoulade Sauce, 188
Ribs, BBQ Seitan, 99, *100*
Rice
   Jambalaya, 120, *121*
   No-Meat Loaf, 126
Ricotta, Seasoned Tofu, 41
Roast, Baked Seitan, 92–93
Roasted Cauliflower Piccata, 166, *167*
Roasted Garlic, 227
Rotini with Roasted Garlic Alfredo Sauce, 226

S

Sage
   Home-Style Marinade, 75
   Maple Breakfast Sausage, 123
   No-Meat Loaf, 126
   Veganized Scrapple, 122
Salad dressing
   Creamy Ranch, 196, *207*
   Goddess, 199
   Hail Caesar, 200
Salad(s)
   California Caesar, 213
   Chickpea and Artichoke Tuna, 154
   Creamy Coleslaw, 212
   Creamy Pesto Pasta, 201
   Deviled Hamish, 131
   My Kinda Chef's, 208
   Niçoise Goddess, 210, *211*
   Pasta Slaw, 212
   Potato Slaw, 212
   Vegan Crab Louis, *156*, 157
Sandwich(es)
   Banh Mi, *114*, 115
   Best Bean Burgers, 84, *85*
   Beyond BLT, 127
   Cheesy Steak-Out, *176*, 177
   Haute Dogs, 128, *129*
   Join the Club, *132*, 133
   Palm-Crab Po'boys, 149
   Pulled Jackfruit BBQ, 172, *173*
   Seitan Gyros with Tzatziki Sauce, *204*, 205

Sauce(s)
  Barbecue, 101
  Basic White, 39
  Basil Pesto, 194
  Better Béarnaise, 190
  Cashew Chantilly Cream, 249
  Cheddary, 44
  Cheesy White, 39
  Curry White, 39
  Date-Caramel Sauce, 250
  Fudgy Chocolate, 251
  Great Brown Gravy, 191
  Hollandaise, 185
  Hot and Spicy White, 39
  Oven-Roasted Tomato, 197
  Pumpkin-y White, 39
  Red Wine, with Mushrooms, 184
  Remoulade, 188
  Shortcut Hollandaise, 185
  Smoky Queso, 45
  Tzatziki, 195
  Whipped Coconut Cream, 248
Saucepans, 20
Sausage(s)
  Andouille, 118
  Cassoulet, 124, 125
  Cheesy Mushroom Scramble, 66
  Cheesy Sausage Biscuits, 232, 233
  Handcrafted Pepperoni, 116
  Haute Dogs, 128, 129
  Haute Dogs Wellington, 130
  Maple Breakfast, 123
  Quiche, Broccoli and, 61
  Spicy Italian, 117
Say (Veganized) Cheese!, 46–47
Scallions
  Chickpea and Artichoke Tuna
    Salad, 154
  Chickpea Flour Omelets, 63
  Creamy Ranch Dressing, 196, 207
  Easy Kimchi, 209
  Goddess Dressing, 199
  Loaded Baked Potatoes, 57–58, 59
  Palm-Crab Imperial, 155
  Pretzel-Crusted Cheddary Log, 52, 53
  Spinach-Artichoke Dip, 50, 51
  Summer Rolls with Fish-Free Nuoc
    Cham, 202, 203
  Tuesday Tacos with Avocado
    Crema, 90, 91
Scallops, Creamy Sriracha See, 152,
  153
Scallops, See, 148

Scones, Cranberry-Walnut, 243
Scramble, Cheesy Mushroom, 66
Scrapple, Veganized, 122
Scratch Biscuits, 236
Scratch Cake
  basic recipe, 260
  Bellini Trifle, 265
  Strawberry Shortcake, 262, 263
  Tiramisu, 261
Sea vegetables, 18
Seafood alternatives
  Chickpea and Artichoke Tuna
    Salad, 154
  Clam-Free Chowder, 138, 139
  Creamy Sriracha See Scallops, 152,
    153
  Fish-Free Fillets, 146
  Fish-Free Sticks, 147
  Fish-Free Tacos, 142, 143
  Hearts of Palm and Artichoke
    Cakes, 150, 151
  Lobster Mushroom Bisque, 140–141
  Palm-Crab Imperial, 155
  Palm-Crab Po'boys, 149
  See Scallops, 148
  Vegan Crab Louis, 156, 157
  Vegan Fish and Chips with Tartar
    Sauce, 144, 145
Seasoned Tofu Ricotta
  Baked Eggplant Italian Style, 162,
    163
  basic recipe, 41
  Handcrafted Lasagna, 220, 221
See Scallops
  basic recipe, 148
  Creamy Sriracha, 152, 153
Seitan
  Banh Mi, 114, 115
  characteristics of, 12
  Cutlets, Oven-Baked, 94–95
  Fettuccine Bolognese, 222
  Gyros with Tzatziki Sauce, 204,
    205
  Haute Dogs Wellington, 130
  Iron Kettle Chili, 83
  Mushroom Stroganoff, 170
  Oscar with Béarnaise Sauce, 96, 97
  Perfect Pot Pie, 230, 231
  preparing at home, 12
  Pulled Jackfruit BBQ Sandwiches,
    172, 173
  Ribs, BBQ, 99, 100
  Roast, Baked, 92–93

Shallots
  Better Béarnaise Sauce, 190
  Creamy Spinach Potatoes, 58
  French-Style Asparagus Omelet,
    65
  Pan-Seared Portobello Strips, 175
  Red Wine Sauce with Mushrooms,
    184
  Wellington, The, 98
Shepherd's Pie, Vegetable, 168, 169
Sherry
  Cheddary Sauce, 44
  Palm-Crab Imperial, 155
Shortcake, Strawberry, 262, 263
Shortcut Hollandaise, 185
Skillet dishes
  Banh Mi, 114, 115
  Best Bean Burgers, 84, 85
  Breakfast Nachos, 68, 69
  Cheesy Mushroom Scramble, 66
  Cheesy Steak-Out Sandwiches,
    176, 177
  Chickpea Flour Omelets, 63
  Creamy Sriracha See Scallops, 152,
    153
  French-Style Asparagus Omelet,
    65
  Hearts of Palm and Artichoke
    Cakes, 150, 151
  Loaded Frittata, 64, 65
  Mushroom Stroganoff, 170
  Palm-Crab Po'boys, 149
  Pan-Seared Portobello Strips, 175
  Piccata Meatballs with Penne and
    Asparagus, 88, 89
  Pulled Jackfruit BBQ Sandwiches,
    172, 173
  Roasted Cauliflower Piccata, 166,
    167
  Spaghetti Carbonara, 223
  Spinach-Feta Quesadillas, 62
  Tuesday Tacos with Avocado
    Crema, 90, 91
  Vive la French Toast, 67
Skillets, 21
Slaw(s)
  Creamy Coleslaw, 212
  Pasta, 212
  Potato, 212
Slow cooker recipes
  Beans from Scratch, 80–81
  Seitan Roast, 93
  Vegetable Broth, 182

Smoky Black Bean Soup, 82
Smoky Chickpeas
    basic recipe, 111
    Loaded Polenta Pizza, 242
Smoky Black Bean Soup, 82
Smoky Queso Sauce
    basic recipe, 45
    Breakfast Nachos, 68, 69
Snacks
    Buffalo Cauliflower with Ranch
        Dressing, 206, 207
    Cheesy Crackers, 234, 235
    Chocolate Truffles, 267
    Chocolate–Chocolate Chip
        Brownies, 271
    Chocolate–Peanut Butter
        Milkshake, 276, 277
    Country-Style Pâté, 119
    Cranberry Oatmeal Cookies,
        266
    Pretzel-Crusted Cheddary Log,
        52, 53
    Spinach-Feta Quesadillas, 62
    Strawberry Shake, 276, 277
    Vanilla Shake, 276, 277
Soup(s)
    Cheesy Broccoli, 56
    Clam-Free Chowder, 138, 139
    Lobster Mushroom Bisque,
        140–141
    Smoky Black Bean, 82
    Vegetable Broth, 182
Sour Cream, Cashew, 33
Soy-free vegan cooking, 20
Spaghetti Carbonara, 223
Spicy Italian Sausage, 117
Spinach
    -Artichoke Dip, 50, 51
    -Feta Quesadillas, 62
    Benedict Pizza, 239
    Beyond BLT, 127
    Greens with Feta and Pecans
        Potato Topper, 58
    Handcrafted Lasagna, 220, 221
    Loaded Frittata, 64, 65
    and Mushroom-Bacon Quiche,
        60–61
    Potatoes, Creamy, 58
Spinach-Feta Quesadillas, 62
Spreads
    Country-Style Pâté, 119
    Deviled Hamish Salad, 131
    Tapenade, 192

Strawberry(ies)
    Banana Split Soft-Serve Sundaes,
        280, 281
    Ice Cream Sundae Cake, 278–279
    Mango Fro-Yo, 264
    Shake, 276, 277
    Shortcake, 262, 263
Stroganoff, Mushroom, 170
Sugars, refined, 17
Summer Rolls with Fish-Free Nuoc
    Cham, 202, 203
Sundaes, Banana Split Soft-Serve,
    280, 281
Sunflower seeds
    All-in-One Cauliflower Pizza, 237
    Chickpea and Artichoke Tuna
        Salad, 154
    Country-Style Pâté, 119
    My Kinda Chef's Salad, 208
    No-Meat Loaf, 126
Sweeteners, 17

T
Tacos
    with Avocado Crema, Tuesday,
        90, 91
    Fish-Free, 142, 143
Tamari, 18
Tapenade, 192
Tapenade–Sour Cream Potato Topper,
    58
Tapioca starch or flour, 18, 48
Tarragon
    Better Béarnaise Sauce, 190
    French-Style Asparagus Omelet,
        65
    Goddess Dressing, 199
Tempeh
    Bacon, 106
    buying, 14
    characteristics of, 13–14
    cooking with, 14
    Fettuccine Bolognese, 222
    Fish-Free Sticks, 147
    Iron Kettle Chili, 83
    Perfect Pot Pie, 230, 231
    Pulled Jackfruit BBQ Sandwiches,
        172, 173
    storing, 14
    Totally Tempting, 79
Tempeh Bacon
    basic recipe, 106
    Beyond BLT, 127

Smoky Black Bean Soup, 82
Thickeners, 48
Thyme
    Andouille Sausage, 118
    Cassoulet, 125
    Clam-Free Chowder, 138, 139
    Country-Style Pâté, 119
    Great Brown Gravy, 191
    Home-Style Marinade, 75
    Homemade Vegetable Base, 183
    Jambalaya, 120
    Maple Breakfast Sausage, 123
    No-Meat Loaf, 126
    Pan-Seared Portobello Strips, 175
    Perfect Pot Pie, 230, 231
    Red Wine Sauce with Mushrooms,
        184
    Vegan Aioli, 193
    Veganized Scrapple, 122
    Vegetable Broth, 182
    Wellington, The, 98
Tiramisu, 261
Tofu
    Bacon, 107
    Banh Mi, 114, 115
    Benedict Pizza, 239
    Breakfast Nachos, 68, 69
    Burmese, 76
    characteristics of, 12
    Cheesy Mushroom Scramble, 66
    Crispy, 77
    Crispy Crumbles, 78
    DIY Jerky, 113
    draining, 13
    Easy Vegan Yogurt, 34
    as egg substitute in baking, 257
    Feta, 48
    firm and extra-firm, 12–13
    Fish-Free Fillets, 146
    Haute Dogs, 128, 129
    Marinated Baked, 74–75
    My Kinda Chef's Salad, 208
    Oven-Fried Crispy, 77
    pressing liquid from, 113
    regular versus silken, 12–13
    Ricotta, Seasoned, 41
    See Scallops, 148
    silken, in recipes, 13
    Spinach and Mushroom-Bacon
        Quiche, 60–61
    Spinach-Feta Quesadillas, 62
    Summer Rolls with Fish-Free Nuoc
        Cham, 202, 203

Tofu (cont)
　Vegan Mascarpone, 253
　Veganized Scrapple, 122
Tofu Feta
　basic recipe, 48
　Htipiti (Feta Spread), 49
　Spinach-Feta Quesadillas, 62
Tomato(es)
　All-in-One Cauliflower Pizza, 237
　Baked Eggplant Italian Style, *162*, 163
　Benedict Pizza, 239
　Beyond BLT, 127
　Breakfast Nachos, *68*, 69
　Cassoulet, *124*, 125
　Cheesy Mushroom Scramble, 66
　Creamy Pesto Pasta Salad, 201
　Eggplant Paprikash, 174
　Fettuccine Bolognese, 222
　Fish-Free Tacos, 142, *143*
　Iron Kettle Chili, 83
　Jambalaya, 120, *121*
　Join the Club Sandwich, *132*, 133
　Jumpin' Jackfruit Chili, 165
　My Kinda Chef's Salad, 208
　Niçoise Goddess Salad, 210, *211*
　Palm-Crab Po'boys, 149
　Rotini with Roasted Garlic Alfredo Sauce, 226
　Sauce, Oven-Roasted, 197
　Seitan Gyros with Tzatziki Sauce, *204*, 205
Tortillas
　Fish-Free Tacos, 142, *143*
　Spinach-Feta Quesadillas, 62
　Tuesday Tacos with Avocado Crema, 90, *91*
Totally Tempting Tempeh, 79
Truffles, Chocolate, 267
Tuesday Tacos with Avocado Crema, 90, *91*
Tuna Salad, Chickpea and Artichoke, 154
Two-for-One Cheesy Wheels, 47

Tzatziki Sauce
　basic recipe, 195
　Seitan Gyros with, *204*, 205

V
Vanilla Shake, 276, *277*
Vegan Aioli, 193
Vegan Crab Louis, *156*, 157
Vegan diet, benefits of, 7
Vegan Fish and Chips with Tartar Sauce, 144, *145*
Vegan Mascarpone
　basic recipe, 253
　Tiramisu, 261
Vegan terminology, 21–22
Vegan Worcestershire Sauce, 186
Veganized Marshmallow Fluff, 255
Veganized Scrapple, 122
Vegetable Base, Homemade, 183
Vegetable Broth, 182
Vegetable Shepherd's Pie, *168*, 169
Vital wheat gluten, 12
　Andouille Sausage, 118
　Baked Seitan Roast, 92–93
　BBQ Seitan Ribs, 99, *100*
　Glazed Hamish Loaf, 112
　Hamish Loaf, 112
　Handcrafted Pepperoni, 116
　Haute Dogs, 128, *129*
　Mama's Meatballs, 86
　Maple Breakfast Sausage, 123
　Oven-Baked Seitan Cutlets, 94–95
　Spicy Italian Sausage, 117
　White Bean Cutlets, 87
Vitamin D, 10
Vive la French Toast, 67

W
Walnut(s)
　Basil Pesto, 194
　Best Bean Burgers, 84, *85*
　Country-Style Pâté, 119
　Cranberry Oatmeal Cookies, 266
　DIY Granola, 218

No-Bake Nut Lover's Cheesecake, 274
No-Meat Loaf, 126
Nut-Parm, 42
Say (Veganized) Cheese!, 46
Scones, Cranberry-, 243
Wellington, Haute Dogs, 130
Wellington, The, 98
Wheat-meat, 12
Whipped Coconut Cream
　basic recipe, 248
　Ice Cream Sundae Cake, 278–279
White Bean Cutlets, 87
White Sauce, Basic, 39
Wine
　Bellini Trifle, 265
　Better Béarnaise Sauce, 190
　Cheddary Sauce, 44
　Eggplant Paprikash, 174
　Fettuccine Bolognese, 222
　Home-Style Marinade, 75
　Lobster Mushroom Bisque, 140–141
　Pan-Seared Portobello Strips, 175
　Piccata Meatballs with Penne and Asparagus, *88*, 89
　Red Wine Sauce with Mushrooms, 184
　Roasted Cauliflower Piccata, 166, *167*
　Say (Veganized) Cheese!, 46
Worcestershire Sauce, Vegan, 186

Y
Yogurt
　Easy Vegan, 34
　as egg substitute in baking, 257
　Mango Fro-Yo, 264
　Tzatziki Sauce, 195

Z
Zucchini
　Cheesy Mushroom Scramble, 66
　Loaded Frittata, *64*, 65
　Mediterranean Quiche, 61